THE HIGH MOUNTAINS
OF CRETE

About the Author

In 1979, after returning from a spell in Dubai during the early building boom, Loraine Wilson swapped life as an architectural assistant for that of trek leader, mainly in the mountains of Greece. A lifelong hillwalker and backpacker, she has been walking the Cretan mountains since 1982. In 1995 a course in heritage management alerted her in a more formal way to the necessity of encouraging 'inland tourism' in Crete, and places like it. Since that so often concerns walking and trekking, Loraine's guidebooks are written to make a positive contribution.

Other Cicerone guides by Loraine Wilson
Crete – The White Mountains

THE HIGH MOUNTAINS
OF CRETE
THE WHITE MOUNTAINS AND SOUTH COAST,
PSILORITIS AND LASSITHI

by

Loraine Wilson

2 POLICE SQUARE, MILNTHORPE, CUMBRIA LA7 7PY
www.cicerone.co.uk

Second edition 2008
ISBN-13: 978 185284 525 4

© Loraine Wilson 2000, 2008

First edition (Crete – The White Mountains) 2000
ISBN-10: 1 85284 298 9
Reprinted 2002

British Library Cataloguing-in-Publication Data
A catalogue record for this book is available from the British Library.

All photographs, route diagrams and legend by the author.

This book is dedicated to all those who enjoy the challenge of exploring mountains that are not, as yet, highly developed for recreational walking.

Acknowledgements

Time has moved on since my first guidebook to the White Mountains was published but I need hardly change my list of acknowledgements, since in Crete the same welcome sustains. However, my special thanks this time go to readers who have sent me their comments, observations and new information for this second edition. I am particularly indebted to Jan and Barry Cropper for accompanying me on Walk 6 (E4), Charles and Linda Wilkinson for the same on Trek 1, and to Roger de Freitas for his enthusiasm for the project and lots of weight-carrying on Mount Ida and Lassithi backpacking routes, and to Jean Bienvenu for his ongoing interest and useful observations.

Advice to Readers

Readers are advised that while every effort is taken by the author to ensure the accuracy of this guidebook, changes can occur which may affect the contents. It is advisable to check locally on transport, accommodation, shops and so on, but even rights of way can be altered. The publisher would welcome notes of any such changes.

Front cover: A trekker pauses on the 'viewpoint rock' high above Kamares, Psiloritis

CONTENTS

PART 2 PSILORITIS – MOUNT IDA

Warning

Mountaineering and wilderness trekking can be dangerous activities carrying a risk of personal injury or death. They should be undertaken only by those with a full understanding of the risks and with the training and/or experience to evaluate them. Mountaineers and trekkers should be appropriately equipped for the routes. Whilst every care and effort has been taken in the preparation of this book, the user should be aware that conditions can be highly variable and can change quickly, thus materially affecting the seriousness of a climb, tour or expedition.

Therefore, except for any liability which cannot be excluded by law, neither Cicerone nor the author accept liability for damage of any nature (including damage to property, personal injury or death) arising directly or indirectly from the information in this book.

Map Key

═══════	north coast highway
────────	surfaced road
------------	unsurfaced road
← W9	walk route, number, direction
• • • • • • •	alternative walk route
○	village
♠	taverna
⌂	open hut
⟡	locked hut
◓	shepherd s hut
©	cave
⌣	pass
▥	archaeological site
⬧	monastery
⬧	chapel
▲	peak
⬛	bus
P	parking
▢ ○ ⚲	water tank, cistern, spring
- - - - -	ferry route
◇	river/sea/lake
⊞	cemetery
♣	forest
⬓	castle
ﮞﮞﮞ	gorge
XXXX	rock scramble
⠂⠂⠂	plain (plateau)
◐ ○ ●	start/finish, start, finish points

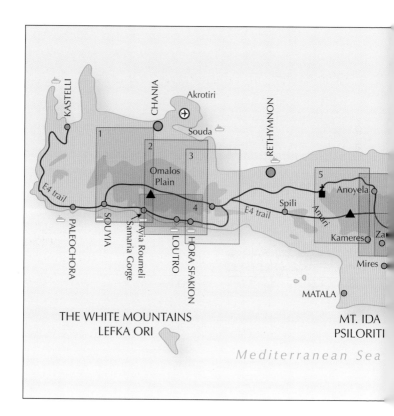

THE WHITE MOUNTAINS
LEFKA ORI

MT. IDA
PSILORITI

Mediterranean Sea

Town Maps

The Mountain Ranges covered in this book

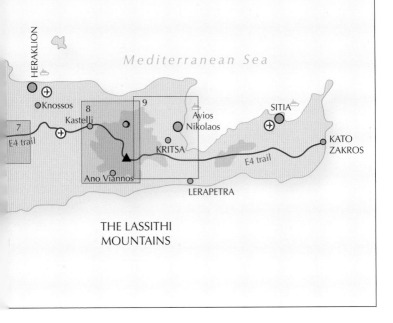

Route Maps

Sunshine and shade as the Samaria Gorge narrows (Walk 2)

INTRODUCTION

The Greek island of Crete, extending for about 250km (155 miles) west to east, is well known for its sunny climate and beautiful natural scenery so typical of the lands of the Mediterranean. Relics of a long and richly varied history dot town and countryside, and botanists find much of interest almost everywhere they look.

But there is also another side to Crete. Visible everywhere as a striking backdrop to the beaches and coastal plains an almost continuous spine of rugged limestone mountains runs along the length of the island. Frequented only by a few shepherds, the wilder regions of this interior offer challenging trekking routes of two or three days' duration. At lower, more hospitable levels, walkers can follow old mule tracks and paths beween foothill villages where a range of facilities can be found.

Throughout Crete an efficient public bus service links towns, villages and trailheads. This guidebook covers walks and treks in the main mountain ranges in west, central and eastern Crete, including the south coast of Sfakia in the west.

Although readily accessible, Cretan mountain ranges are very rugged and potentially hazardous. Route-finding is not easy due to the many spectacular limestone features that are typical of Greek mountains. There are 1:25,000 contour maps covering selected areas, but for full coverage of the island only 1:100,000 contour maps are currently available. This guidebook aims to pro-vide you with the additional information you need to follow the routes of your choice.

Crete is the largest and most pros-perous of the Greek islands, thanks, in part, to the many beaches that attract summer tourism. In addition, fertile coastal plains and valleys allow a thriv-ing agricultural industry, and Athens, for example, provides a ready market for produce (by overnight ferryboat). Cretans and visitors alike enjoy an abun-dance of good home-produced food and wine.

The island is busy: there are three main towns – Chania, Heraklion and Rethymnon – with both fashionable and traditional-style shops, together with harbours, markets, universities and museums. Crete is easy to reach by air or by sea from Athens or by direct charter flight to Chania or Heraklion airports. Happily for walkers, 'getting to the trail-head' is also easy using KTEL, the public bus service, or local taxis.

HILLWALKING AND TREKKING REGIONS

The walks and mountain treks suggested in this guide are grouped under three main headings. In the west, the **Lefka Ori (White Mountains)** (Part 1) cover 960km^2, and include over 20 peaks ris-ing above 2000m (6560ft); Pachnes (2453m/8047ft) is the highest. There are five good walking areas – the Omalos Plain, the Northern Foothills, the Askifou

Making graviera cheese in Askifou

Plain, Anopolis and the South Coast of Sfakia – all with trailheads served by bus from Chania. Since many of the best walking routes are linear, a hired car can be limiting especially as much of the rugged south coast, having no roads, is only served by boat. Fortunately villages on many of the walking routes offer plentiful accommodation, not all of which is pre-booked, enabling a flexible itinerary. Town bus stations have left luggage facilities, useful for those who wish to travel without a particular base.

In the region of Sfakia, the southern flank of the Lefka Ori rises very abruptly above the coast to over 1000m (3280ft). Thirteen gorges split this steep escarpment, the largest of which – 18km long and over 1000m deep – is the Gorge of Samaria. The huge and inaccessible forested crags of this gorge and its neigh-

bour, the Tripiti Gorge, form a refuge for a treasure that is unique to Crete: a little ibex goat, the kri-kri, which has survived here since ancient times.

All the mountain ranges of Crete feature high plains, gorges and ravines, but in the heart of the Lefka Ori there is something else. High above the treeline snow thaws by July to reveal a great circle of massive barren peaks, interspersed with 'moonscape' outcrops, or depressions, of sinkholes in black, grey or red rock. This high desert wilderness is seldom visited, even by Cretans. Old trails across this interior never fail to impress those who venture to walk them.

In central Crete, where the island is at its widest, the huge mass of **Psiloritis (Mount Ida)** (Part 2) dominates the whole region. Covering about 560km², this massif is different in that a single huge, partly scree-surfaced summit ridge rises above massive cliffs on one side and a large area of lower peaks and forested foothills on the other. The summit of Mount Ida has always attracted peak-baggers because, at 2456m (8057ft), it is the highest point in Crete. At lower levels the forests, freshwater springs, and accessible foothills sustain a strong shepherding tradition and large flocks of sheep, together with goats, are still a regular sight.

Psiloritis offers several challenging linear walking routes with the high level Nida Plain as a fulcrum. In the foothills, trailhead villages, all of which have tourist facilities, are served by bus from either Rethymnon or Heraklion. However, for walks starting from the Nida Plain, such as the day-walk to the summit, there is no public bus service and alternative plans must be made (see individual route descriptions).

The **Dikti** or **Lassithi Mountains** (Part 3) cover about 780km² and virtually divide central Crete from the eastern end of the island. The dominant feature here is the Lassithi Plain (formerly famous for its hundreds of windmill water pumps), which is surrounded by a series of peaks including Mount Dikti, at 2147m (7047ft) the highest summit of eastern Crete.

Although the European long-distance walking route the E4 Trail crosses Lassithi as an interesting and, in some places, challenging linear route – and is readily accessible by public bus – a few day-walks from the plain (which is very large) are best reached by car. Lassithi

Aravanes 'Old Mitato' in May (Walk P7)

has several important Neolithic and Bronze Age sites which attract visitors: villages on the plain offer facilities during the tourist season.

GETTING THERE

There are two ways of getting to Crete by air:

- by direct charter flight to a Cretan airport, and
- by scheduled flight (or charter flight) to Athens International Airport, followed by an internal (domestic) flight to Crete, or a ferryboat from Piraeus (the port of Athens) to a Cretan port.

At busy periods you may not be able to book the travel route or method of your choice. The following information should help to simplify arrival proce-

dures and reduce the time it takes to get to the trailhead, but be aware that arrangements can change at any time.

Flying to Athens

Athens Eleutherios Venizelos International Airport, with bus and train connections to Athens city and the port of Piraeus, was fully completed by 2004, the year of the Olympic Games. It is located 20km north of the city near the village of Spata (not the town of Sparta in the Peloponese); locally the location is sometimes still called 'Spata'. Olympic Airways (and possibly other airline partnerships) will send your luggage right through to destination if you are transferring at Athens onto an ongoing internal flight. **Note** Internal flights are quite often delayed because of bad weather in the Aegean, causing, for

Heading towards the Eligas Gorge from Ay. Pavlos (Walk 49)

example, strong winds at the destination airport; if you have accommodation booked, telephone ahead to advise of your late arrival.

Information leaflets are available from racks in the thoroughfares and in the Arrivals hall; the 'Timetable Information' booklet has full details of bus or train connections. Read this in conjunction with the leaflet map 'Airport Access'. This is a busy workaday airport with only one outside terrace, at Departures level. The 5min walk to the Athens Airport metro station (the subway – city rail transport) is well signposted. An hourly express direct Airport–Piraeus Harbour metro service (enquire) takes one hour (fare €6 in 2007). There is a Sofitel airport hotel, which is cheaper if booked on the internet.

If you have a long wait between flights, one solution is to take a bus or taxi to the nearby seaside resorts of either Loutro or Rafina. The Rafina bus stop is found by crossing the Arrivals-level road on the walking route to the metro station. The airport has a pricey but useful left luggage store at the southwest end of the Arrivals-level pavement.

An information desk can be found near the main exit of the Arrivals hall. Taxis and buses to central Athens, Syntagma Square (Service 95, 24hr), and Piraeus, the port of Athens (Service 96, 24hr) draw in here. These are town buses: buy a ticket at the kiosk beside the bus stops (budget €3 in 2008). Date stamp your ticket using the device found in the centre of the bus. Taxis take up to four passengers and charge extra for luggage and night work. Ask the expected fare and check that the meter is turned on.

Ferryboat from Piraeus

A passenger-and-vehicle ferryboat vessel is, usefully for visitors, understood as 'ferryboat' by the Greeks, although they will call it a *ka-rar-vee*.

Greece has many islands, and many competing shipping lines, so that modern ferryboat travel is very complex. There are fast, moderate and slow services, and at busy periods all three types may depart for the same destination almost at the same time. Boat travel is time-consuming and tiring but (unless you take a cabin) is much cheaper than flying. However, that may only work out if you travel overnight and can sleep well enough in the reclining seats of 'deck class', in the hallways, or on deck (although modern ferryboats have very little outside deck space). Daytime departures to Crete arrive at busy destination ports in the evening, after dark, which is hardly convenient unless you know your way around and are prepared to compete for nearby accommodation, taxis and buses. It may be easier to arrive in the early morning and then make your way to the town bus station to pick up the first buses to the countryside.

As Crete is a large and busy island there are regular overnight ferryboat sailings, seven days a week, between Piraeus (the port of Athens) and Heraklion, Rethymnon, and Souda (the port of Chania), the towns that give you access to the mountain trailheads. These ferries arrive at destination ports early in the morning, the exact time depending on the weather during the crossing. For

Ruined houses of Aradena (Walk 40)

Souda (Chania) and Rethymnon, ANEK Line vessels are likely to depart Piraeus between 20.00 and 21.00, and for Heraklion, Minoan Line departs 22.00. (The return journey has later departure times.) There will also be a daytime departure, such as the 16.15 (2004) Blue Star Line to Chania, or even hydrofoil departures from Rafina port (on the north coast, 20min bus ride from the airport) to Paros, for connections to Santorini, from where there are connections to Heraklion (see Appendix 3).

For basic journey planning note that most daytime ferries to the Aegean islands (not Crete direct) depart 07.30 and that 'fast' boats, catamarans and hydrofoils, cannot travel if the sea is very rough. After a night flight, if you are aiming for a 07.30 Piraeus departure, be sure to catch the 05.20 bus Airport–Piraeus as the journey time can be 1hr 30min. There are several ticket agencies alongside the Piraeus bus station (terminus), which is just beside the ferryboat dock. However, note that the Blue Star Line uses a newer dock that is served by free shuttle bus – check these details with the ticket agents. (Similarly, Blue Star Line's dock at Souda is some distance west of the ANEK dock.)

Note that it is no longer possible to board an 'overnight' vessel more than a couple of hours before departure time, and that not all vessels have shower facilities for deck class passengers, although there are always lounges, bars and restaurants.

Alternatively, if you have reached central Athens via the subway 'metro line 3' to Monasteraki (for the Plaka and the Acropolis) change at that station onto a 'metro line 1' train for Piraeus. Conveniently, Piraeus metro station (the terminus) is just across the road from the ferryboat dock and there are ticket agents near the station.

The Aradena Gorge from the ferryboat (Walk 49)

Chania

Chania Airport is located 12km out of town on the Akrotiri peninsula. KTEL operates three buses daily: Airport to Chania: 07.15, 10.30, 19.30; Chania to Airport: 06.00, 10.30, 19.30. Budget about €20 (2008) for the 20min taxi ride. Charter flights' package tour operators' buses are not available to 'flight only' passengers.

Heraklion

A new airport is under construction (2007, see below). The current Heraklion Airport is close to town, although busy traffic lanes may delay what was once a 7min taxi ride to, perhaps, the bus station of your choice (airport taxi €10 in 2007) – see ferryboat arrivals information below. Town bus No. 1 serves the airport – the stop is not far from the taxi rank near the pitched-roof left luggage building across the car park. You need to buy a ticket (€0.80 in 2007) in advance – enquire in the airport shops. Buy a couple of tickets if you intend to return to the airport by bus.

For the return journey, get to the airport bus stop (7min walk) as follows: walk east out of Heraklion main bus station and bear right uphill to the main road. The bus stop/shelter is almost opposite, outside a petrol station adjacent to a McDonalds outlet. Buy your ticket in advance, for example from the kiosk at the main bus station (which also sells tickets for the Knossos town bus). The No. 1 bus runs every 10mins or so.

At the main bus station, KTEL buses for Chania (2hrs 30mins), Rethymnon (1hr 30mins) and Ay. Nikolaos (1hr 30mins) are likely to depart every 30mins up to 20.30. Alternatively, taxi drivers may be eager to get long-distance jobs between the Cretan towns because a good main road links them all (budget about €100 for Heraklion–Chania [2008]). Note that the **new Heraklion Airport** and related infrastructure is scheduled to open around 2010. The location is near Kastelli in the Lassithi foothills, so it may be prudent to allow at least 30mins for the transfer to Heraklion town. There willl be a different airport bus service – enquire at the bus station.

Souda (for Chania)

Depending on sea conditions, overnight ferries arrive at Souda at 06.00 (before dawn in autumn/winter). The bus stop for **Chania** ('Han-YA') town buses (blue and white), a circular route from the Agora, is just outside the dock gate, beside an ATM and Souda's pleasant main square. Tickets for the town bus are purchased in advance from a nearby kiosk. For journeys to **Rethymnon/ Heraklion**, KTEL buses pass along Souda's main street, which is on the main road, at the top of the square. **Note** There may also be KTEL Rethymnon direct buses waiting on the dock – this service is popular with ferryboat passengers.

Heraklion (and bus stations)

The **Chania–Rethymnon** and **Lassithi** (east) bus stations are currently (2007)

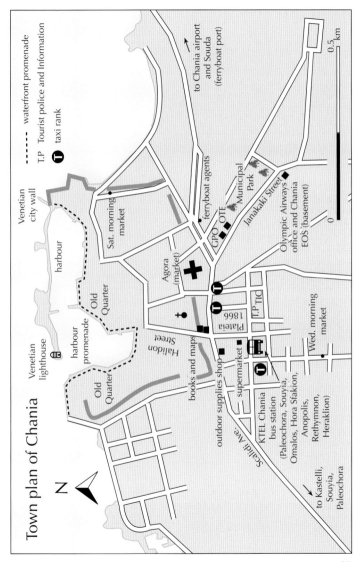

Town plan of Chania

N

----- waterfront promenade

T.P Tourist police and Information

🅣 taxi rank

Venetian city wall

harbour

Old Quarter

Venetian lighthouse

harbour promenade

Old Quarter

harbour promenade

Sat. morning market

Agora (market)

Haldion Street

books and maps

outdoor supplies shop

supermarket

Plateia 1866

T.P TIC

ferryboat agents

GPO OTE

Janakaki Street

Municipal Park

Olympic Airways office and Chania
EOS (basement)

Wed. morning market

to Chania airport
and Souda
(ferryboat port)

Sealidi Ave.

KTEL Chania
bus station
(Paleochora, Souyia,
Omalos, Hora Sfakion,
Anopolis,
Rethymnon,
Heraklion)

to Kastelli,
Souyia,
Paleochora

0   0.5 km

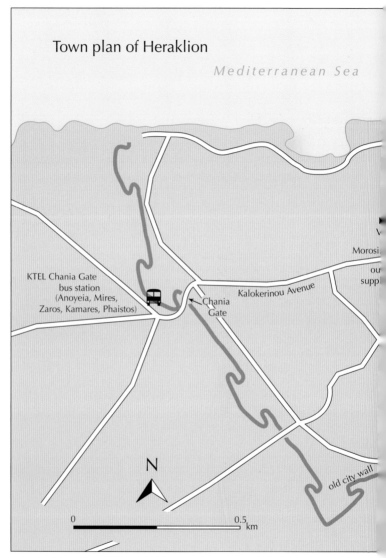

Town plan of Heraklion

Mediterranean Sea

KTEL Chania Gate
bus station
(Anoyeia, Mires,
Zaros, Kamares, Phaistos)

Chania
Gate

Kalokerinou Avenue

Morosi

ou
supp

N

old city wall

0   0.5
          km

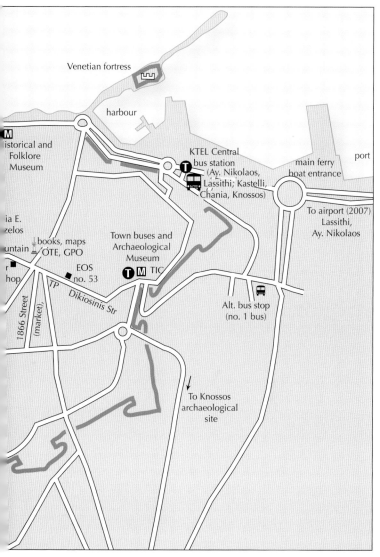

Venetian fortress

harbour

M istorical and
Folklore
Museum

KTEL Central
bus station
T (Ay. Nikolaos,
Lassithi; Kastelli,
Chánia, Knossos)

main ferry
boat entrance

port

To airport (2007)
Lassithi,
Ay. Nikolaos

ia E.
zelos

untain ↓ books, maps
OTE, GPO

EOS
no. 53

T **M** TIC

Town buses and
Archaeological
Museum

r
hop

TP *Dikiosinis Str*

1866 Street
(market)

Alt. bus stop
(no. 1 bus)

↓
To Knossos
archaeological
site

25

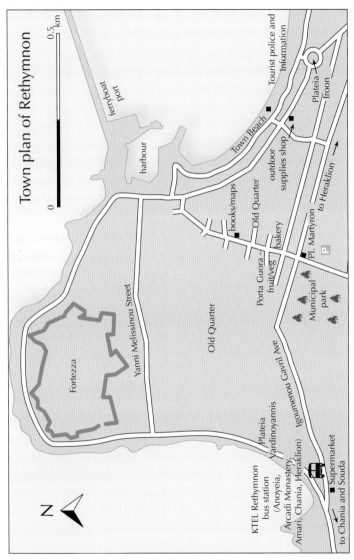

Town plan of Rethymnon

combined. Facilities include a left luggage store and refreshments outlets, but there are no shops nearby. For this bus station, from the ferry, turn right along the main road outside the dock gates. The frequent town bus service direct to Knossos village and archaeological site (30mins) also terminates here. However, KTEL buses for Mount Ida trailheads featured in this guidebook (Anoyeia, Zaros and Kamares) depart from the **Chania Gate bus station** which is just outside the old city wall to the west.

Unless you take a taxi or consult a street plan for the best shortcut, the easiest way to get to the Chania Gate is to walk straight down the main street, Kalokerinou, from Eleutherios Square in front of the Archaeological Museum or from just beyond (pedestrian precinct) E. Venizelos Square, with its Morosini fountain. A flight of stone steps to the right, behind the town bus station, is the most direct pedestrian route up to the centre of town – turn right at the top of the stairs.

Note Mainline buses heading for Rethymnon and Chania also pick up passengers at the roadside bus stop just outside the Chania Gate. Also, if travelling to Rethymnon or Chania from Mires on the Messara, you can alight at a main road stop on the outskirts of Heraklion and then cross the busy road to pick up the next mainline service going west. This saves having to go right into Heraklion. Enquire about this when you buy your ticket, and again with the bus conductor who will be familiar with this procedure.

Rethymnon (and bus station)
Rethymnon ('Reth-theem-no') old town is very compact. The bus station is about 15mins walking distance from the dock. A Venetian walled citadel, the Fortezza, dominates the town. Keeping this on your right, make your way southwest across town. The bus station, already relocated from a more central position, is once again too small (2007) and an extension, or perhaps another relocation, is planned. For the large supermarket on the main road take a flight of steps at the back of the building.

Note Although the 14.00 bus to Anoyeia stops to pick up passengers at the *plateia* Iroon (at the eastern end of the old town), the early morning departure to Anoyeia does not, as it is a school bus.

Arriving in the Evening
Flights may arrive after the last KTEL buses to trailhead destinations have left, and after town shops have closed. Immediate taxi transfers to the countryside save time, but mountain trekkers and campers arriving late will need to bring Euros in cash with them and start from villages with supermarkets (see individual route notes), or bring their own food supplies. Informal accommodation in mountain villages closes up at about 22.00. In general, from Chania airport allow 1hr 30mins for taxi journeys to Omalos or Askifou, and 2hrs 30mins to Anopolis. From Heraklion Airport allow 1hr 30mins for a taxi transfer to Zaros, and 1hr for Anoyeia.

Consult latest editions of touring guidebooks for accommodation recommendations but remember that hotels can be block-booked during the tourist season from May to September (see also Appendix 3). There are youth hostels in

A shepherd and EOS members at Katsiveli

Chania, Rethymnon and Heraklion. There is a town campsite along the coast west of Chania near Platanas (ask the bus driver for 'Chania camping').

In **Chania** hotels and rooming houses around the bus station are useful for early morning departures. There is a variety of accommodation along with restaurants, coffee bars and fast-food outlets on the waterfront and around the harbour area. In **Heraklion** finding mid- or budget-priced accommodation near the bus station is less easy; Hotel Rea (www.hotelrea.gr) in a street just behind the Historical Museum is offered as a suggestion. If you have booked into a small hotel, telephone ahead if your arrival is delayed so they know to wait up for you. **Rethymnon** old quarter, a semi-pedestrian precinct around the harbour, has rooming houses (and all other amenities). Unfortunately, late-night scooter riders tend not to respect its pedestrian-precinct status.

LOST LUGGAGE

What really matters on any walking trip are your boots and socks – **always** travel with them, or wear them on the plane. If you have to replace lost outdoor gear, Chania, Rethymnon and Heraklion have relevant shops (but choices are limited).

GETTING TO THE TRAILHEAD

Public Transport
KTEL (referred to in Crete as 'K'tel'), the Greek Public Bus Association, operates an extensive network nationwide. KTEL buses are cream and turquoise – learn to recognise them because there are lots of 'touristico' private tour buses that look similar from a distance. Recognising KTEL is less easy since 2004, as new buses in the fleet display a variety of cream and turquoise livery styles, together with advertisements for ANEK or MINOAN ferryboat lines.

Town bus stations have information kiosks and English is widely spoken. Latest timetable sheets (the schedule can change weekly) are available in the tourist season, and timetable boards list the busiest destinations in Greek and English. Departures are announced in Greek, English, and sometimes German, together with the bus number: for example 'Heraklion – bus no. 78'. Left luggage stores are rather informally run, so do not leave obvious 'valuables'. Opening hours are likely to be 07.00–20.00, but check. Note that staff may lock up for a few minutes at a time when they are out loading goods onto buses; unaccompanied parcel consignment is a KTEL service. You can only do this – for example with camping food supplies – if you arrange for someone (preferably a local) to meet the bus at the other end and collect it – and assure the staff that this is going to happen.

Small daysacks are allowed inside the bus; other luggage is put in the hold. Tell the conductor your destination as you load it. Carry your valuables with you and (as with air travel) remove items like karabiners from your rucksack. Thefts very occasionally occur at bus stations; expensive rucksacks may be coveted by certain other travellers, so keep an eye on the hold until it is closed for departure. Monitor the unloading of bags at busy bus stops en route, especially when the hold is full – innocent mistakes do sometimes occur. Note the conditions of your travel insurance concerning luggage in transit. As a rule losses must be reported to the relevant local police station within 24hrs, a very time-consuming procedure.

Village Bus
Depending on the distance from town, weekday services doubling as school buses may operate from bus stations rather than from specific villages. Typically, a village bus departs about 06.00 and returns from a village at about 07.00, and repeats that run in the early afternoon. During school holidays a different service may operate. Ask at information kiosks for services to villages not listed on the main board – they may run, but not on every day of the week and seldom at weekends. It is wise to be early for village buses as the driver may depart when he sees that all local passengers are aboard.

Chania Bus Station
Chania bus station is just a few minutes' walk from all other places useful to visitors. It has an authentic workaday-style restaurant (2007), open to about 15.00, and also a snack bar. As a rule, tickets should be bought inside the hall, although almost all buses carry both

A kafeneon *in Koustoyerako (Walks 6, 7)*

driver and conductor. The only return ticket issued is the KTEL special for the 'Samaria Gorge' round excursion.

Vrisses

Secondary roads branch south over the mountains from the main north coast road that links Heraklion, Rethymnon, Chania and Kastelli. In western Crete there is an important road junction at Vrisses ('Vree-siss'), since this is the road to Hora Sfakion and the Sfakiot south coast. The Vrisses bus stop is at a *kafeneon* in the main street west of the bridge. Vrisses supermarkets are open all week. Expect buses departing from Chania to arrive in Vrisses 40mins later, and from Rethymnon 25mins later.

Bus Routes

In western Crete the following year-round main bus routes are particularly useful.

Times listed are a guide only, since schedules could change. Services expand during the tourist season. On all runs note any Saturday and Sunday variations.

Chania – Hora Sfakion and Anopolis
Daily, except Orthodox Easter Sunday and Monday, and Christmas Day. Departs Chania at 14.00 and, going via Vrisses, serves Askifou, Imbros, Hora Sfakion (on the south coast) and terminates at Anopolis about 17.00. This bus returns from Anopolis in the early morning (see the Anopolis section) to arrive at Chania bus station by 09.15.

Depending on the season, other buses to the south coast depart 08.30 and 11.00 and return in the afternoon and early evening.

Note Hora Sfakion is called 'Sfakia' locally.

Chania – Souyia

At certain times (enquire) this service will include Koustoyerako as its terminus destination. The basic timetable (a midday departure from Chania about 13.45 and an 07.00 departure from Souyia) expands during the tourist season. Weekends vary. Note that there is no early Sunday morning departure from Souyia to Chania. For this, walk the E4 Trail footpath or take the ferryboat to Paleochora on Saturday, as there are all-day Sunday departures from that much larger village.

The Souyia–Chania 07.00 bus climbs to the watershed at Seli pass ('sell-LEE' – see Walk 8), where it connects, in the tourist season, with a bus to Xyloscala for the Samaria Gorge trailhead. This allows those who are staying at Souyia to walk down the gorge and return to Souyia by afternoon ferryboat

from Ay. Roumeli. These connections must be checked in advance since they may not operate on every day of the week.

Chania – Omalos and Xyloscala

This run needs special attention: an all-year village service to Lakki (on the Omalos road) terminates there outside the tourist season, when the Samaria Gorge is closed. However, when the gorge is being prepared for opening, normally by 1 May, a skeleton service reaches Xyloscala (see Omalos section). The service expands a little when the gorge is busy. Check the timetable (including return times) in advance at Chania bus station: people working on the Omalos route are uncertain of the changing timetable. KTEL buses pass through Omalos hamlet (also known as 'Omalos hotels') on the way to and from

Trekkers starting along the south end of the Zaranokefala crag (Trek 7a)

Xyloscala (3km), but not all drivers will stop there to pick up passengers. Certain Omalos proprietors run a convenient 'trailhead' mini-bus service for their guests and if there are spare seats they will sell tickets to non-guests.

KTEL sells a round-tour ticket for the Samaria Gorge excursion which covers Chania–Xyloscala and Hora Sfakion–Chania. The boat trip Ay. Roumeli to Hora Sfakion is separate (purchase tickets at Ay. Roumeli). On a single-day trip buy this ticket, with its reserved seat from Hora Sfakion and, during busy periods, buy it the night before. The KTEL round should give you more time in the gorge than an organised tour, although this depends on the boat schedule from Ay. Roumeli, which also varies according to demand. Eliminate these unwelcome pressures by staying overnight in Ay. Roumeli (Walk 2), where there are plenty of facilities. The first boat leaves Ay. Roumeli for Hora Sfakion (via Loutro) at about noon; journey time is 50mins.

Taxis

Taxis are metered according to a government-regulated charge per kilometre which – according to drivers – needs to be reviewed annually. If it is not, they may seek to charge what they calculate to be fair. Agree the fare in advance and/or check that the meter is turned on. Extra is chargeable for luggage, and up to four passengers are allowed (certain taxis hold seven). For a party of four, long-distance taxi transfers can be very economical.

In general, taxi drivers dread unmade roads because of the dust and the extra driving effort needed on many inland, winding mountain roads; some may avoid these jobs. In the countryside, if you arrange a lift in a private vehicle, expect the driver to drop you just outside your destination to avoid offending local taxi drivers. In Chania, the Roussos & Manouli Marianakis taxi agency (tel: 28210.92122, mob: 697403.4453) is familiar with walkers' needs in relation to remote trailheads and advance luggage transfers.

Taxi Availability
Chania
Chania airport, Chania bus station exit west side, *Plateia* 1866 east side, *Plateia* Makris Kritis west side.

Rethymnon
Taxis regularly drive by the entrance to the bus station and the main road above it; unfortunately (2007) there is not enough space for a taxi rank.

Heraklion
There is a taxi rank and shelter to the right (west) of the Arrivals exit at the airport. Taxis regularly pass by the two bus stations, Knossos archaeological site, and the city Archaeological Museum.

SHOPPING AND ACCOMMODATION

Shopping in Towns
Whilst shops in the countryside stay open most of the time, in towns there are midday closing hours, three late-night shopping days and two early-closing days: Tuesday, Thursday and Friday 08.30–13.30 and 17.00–20.00; Monday

On the ascent of Gingilos the path turns into the re-entrant, heading for the rocky pinnacles (Walk 3)

and Wednesday 08.30–13.30; Saturday 08.30–15.00. On Sundays only patisseries and tourist souvenir shops will be open.

Chania
Including Sundays, a small fruit and vegetable wagon may be found outside the bus station, northeast corner. A farmers' market (and cheap clothing) operates on Saturday morning in Minos Street beside the old city wall, east side, and on Wednesday mornings in Solomou about three blocks south from the KTEL bus station; anyone will direct you since Chaniots are very keen on home-grown produce. All food supplies are available in the Agora and the supermarket opposite its west-facing entrance. Convenient to the bus station is a branch of Inka supermarkets on the west side of *Plateia* 1866.

Karistiyannis has a selection of mountaineering equipment as does a 'survival' shop opposite, in Skalidi, one block west of *Plateia* 1866. A cheap clothing shop can be found opposite the north entrance of the bus station. A plastics shop that sells sheet polythene by the metre (camping mattress protection) is found opposite the bus station pedestrian entrance, northeast corner. Mountain trekkers are advised to bring their own cooking pans since cheap lightweight pans are not easy to find nowadays. For tools, gas stoves and cylinders there are various household goods shops near the bus station, such as Ziroukakis in Sfakianaki. A foreign books and newspapers shop is near the corner of Skalidi with Halidon. Also at the top of Halidon there is an ATM and several money-change agents. A short way down on the right the bookshop

Pelekanakis stocks contour maps and foreign books. There are various travel agents for flights and ferryboat reservations in the downtown area (enquire).

The Tourist Information and Tourist Police office is in the Town Hall, a modern building in Kydonias, east of *Plateia 1866*. The National Bank of Greece, opposite the Agora, has an ATM; the GPO and OTE (public telephones) are close by in Janakaki Street. OTE operates telephone booths: street kiosks sell phone cards, as well as stamps – postal charges are similar throughout the EU. Germanos, just west of *Plateia* Makris Kritis (Battle of Crete Square) deals with mobile phone requirements as does Vodafone, in Skalidi.

Walking sticks, or *katsounas*, shepherds' crooks, traditional to Sfakia, are on sale in souvenir shops in or near Halidon. When choosing one, turn it upside down to check the length from the handle. Even if cut down, it should be a minimum of 5cm (2ins) above the waist to be useful on descents.

Heraklion

A range of similar shops, including a fruit and vegetable street market, are found in and around the 'honeypot' downtown area of Dikiosinis Street and Plateia Venizelou (Morosini fountain).

Rethymnon

In the old quarter head for the Porta Guora (Plateia Martyron) to find a useful bunch of shops: household goods, fruit and vegetables, a bakery and a bookshop nearby stocking maps and foreign language books. **Note** Be aware that shops and other commercial enterprises in all the Cretan downtown areas can change from year to year. This is partly

Chania: the old harbour

Roussies, showing the cistern and stone-built shelter hut (Trek 8)

due to proprietors reaching retirement age and partly to rapidly changing customer requirements.

Shopping in the Countryside
With the exception of bakeries (which close on Sundays) village shops stay open every day, and close at about 22.00. In **western Crete**, Sfakia district has several village bakeries, which together supply the busy south coast with its massive daily needs. This could change when Hora Sfakion opens a large new bakery (under construction in 2007). The boat service transports fresh food supplies daily from Hora Sfakion to Loutro and Ay. Roumeli. Currently there is no pharmacy in the district, but village supermarkets stock non-prescription essentials. For **Mount Ida,** villages of the foothills all have grocery shops although, to the south, Mires may be the

only place large enough to support a pharmacy. The larger villages of the **Lassithi Plain** all have grocery shops, but Tzermiado is the only one to have banks, ATMs and a pharmacy.

Accommodation in the Countryside
Tourist accommodation is inspected, graded and price-regulated by the Ministry of Tourism. Proprietors are permitted to drop a price grade at their discretion; in the countryside there is certainly a better chance of this during non-busy periods. Discounts for large groups may be offered. Prices in rooming houses ranged from €20–35 in 2007. All the walking areas featured in this guide offer family-run lodging houses ('rooms') or hotels (or both) with hot water, so long as sunshine heats rooftop solar panels. If it does not, hot water supplies will sustain for one further day

(depending on demand). Certain hotels, such as those that are open in the winter, are equipped to switch to alternative power if rain sets in for several days.

Note Whilst much of the following information applies to the Cretan countryside as a whole, please also see relevant chapters for notes specific to Mount Ida and Lassithi.

In and around the White Mountains walkers on a continuous route need not necessarily make reservations, because it is unlikely that all village accommodation will be full at any one time. Omalos hotels, for the Samaria Gorge, could be full on certain days of the week with group bookings, but the hamlet also has rooming houses.

If your overnight accommodation does not provide meals, there is normally somewhere nearby which does. In villages where customer turnover is not continuous, landladies produce simple home-cooked meals to order. The choice will be limited, but the food will be wholesome – eat what is on offer. Travelling food vans supply villages with fresh produce to supplement what is home-grown. Order chickpeas, beans or lentils in advance, but spaghetti and cheese or omelette and pork grills with chips are almost always available. Salad, fruit and vegetables vary in availability. Homemade wine is locally preferred, but if none other is available your own wine bought elsewhere would not offend in an informal village *taverna* (but ask). In mountain villages sheep's milk yoghurt (all milk is boiled) is made in the spring. Breakfast, not usually included, will be bread and jam, tea or coffee, or 'mountain tea' (made from local herbs).

Fresh orange juice, commercially made yoghurt, eggs and local honey may also be available.

Since the mountains are unfrequented, except by shepherds, 'wild camping' is not a problem. However, remember not to get in the way of shepherds and their work. Cretan sheep move around in close-knit flocks. They are gentle, nervous creatures and will be afraid to come to drink (which they should do) if they see something unusual beside the cistern or on the footpath.

Noise Pollution

Thanks to traffic, two-stroke engines, live music, revellers, and pre-dawn garbage collections, Cretan towns are noisy at night. Coastal villages, and some mountain villages, tend to be free of church clocks, and traffic noise in the countryside ceases quite early. However, this is likely to be replaced by a cacophony of barking dogs, crowing roosters and, in the autumn, chainsaws by day. In general, loss of tranquillity due to the modern faster pace of life is fully acknowledged by all Cretans.

Backpackers could think they have solved it, camping out in the mountains, but as sheep graze after dark when it is cool flocks may pass back and forth all night, ringing their bells. To be sure of the rare luxury of silence, aim for the high mountains in the spring before the sheep arrive, or in the late autumn, after they have gone.

Mountain Refuges

Other than Kallergi refuge, above the Samaria Gorge in the Lefka Ori (Walk 4), which is run as a commercial enterprise,

Crossing the Gougoutha tou Spathiou: nearing Stavrou Seli pass (Trek 2)

mountain refuges are operated by the Hellenic Alpine Association (EOS), which has branches in Chania, Rethymnon and Heraklion. The refuges are unwardened, but kitted out with bunks, mattresses, blankets (take a sheet liner), kitchens (bottled gas), washrooms and wood stoves, and so have to be kept locked. These refuges can be useful for groups – perhaps those based in Cretan towns – but otherwise booking arrangements (with local EOS branches) are not convenient for visitors who are travelling about.

The EOS of Chania club premises (tel: 28210.44647) is in the basement of the same block as the Olympic Airways office opposite the Municipal Gardens. It is usually open on weekdays 19.00–22.00. In the **Lefka Ori** the refuges are Volikas above Kambi (Walk 13, Trek 2), Takis Houliopoulos near Katsiveli (see Mountain Treks 4, 5 and 6) and Tavri near Niato (Walk 30). On **Psiloritis**, Rethymnon branch (tel: 28310.23666, Tuesdays after 21.00) runs Toumbotos Prinos above Kouroutes (Walk P10), and Heraklion branch, 53 Dikiosinis Avenue (tel: 2810.227609), operates Prinos above Avgeniki, and the refuge above Limnakarou (Walk L5) in the **Lassithi Mountains**. Nowadays, Greek mountaineers visit mountain ranges worldwide and local refuges tend to be used, if at all, for club meets in the winter.

For details on backpacking and camping in the Cretan mountains see below.

GENERAL INFORMATION, SKILLS AND EQUIPMENT

Public Holidays

Orthodox Easter weekend (April or May, dates vary each year) is the most important holiday in Greece. All public transport is crowded as people visit relatives around the country. Other holidays include Independence Day on 25 March (town parades) and l May, 15 August, 28 October. Main route bus services will operate. Tourist shops and village shops will stay open.

Time Difference

Greece is on Eastern European Time.
• Summer: GMT plus 3hrs
• Winter: GMT plus 2hrs.

The 'Language Barrier'

Like all Greeks, Cretans communicate easily with foreigners. Older people involved in the tourism business have learnt foreign words and phrases by ear. Nowadays English is seen as important for getting on in life and is taught in schools and widely spoken at least by the younger generation as well as by the many returnee emigrants from the US, Canada and Australia.

For travellers, prices are what really matter. Shopkeepers not fluent in foreign languages will write down price totals for tourists. To avoid misunderstandings use a notebook and pen for this purpose. Almost all place names are written in both Greek and English. A small dictionary is useful if you are travelling in the countryside.

Weather

The island of Crete may be a Mediterranean beach holiday destination, but it does not have a particularly 'easy' climate. Extremes of temperature – including enervating heatwaves – high humidity, aggravating hot or cold winds, heavy rain and penetrating dampness, and days – or months – of snow in the mountains are all characteristic of the yearly round.

During spring and autumn temperatures for walking are usually pleasant but conditions likely to be unsettled. From April to mid-June it could be cold and wet, fresh and sunny, or warm, overcast and humid – all within the space of 10 days. Normally by June temperatures, including sea temperatures, have warmed up considerably and should last until the end of October (outside of autumn deluges). In midsummer daytime temperatures of 28–33°C (80–90°F) are normal, and heatwaves can reach more than 40°C (104°F).

Heatwaves are very difficult to cope with, as even just before dawn there is little respite. Look for accommodation with rooms (and balconies) orientated north, east or west, rather than south. Nowadays many hotels and rooming houses on the coast, and in the towns, provide air-conditioning units. The high mountains get breezes – plan high-level walks (perhaps not Walk 43 because it is in pine forest and so vulnerable to fires) and long midday breaks.

For campers on the **south coast of Sfakia**, the Samaria Gorge river estuary beside Ay. Roumeli offers sea breezes and shady pine trees and, in a good year,

A group heading for Zaranokefala stocks up with water in the Potamos Valley (Trek 7, 7a)

freshwater bathing. The Omalos Plain and the mountain villages of Askifou, Imbros and Anopolis are cooler at night.

Mount Ida has no coastline although Matala, a scenically interesting resort on the Bay of Messara, is within easy reach by bus from Mires. Either side of Matala Bay walkers can find crags and unfrequented walking terrain. However, inland at Zaros – where there are gushing aqueducts, a mid-priced hotel with a pool, shady trees and a pleasant freshwater lake (for fish – no swimming) on a cul-de-sac – could be the best place to linger during a heatwave (unless you have already escaped to high level). **Lassithi** has always been a refuge from the summer heat and several villages of the plateau offer accommodation. New building developments may result in a hotel with a pool.

Rainfall

December, January and February are rated the wettest months, but three-day periods of rain, and snow blizzards above 1000m, may occur as late as mid-June. At summer's end the hot weather should break in stages as from late September, but this can vary. After bursts of rain, fine weather should return, making October a good month for walking. Sea temperatures remain warm until after the second period of autumn rain. Daylight hours are shorter, but sufficient for a good day out. Snow may cover the mountains from the end of November; the thaw should be well advanced by mid-April.

Wind

Crete lies in the path of various winds that can change the weather in half a day. A long-lasting warm south wind in spring will thaw the snow too quickly, resulting in quite spectacular natural erosion in the gorges. Similarly, localised flash flooding from thunderstorms sometimes occurs and this too, causes massive erosion. The mountains can attract fierce gales, even in summer. Strong billowing gusts hit below the knee and toss you over. Do as the locals do – wait out the worst of the storm since, with any luck, it should ease in half a day. Alternatively, in summer, ordinary northwesterlies cool the mountains, making trekking routes and summit ascents more attractive than low-level walks.

Mist

When the *notos* or the *sirocco* – warm winds from the south – reach mountains recently cooled by a north wind, or vice versa, a period of up to three days of mist and rain may follow. (Northern slopes are more prone to mist.) In the high mountains, always assess your next day's route and the whereabouts of the next shelter and water source. From June to October shepherds' huts may be in use. Some shepherds are more sociable and welcoming than others, but all would make space for walkers in bad weather.

The Winter Months

Although Askifou, Anopolis and Hora Sfakion are inhabited all year, many coastal facilities in the **White Mountains** will close after October. Building construction and maintenance goes on at this time, so some facilities need to remain open. However, for accommodation it would be wise to expect to camp.

Depending on conditions, the Gorge of Samaria National Park will close to the public from mid- to late October, and will

On the path to the Katheros Plain in April: a short-lived springtime snowfall has transformed the landscape (Walk L4)

reopen on 1 May (but this, too, can vary by a week either way). The New Omalos Hotel (www.neos-omalos.gr) is open at weekends in winter. Although November is a good month for off-season walking in Crete, it is also the kri-kris' mating time, which can be dangerous because they may disturb loose rocks on the high crags. Whatever the regulations of this National Park, the gorge will always be tempting to walkers as a north–south through route and it is not fenced off. Omalos and Ay. Roumeli people are very knowledgeable about the gorge and its hazards; listen to their advice. Conditions in the gorge can change at any time, but it is seriously impassable when winter snow starts to thaw. Flash flooding due to thunderstorms is now a potential danger all year. Do not start up (or down) it unless you are fully prepared to retrace your steps. The best secondary trail has long been closed to the public as a result of the death of one lone off-season walker who had the misfortune to break his leg.

The **Mount Ida** trailhead villages featured in this guide are all workaday places and at least some facilities will be open all year. The road to the Nida Plain will normally be under snow in winter.

On the **Lassithi Plain** many people escape the winter by moving down to their 'second homes' on the coastal plain. In Ay. Georgios *Pension* Dias remains open, as do some facilities in Tzermiado, and no doubt at least one *kafeneon* in the other villages. The same will apply to Kritsa but Ay. Nikolaos, like all coastal resorts, will be closed up and primarily engaged in maintenance works during the winter. Selakano closes up from December to February. All mountain roads could be blocked with snow at times.

Water

Thanks to winter snowfall in the mountains, towns and villages throughout Crete are supplied with good water from underground sources. Tap water is normally safe to drink, although it may come via a rooftop tank rather than the mains supply. Town supplies are chlorinated. Bottled water is widely available. Route notes in this guide mention shepherds' cisterns, many of which hold palatable water. In the high mountains, after snow has thawed, nothing is more important than the whereabouts of cisterns and springs, and it is useful to learn how to find and take care of this water. You may also be able to collect a litre or two on a waterproof sheet when it rains, helpful if you are delayed by mist.

Thanks to the specialist skills of those who made them, many very old well shafts and cisterns still function throughout Crete, despite earth tremors and the ravages of time. An old cistern may be topped with stone barrel-vaulting (or just a wooden log), blending so well into the surroundings that you may miss it as you pass by. This type is most often sited on small flat plains of alluvial soil (dolines), which provide a run-off for rain and snowmelt. Modern cisterns are of reinforced concrete with or without a cover (which may be locked), and the most recent are large concrete-aproned constructions, blasted into the hillsides. The Psiloritis and Lassithi ranges have more freshwater springs than the Lefka Ori, where

Aravanes spring in autumn (Walk P8)

man-made cisterns for collecting rainwater have been built to substitute.

Drawing up water Always carry 5m of lightweight nylon line and, ideally, a camping pan that doubles as a bucket. Remove your sunglasses or spectacles to a safe place (never on the ground – someone will step on them) and secure the line to your hand or foot before you drop the bucket (especially if you are using the shepherds' bucket). Some cisterns are very deep and it may be impossible to retrieve anything dropped in (a large fish hook, obtainable in coastal resorts, could be your only chance). Up-end the bucket and let it drop down square on, to hit the water face down. It should then collect water as it sinks. If it does not, try again. Shepherds have the better knack of raising water without dropping the bucket face down, but this takes practice. If you use the shepherds' bucket, do not allow it

to overfill unless you can raise this heavy weight easily – this is not the moment to wrench your back.

If you do not have a bucket, form one by putting a plastic-bag-wrapped stone into a carrier bag and, using your length of line, lower this down the well. Water can be strained through a handkerchief or cotton scarf, then filtered, or boiled, or drunk straight off – use your own judgement. However, as worldwide travel and recreational use increases, contamination becomes more likely. Droppings from (chemically treated) sheep may be around the collection area. Some water is clear and tastes good; some tastes awful. Vegetation near the cistern may have unattractively coloured the run-off, but in these dry mountains water of *any* sort is precious. Replace the logs, or other devices, put there to stop animals from falling in, and re-secure the shepherds' bucket if you have used it. Buckets are tied up because strong winds can occur at any time.

Be careful not to contaminate or waste any water. If supplies dry out too soon flocks must be taken down to be fed on (stinted) supplies of purchased fodder. If a water trough is empty, goats will let you know if they are thirsty more readily than sheep. They emerge from the shade and look at you with big, pleading eyes. Unless the place is obviously very remote, give them no more than a bucket or two, in case the shepherd is saving this particular cistern for supplies later in the year.

Shepherds may call any water supply simply 'nero' ('neh-RO'), so you may not know whether to look out for a well, cistern or spring. They will warn you by saying 'it isn't good' ('then ee-neh ka-lo')

if it is only fit for animals, in which case you would have to boil it thoroughly.

Water allowance In hot weather and on backpacking treks make a point of replenishing your body reservoir, like a camel, before you set off. Start drinking water, or other liquids, from the time you get up. Supplement your morning tea or coffee with glasses of water. During the day, top up your body reservoir with 100ml gulps, rather than small sips to alleviate a dry mouth. If this is an uncomfortable problem, suck a small (smooth) fruit stone or similar to keep producing saliva in your mouth.

Backpackers especially need to rehydrate in the evening. For an overnight camp between water sources, allow a minimum of three litres per person. This has to cover dinner, breakfast, hot drinks, ordinary drinking, teeth cleaning and minimal washing, so there

The path in the Samaria Gorge crosses the river in many places (Walk 2)

will not be much left for your start next morning. Plan to stop at the next water source for a big brew up.

Along with your water supply, plan your food. For example, a staple like pasta needs more water (and gas cylinder time) for cooking than couscous. (Couscous is seldom found locally – bring your own if you want it.) In remote places aim to keep 1 litre of water in reserve in case of mishaps or delays. If you are short of water do not eat as this draws on body moisture reserves – being hydrated is much more important than being well fed. Plan gas cylinder supplies to cover daytime brew ups or water boiling as well as cooking.

Shelter
Mitata

Shepherds' huts, variously called *mitata* or *koumoi*, feature throughout the Cretan mountains. Pre-1940s huts are made of drystone walling and corbelling. These workstation complexes look like piles of rocks in the landscape, or on the skyline, as they are often located overlooking views of the trail. Some *mitata* are still used during the grazing season (about mid-June to mid-October) as shepherds' overnight shelters, or fodder storage huts, but off-season, with no desirable possessions inside – old tools, old clothes and perhaps old food – they are often left unlocked, perhaps in case passers-by need shelter. After the winter interiors are a real mess, but they can be cleaned up and left in a better state when you depart.

Note that disused *mitata* may be structurally unsound; approach these interiors with care. *Mitata* are usually (but not always) near a water supply.

Whether abandoned or not, they remain the property of the families, or the descendents, of those who built them. Most grazing areas are now accessed by road, but the old huts may still be used at times, especially as shelter from the midday heat in summer.

Caves

Potholes are more common than caves; there are few accessible open-sided caves that provide shelter. As a rule, those that do exist are much used by (flea-ridden) sheep and goats eager for shade.

Types of Pathways

Wherever possible, walks in this guide follow footpaths or mule tracks rather than roads.

Unsurfaced shepherds' roads

These link shepherding villages to traditional grazing pastures in the mountains. They enable shepherds to pursue a modern lifestyle: instead of staying up in the mountains for long periods, especially during the milking season, they can drive up in the early morning and bring down the day's milk yield to the village dairy in the evening. Presumably mountain-road-cutting will continue in line with EU funding for this type of development. On south-facing barren hillsides new roads take about 40 years to blend into the landscape, but in places where rainfall is higher this process is much faster; any disused tracks are soon overgrown and so become pleasant walking routes.

Major road building in the Cretan mountains includes a south–north road under construction in the **Lefka Ori**, bit by bit from Anopolis. It may be designed

Looking east on the climb to Vitsinela pass (Walk P17)

to access the main high-level grazing pastures around Katsiveli (Trek 8), Livada and Potamos, and to provide a link to the Omalos Plain, with a branch to meet the Theriso shepherds' road (Trek 1). However, for many years it has terminated at Roussies and its extension no doubt depends on various factors. Many Cretans, aware of beach areas already 'ruined', regret this type of project. The Lefka Ori central massif, which is roughly circular in shape, is the last wilderness area in Greece yet to be crossed by a road. On **Psiloritis** the 18km road from Anoyeia to the Nida Plain is surfaced throughout, and new road access to the Amoudara Valley, southwest of the plain (Walks P3 and P15), was made in 2005. In 2004 an unsurfaced road linking the **Lassithi** and **Kathoros Plains** was completed. This forms a direct road connection between Kritsa and Lassithi.

Roads between villages

Naturally, these roads have qualified for asphalting before the shepherds' roads and it is now unusual to find one that is unsurfaced. Taxi drivers are relieved, but walkers must now find alternative routes.

Cobbled mule tracks

In their heyday during the Turkish occupation (1669–1898) these *kalderimia* served villages, terracing and grazing pastures. Nowadays most of these old trails, which so delightfully followed the lie of the land, are in a broken-up state. Sections with gradients suitable for vehicles have often been replaced by new roads. This policy spares mule tracks routed up steep ravines, or crags (for example Walks 12, 41 and 47) but these, in turn, are subject to weather erosion.

Old roads in Greece were always made with zigzags at gradients suitable for pack animals. Therefore, if you are following this type of trail and find yourself climbing straight up or down a steep hill check the route again, since you may well have missed the path. Two examples of old mule tracks still in practical use, and in need of repair, are found on Walk 41 and Trek 7. The Zaranokefala location is too remote and almost disused nowadays, but Sellouda might eventually qualify (assuming it is not replaced by a road). Hopefully (for walkers) the shoreline is too unstable to make such a project worthwhile.

Footpaths

These are footpaths used by local, or recreational, walkers, as well as animals. Nowadays many old paths have become overgrown and disused. Sheep or goat paths are small paths made by these animals, such as those seen on large scree slopes. They may be unsafe for walkers. 'Splintered paths' are formed by flocks of sheep and goats as they pass up and down the mountainsides; they may also split a main footpath into several small paths.

The E4 Trail

This is the European long-distance walking Route No. 4. It starts in Gibraltar and goes via Andalucia, southern France, eastern Europe including Bulgaria, the Pindos mountains of northern Greece and the Peloponese, and ends (before continuing in Cyprus) on Crete's eastern shore at the archaeological site of Kato Zakros. In Greece the E4 Trail (*Epsilon Tessera*) is all too often routed along roads more suitable for mountain bikers than walkers. Also, whilst some footpath sections are a delight, others involve crags and are quite hazardous; there is no basic standard of safety, and you must use your own judgement. All you can be really sure of is that a waymarked trail is a walking route of some sort.

In Crete the E4 starts at Kastelli and takes in several of the less-visited archaeological sites on its journey east. Although the main trail follows the mountainous backbone of Crete, Cretan branches of the Hellenic Alpine Association (EOS) have also designated good route 'variations' either along the coast, or as branches that lead to the main trail (see contour maps).

The E4 is waymarked with aluminium yellow and black poles supplemented in places with diamond-shaped paint-enamelled aluminium signs nailed to trees, or simply with paint-marked rocks. Unfortunately, winter storms strip the poles, shotgun owners use them as targets, souvenir hunters remove the signs, and sheep and goats tramp over the painted rocks. Positioning trail markers needs a practised understanding of sightlines, and of other people's thought processes, so that getting it exactly right is not easy. Even where sightlines have been carefully considered, route choices at possible path junctions may still be 'left open'. Relying on the waymarks to show you the route can be stressful and frustrating, although in some places it is difficult to manage without them. Even so, try not to be deskilled by the E4! With your contour map, compass and altimeter – and perhaps GPS (with the Anavasi maps) – take time to consider

E4 Trail: Nida Plain from the ridge above the taverna and car park in autumn (Walk P12)

the lie of the land, looking for likely footpath or mule track routes, as you would have to do if the E4 Trail did not exist. Hopefully, when it appears, a marker will come as welcome confirmation that you have got it right.

Walking Technique

The mountains of Crete are very rugged. Footpaths are endlessly rocky, obliging you to concentrate at almost every step. Tripping when facing downhill, and stepping on a rock which then rolls over, are the most common hazards. You will land on a thorn bush if you are lucky, otherwise it will be on rocks. Don't let this happen: be patient. Adjust your walking style – learn to lift your feet and discipline yourself to slow down immediately you feel yourself stumbling. It may be galling if your companions are faster than you, but accept this and stick to your own safe pace. In this way you will be a competent walker. Shepherds use *katsounas* (long sticks) in the mountains. Buy one or bring a trekking pole with you or – even better – a pair of poles.

Exploring

If you go exploring – especially in and around the many gorges – be aware that weather erosion has reduced many old footpaths, which may be marked on maps yet unmaintained for decades, to a dangerous or even non-existent state – BE CAREFUL.

E4 Trail: damaged wire handrail on the 'horizontal' slab of rock (Walk 6b)

Rock scrambling The walks in this guide do not involve scrambling unless this is mentioned, but as a reminder the basic rules are:
- do not explore **down** unless you are absolutely sure you can get back up again, and
- do do not explore **up** unless you can get down again.

Note Scrambling (unroped) is the most dangerous form of mountaineering.

Backpacking and Camping

In wilderness situations the loss of any item will be inconvenient. After any stop during the day always look behind as you leave to check that you have not forgotten anything.

Sleeping bags Many lodging houses have easy-care nylon blankets that are hardly warm enough in early spring or when rain sets in. In case of this (and for general mountain use) bring thermal underwear. Similarly, for indoor use, a one-season bag or a warm liner can be a welcome (but not essential) luxury.

For camping in the mountains, a full-length-zipped three-season bag is the good all-rounder. However, from July to September, a one-season bag may suit even at altitude, especially if it is upgraded with a Gortex 'bivi' bag. In the warmer months nylon materials are uncomfortable: bring a cotton or silk inner liner. This is also useful against insects, although not as good as a mosquito net (see Insects and Other Hazards section below).

Mattresses Lightest and most comfortable of the insulation mats are Cascade

Designs' Z-Rest and Ridgerest. Self-inflatables are greatly at risk from thorns and thistles. Protect your expensive mattress with a piece of tough poly-thene DPM (damp-proof membrane) undersheet (from any builders' sup-plies). This also works as a shower and washing mat and, supported with rocks, makes a bowl for clothes washing (do not contaminate any water trough with soap).

Tents In rocky terrain, the more self-sup-porting your tent, the more convenient it is likely to be.

'Bivi' bags On two-day treks – with one overnight out – a non-breathable poly-thene survival bag will do. On longer-range treks you need a breathable 'bivi' bag. Camping with a 'bivi' bag in the rain is not easy – an umbrella is useful. You will view a squalid *mitato* interior, overhang or cave, in a new light if mist and rain sets in for three days.

Cooking stoves Small gas stoves that take the fixed, non-valved 190g gas cylinder are popular throughout Greece. Greek-manufactured cylinders are avail-able in remote places, and Camping Gaz C206 supplies are available in towns. Note that valved (removable and resealable) gas cylinders are not avail-able, and also that you cannot take gas cylinders (or liquid fuel of any sort) on an aircraft. One 190g gas cylinder is reckoned to last for about 2hrs 30mins, but this depends on conditions – use a windshield. Three slim-profile stoves grouped together are good for melting snow in a large pan. The Camping Gaz

C206 stove head needs checking for tightness each time before it is lit. Practise cylinder changing in advance of your trip. Carry a 'last resort' set of matches encased with their striker in a waterproof container.

Cooking pans Wherever drinking water has to be boiled or filtered, or carried from source, a cooking pan of minimum 1 litre capacity is an essential tool. It's good to have your own bucket for the cisterns. A loop-handled billycan is the best choice for this although this type of cooking pan is currently out of fashion.

Rucksacks/Daysacks In summer, back-packers might avoid specialist alpinists' sacks, since they are designed to fit close to the back. If you are caught in a storm without a waterproof liner, use your 'bivi' bag for this job.

Water bottles On mountain treks your main water bottle needs to be 100 per-cent reliable. The easy-fill, lid-attached, wide-mouth, easy-clean, transparent, non-tasting, high-impact Lexan 1 litre Nalgene or Coleman water bottle must be the best design yet. Bladder-type bot-tles in new condition, with drinking tubes, are useful for immediate use, but secure the mouthpiece with adhesive tape and fix it facing upright – you can lose the lot if it siphons out, which on some routes is a risk not worth taking. Those on a budget could use fizzy drink bottles as these are very tough (mineral water bottles may split if dropped).

Blisters and first aid Zinc oxide plaster applied directly to the skin (check first

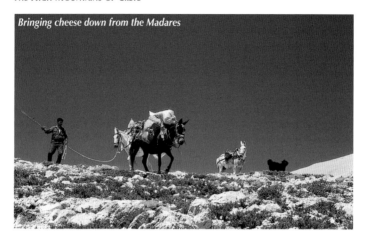

Bringing cheese down from the Madares

for allergy) protects against foot burn, rubbing and chafing, the skin conditions that precede blisters. Unlike moleskin, zinc oxide can be removed (with care) overnight. Most importantly, if blisters do develop, proprietary dressings such as Compeed will enable you to continue walking. On the mountain, a get-you-home aid is sheep or goats' wool as it makes resilient padding – but not next to broken skin. It is always wise to take your own knee and ankle support tubes. Include a menthol inhaler (or similar) in your first aid kit in case a thick head cold is going around, and also travel sickness and hay fever pills if you usually need these.

Litter
There is an abundance of product packaging in Greece. As recreational walkers, set an example and bring all your rubbish out of the mountains and countryside. Villagers recognise the problem

– even if visiting Cretan town-dwellers apparently do not – and most villages are supplied with large rubbish trolleys. Win local approval by putting your rubbish in the village bins. Women should note that buried sanitary materials will be dug up by animals. Boat service notices ask passengers not to throw litter into the sea.

Daysack and Trekking Essentials
'Daysack essentials' are contingency plan items that each individual hill-walker should carry in case of sudden changes in the weather, changes of plan, or unfortunate mishaps. Hikers of the Sierra Club of California neatly call these 'The Twelve Essentials':

- rain shell clothing
- spare warm layer
- warm hat
- gloves
- water bottle
- spare food

- map
- compass
- torch
- whistle
- pocket knife
- survival bag.

Think this through as: spare clothing, sustenance, navigation aids, means of attracting attention, a minimum of one useful tool, and shelter. Mobile phones are another means of attracting attention (see below).

In Crete take daysack essentials on all summit ascents and mountain walks. Whatever the day looks like when you set off, unpredictable winds can bring mist and heavy rain by the evening. You might extend the list to include the following items:

- blister kit
- knee and ankle support tubes
- sunglasses (your hat counts as an 'everyday' item)
- sun cream
- Greek–English dictionary or vocabulary list.

For communal use, also carry a water kit (see section on Water above), which comprises 5m of string and a plastic carrier bag, a purification outfit or a brew-up kit including matches. Campers note that soft cleaning sponges, if left out overnight, are stolen by animals that live in burrows. Take something to do, or read, so that if thick mist develops you can wait patiently and confidently until it clears.

If most 'essentials' seem a fiddly nuisance, parcel them up into one separate stuff bag and belay this to the inside of your rucksack. Secure your trekking pole(s) to a clip on your rucksack whenever you are not using it (them) to avoid leaving it behind. Trekking poles are most easily forgotten when you are travelling by bus.

On Grade A and low-level Grade B walks, especially during warmer months, you will need fewer items:

- long-sleeved shirt (or rain shell)
- spare warm layer (thermal vest or T-shirt in a plastic bag)
- water bottle
- spare food
- map
- whistle
- sunglasses
- sun cream
- blister kit
- knee and ankle support tubes
- pocket knife
- cotton scarf (always useful).

If walking with a group, do not automatically rely on others. Make sure that you understand the itinerary and know the name of your destination. Carry your own supply of Euros in cash. Sometimes a series of unlucky coincidences can separate you from your companions.

Mobile phones/telephones

Germanos and Vodafone phone shops, with English-speaking staff, can be found in towns throughout Greece. In Greece a mobile phone is called a 'kinny-toe'. Your phone will work in many places in the Cretan mountains, but not all; you will certainly be out of contact when in a gorge. Greece has two-pin EU-style socket outlets. Suitable

Lassithi: milking sheep

charger leads (weight 5oz) are obtainable from phone shops. *Taverna* owners are usually pleased to allow you to plug in during your visit.

The National Telephone service (land line) is called 'OTE'. Phone booths use phone cards, and these can be bought at pavement kiosks. It is useful to have one as an alternative if you intend to make local calls. Most villages have phone booths.

Compass, Altimeter and GPS

Magnetic declination in Greece is zero. Most commercially available contour maps are small scale and not detailed. You will need the additional aid of a compass – preferably a sighting compass – for taking bearings off identifiable mountain summits, passes or plains, and to check the direction of valleys, ravines and paths. An altimeter is also useful in the moun-

tains. Altitude levels listed in the route notes are approximate partly because it is seldom possible to reset the device accurately; a GPS will do better. Maps published by Anavasi (see below) incorporate the new metric grid Greek Geodetic Reference System (GGRS 87) which can

GEODETIC REFERENCES

User Grid

Longitude of origin	+24.00000E
Scale factor	0.9996
False easting	+500000
False northing	+0.0

User Map Datum

Dx	-200
Dy	74
Dz	246
Da	0
Df	0

Nida: 'the Partisan of Peace', photographed in 1992

be added to a GPS as set out in the box.

For final route planning, note the daylight hours as soon as you arrive. By the end of October (when clocks go back) there are 10hrs of daylight.

Contour Maps

Part of the challenge of mountain walking in Crete is that you have to adjust to working with maps that are either small scale, or far less detailed than Ordnance Survey maps. This obliges you to take more time examining the lie of the land.

'Walking' maps show contours, footpaths and the E4 Trail. Contours and mountain summits should be accurate as these are based on up-to-date military surveys or computer-generated technology linked to satellite information. Therefore, as a priority, pay attention to the contours. All other information can vary from map to map. 'Footpaths' may

be district boundaries or notional watercourses and new access roads may be drawn in the wrong place, or not yet built. Budget about £8 for a map.

For the White Mountains, the Sfakiot coast and Mount Ida, four GPS-compatible 1:25,000 scale maps are published (2006) by **Anavasi** of Athens: Greece-Crete, Topo 25 series, scale 1:25,000, No. 10.11 Sfakia, No. 10.12 Pachnes, No. 10.13 Souyia and No. 11.14 Mount Idha. These are a welcome addition but, like other maps, seldom mark cliffs and crags, and some older, unfrequented footpaths and mule tracks (such as Trek 1), springs, cisterns and *mitata* are omitted. This may make certain routes more attractive to those who like to explore for themselves.

Psiloritis is covered by No. 11.14 Mount Idha, but this map does not fully cover Walks P7 and P17. For these you

Avasamai pass from Asfendami, October (Walk L5a)

also need the **Harms Verlag** 'Touring Map with footpaths and the E4 Trail' scale 1:100,000 which is one of the best available, and very useful for back-up reference. Map No. 1 Western Crete covers the White Mountains and Mount Ida, No. 2 Eastern Crete covers Lassithi and Sitia.

A good and more economically priced map sometimes available locally is **Efstathiadis** 'with footpaths' scale 1:79,000 Map No. 1 Chania and No. 3 Heraklion. Less detailed is **Petrakis** 1996 'Trekking and Road Map' scale 1:100,000 No. 1 Chania and No. 2 Rethymnon. The **Freytag & Berndt** Kreta-Crete scale 1:50,000 map and text book, which covers bits of specific walking areas, has its uses but on its own is not the best choice because it does not allow you to identify or take bearings off distant features. It is probably (currently) best for Lassithi, and can be used in conjunction

with the Harms-Verlag 1:100,000 map (of which it is a direct enlargement). **Road Edition**'s 1:100,000 maps, Western and Eastern Crete, show mountain roads apparently researched by motorcyclists (for whom this series is principally designed). Another option for those who wish to reach remote trailheads by car, or ATV, is **Anavasi Digital**'s 2008 'Crete Road and Touring Atlas' scale 1:50,000. This is the latest and best road atlas (price €18), showing contours and almost all the new access roads, with sections of the E4 Trail marked. These are better than average road maps but not walking maps.

Since new maps may appear at any time it is worth asking Stanfords for latest publications, at 12–14 Longacre, London WC2, tel: 0207 836 1321; fax: 0207 236 0189; www.stanfords.co.uk.

In Chania, Pelekanakis on Halidon Street, may have sold out of walkers'

PHOTOGRAPHY

Greece is famous for the quality of its light; photographically speaking, there is 'light in the shadows'. However, there are variations: light is crisp and contrasty early in the year, but in summer a haze develops. In the autumn, as if compensating for the absence of greenery, the haze clears and mellows attractively, offering a wider exposure latitude. In particular, the Madares (Treks 1–9) look their best at this time, but shadows are denser at high altitude. In general, soft early morning light is gone by 08.30 but evenings, after 18.00, offer more scope.

maps by September. Maps of the Anavasi series may be found (at least early in the season) in Hora Sfakion, Loutro and Ay. Roumeli. Rethymnon old town has a well-stocked bookshop near *Plateia* Martyron, as may (2000) Matala, a beach resort on the Bay of Messara. In Heraklion there are likely bookshops in the vicinity of *Plateia* Eleutherios Venizelou, including a foreign-newspaper stockist just near the fountain.

Emergencies

There is no official mountain rescue service in Crete. Expect to pay for local help. Shepherds are best at finding lost people, usually after other search parties have given up. Unfortunate accidents can happen to anyone but, in principle, Cretan opinion on trekking ventures is 'if you can't handle it, you shouldn't be doing it'. This guide has been written to give you the necessary information, but the message must always be to take extra care on all routes. Injuring yourself and then running out of water is the chief danger.

Shepherds would expect you to have a mobile phone – as they now do – especially if you are alone; remember to carry relevant telephone numbers with you. EU Nationals should keep their European Health Insurance card with them (available from the post office before you go to Crete). A tetanus inoculation is advisable since there are many rusty fences and lots of animals. Keep a whistle on your person (although it may be ineffective in a wind); ideally supplement it with a strobe or flares, or at least a good quality torch. Flares are said to be best for attracting attention. The English-speaking staff at Kallergi refuge, Chania (tel: 28210.33199) are knowledgeable about local rescue options.

Mountain villagers are well aware of the risks involved as bad accidents occur even to those well used to the terrain. Before setting off on a mountain trek leave a note of your plans (with dates) in your own language with your rooming house proprietor, or at a central *kafeneon*.

Clothing and Footwear

In spring, autumn (and winter) bring one outfit of lightweight quick-drying synthetic fabric. However, above a certain level of humidity all synthetics are uncomfortable, so you also need a cotton outfit such as shorts and T-shirt. To travel light, consider the versatility of silk which is quick drying, fairly windproof and

55

insectproof, quite warm and yet wearable in the worst humidity (www.patra.com).

Underwear In case of chafing, pack two different types. If underwear incorporates synthetics, bring cotton or silk alternatives.

Warm layers Depending on season and altitude, you need one, two or three warm layers from the following range: thermal underwear, a lightweight wool or fleece pullover and a fleece jacket or light duvet. In rooming houses and hotels, facilities for drying clothes are minimal. Keep dry clothes in reserve. Backpacking trekkers may have to change back into damp clothes, which is why synthetic dry-on-the-body materials are so practical.

Rain shell Insulated waterproof garments are too warm outside the winter months. Lightweight Gortex or similar is best since 'breathable' materials double as windproofs, but any waterproof is better than nothing: at very least kit yourself out with a big dustbin bag. However settled it looks at first, storms can develop in half a day at any time of year. On mountain treks and summit ascents you must have a rain shell. Overtrousers and gaiters are a welcome luxury. An umbrella is always a useful travel item especially now that ultra-light models are readily available.

Protective clothing In summer, wear loose-fitting cottons for protection from the sun and from chafing. Check beforehand that all clothes are comfortable in use, and bring long-sleeved tops and long trousers, which also help protect against insects, levels of which build up over the summer. If you find the heat exhausting, use an umbrella – your own pool of shade makes all the difference.

Boots Cretan footpaths, with loose stones, are relentlessly rough underfoot, but there are also lots of new service tracks in the mountains. Ideally your boots need to provide good ankle- and foot-muscle support and yet also be flexible enough to suit road-tramping. Shock-absorbing footbeds are particularly helpful in Crete. However, in hot weather your feet will seem to swell. You will need generously sized boots; the introduction of either thick insoles or two pairs of socks, or both, could make your boots too tight: consider these options beforehand.

Shoes Velcro-fastening sandals are useful for sea bathing or river crossings. Some cheap varieties are ultra-light.

Socks In principle two pairs of socks, perhaps one soft loop stitch and one loose weave, are best for perspiration-wicking and cushioning. However modern hiking boots are apparently designed for a correct fit with one pair of socks. Cotton has a place, but for walking it soon becomes saturated, which causes chafing. High-wool content socks may work better than the synthetics – skin that causes no trouble at home may react quite differently in the heat. On a first venture bring a variety of sock types, including cotton. Heat rash around the ankles just needs a good re-airing. Long

Xyloscala, near the top of the Samaria Gorge (Walks 2, 50)

socks which can be pulled up against thorns are useful if you wear shorts. Canvas gaiters are a luxury especially on northern footpaths – walkers soon appreciate why knee-high leather boots are part of traditional Cretan dress.

Ultra-light clothing alternatives In the mountains, where storms can occur at any time of year, function-specific clothing is needed in winter, spring and autumn. In summer also you must have a shell jacket and an effective warm layer, but other minimum-weight 'just in case' items could be:

- an elastic chinstrap onto your sun-hat so that it stays on in wind and provides warmth; wear a plastic bag under it (or over it) if it rains.
- cotton or silk scarves are useful and versatile: bring at least two.
- for the hands, latex gloves are wind-proof.

- a ring made out of spare socks (toes inside ankles) makes a warm hat. Spare socks can also be used as gloves.
- nylon tights make effective long johns.
- polythene bags can be formed into boot-top gaiters.
- as a last resort, a large polythene dustbin bag worn next to the skin, under wet clothes, acts as a vapour barrier, helping to conserve body heat (this is for overnight camp – remove it when you move).

For all packing think carefully about reducing weight as on some routes you may need to carry lots of water at 840g (2.4lb) per litre.

Lone women walkers

In Greece there is great respect for the family and, therefore, the role women play within the family. Cretan, and especially Sfakiot, society is very 'macho', but lone women travellers and walkers are as safe in Crete as anywhere.

However, women travelling on their own for pleasure, curiosity or interest should be aware that this could be misconstrued. It has not been a normal part of the local culture, although all such ideas are changing nowadays. In particular, the high pastures of the Lefka Ori are traditionally a men-only workplace. In the other mountain ranges, where either the conditions, or the customs, are a bit different, you may see whole families working together.

Cretan women of the countryside have observed visiting foreign women for many years, so they are well aware of what they miss out on or gain in comparison. In the mountains, meet the culture halfway by creating (if necessary) an impression of community patronage – give the name of an accommodation destination address as every family-run business is known.

In **Sfakia** examples of respected contacts are:

- Anopolis: Poppy Kopasis (fluent English) at The Platanas rooms/ *kafeneon* in the *plateia*
- Askifou-Ammoudari: Pendelis Zoulakis (rooms/restaurant in the *plateia*)
- Ay. Roumeli: Andreas Stavroudaki (fluent English) at the Tara
- Omalos: George Drakoulakis (fluent English) at the New Omalos Hotel

On **Psiloritis** (Mount Ida):

- Anoyeia: Stelios Stavrakakis at the *taverna*, Nida Plain, is very well known since his *taverna* doubles as a shepherds' *kafeneon*.

In **Lassithi:**

- Ay. Georgios: Niki Hatzakis at the *Pension* Dias ('Dee-as') is very well known as a landlady who accommodates walkers.

Manners For both sexes, quiet considerate good manners are noticed and

FOREIGN WORKERS

Many thousands of workers from north Africa, eastern Europe, the Middle East and the Indian sub-continent now live in Greece: even the smallest village may have two or three in temporary residence and a modest cottage, or the old schoolhouse, may be turned into a dormitory for them. In the towns, workers wait at certain spots each day to be hired in accordance with government-directed day rates and conditions. They work in agriculture, construction, in restaurants and as shop assistants and as carers for the elderly, especially in inland villages. Skilled stonemasons, from Albania and Romania particularly, find a rich source of work in the limestone areas. In the mountains some shepherding may be done by non-local men, especially if the place is remote from village amenities. If this is the case see the Lone Women section above, as the 'meet the culture' approach might not be so applicable. Cretans firmly encourage foreign workers to stay out of trouble – which they mostly do.

appreciated. Young Cretans tend not to display affection in public.

Insects and Other Hazards

Mosquitoes These are present from the spring, especially in low-lying areas. Mountain accommodation may be free of them, at least until summer. On white walls, they are fairly easily located and swatted. Supermarkets sell anti-mosquito products – coils are low-tech and lightweight. Some hotels issue plug-in devices on request. If they do not, it is because guests have taken all the stock. Bring a good insect repellent. Alternatively a **mosquito net** can be very useful in the spring and summer months. Micro mosquito nets for travel may need an additional hanging kit. Add a good length of lightweight line, some self-adhesive plastic hooks, pads or clips (from tool shops and ironmongers). Leave the hooks behind – wrenching them off spoils the paint.

Midges Depending on the type of vegetation nearby, midges are found in some low-lying parts of the coast. When these midges bite, the impact will wake you up but the irritation is not long lasting. This insect appears to be unable to get through mosquito netting. If you plan to spend time camping at sea level, consider a hooped self-supporting type of net.

Cockroaches Stepping on a cockroach apparently causes its eggs to disperse in all directions. Shovel it out of the window, in the hope that the cat will get it.

Hornets and wasps Hornets look like large wasps and the locals say their sting is severe. Luckily this insect is not aggressive, but be careful not to provoke it. Wasps, also, do not normally attack.

Fleas and flies Many footpaths are also sheep routes, and from the summer fleas may be in full swing in the shady sections. In the mountains, choose your camp spot carefully away from anywhere that has provided shade for animals during the day. Fleas target the warmest parts of the body and are the worst of any bites because they can irritate badly for several days. You will notice that many chapels and huts are fenced off to keep animals from using adjacent areas of shade. If there is no breeze, flies may also spoil picnic sites which, since the spring, have filled up with droppings. In late September, when shepherds have burnt patches of hillside, these areas are free of insects (other than ants).

Honeybees Beehives are located in groups, usually beside shepherds' roads, remote from the villages. Bees are very active in the spring when flowers appear, and worker bees occasionally sting passing walkers. Protect the back of your neck and, if stung (quite rare), locate and remove the shaft immediately or it will continue to dispense venom.

Sea urchins Sea urchins are small, round, jet-black spiny creatures that live on rocks near the seashore. However, in recent years these environmentally sensitive creatures have been absent from much of the south coast probably as a result of the busy ferryboat schedule. If you do happen to step on one, you will not be walking anywhere for six months as the spines

Anopolis: milking sheep at Limnia

are almost impossible to extract. If in doubt, wear Velcro sandals in the sea.

Dogs In the countryside dogs are regarded as useful tools for guarding premises or livestock. Their need for affection is ignored. Dogs chained up for most of their lives, sometimes out of sight even of stimulating diversions, quite naturally become demented. Therefore, if you feed these dogs (they usually need it) or give them water, take care not to turn your back on them, for some (but not all) will bite you if they can. By law, dogs are inoculated against rabies and other relevant diseases.

Wildlife and Hunting

The *agrimi* ibex – the kri-kri – of the Samaria Gorge is seriously protected from hunting. This is accepted by the gorge community, but pure-bred kri-kri leaving the gorge are probably still at risk. The fairly recent decline of goatherding as a profession has increased the population of feral goats in the mountains. Female ferals interbreed with male *agrimi* so that where once domestic goats were kept out of the gorge, nowadays it is common to see half-breeds tramping about in the lower section. These half-breeds are supposed to be culled in the winter months, but this measure has limited success. Goats live in inaccessible places but, thanks to the female kri-kri's habit of refusing to interbreed, it is hoped that pure-breds – being superb rock-climbers – will sustain at least in the higher reaches of the Samaria Gorge (information from Andreas Stavroudaki of Ay. Roumeli, 2005).

Vultures and eagles are officially protected from hunting, but they, too, remain at risk. The hunting season starts mid-September. The standard prey is chukar (a type of partridge that nests in rocky terrain above 1800m/5905ft) and mountain hare. To the regret of the locals (who hunt) hares are now very rare. New access roads and off-road vehicles exacerbate the situation. You may be asked if you saw a hare or heard chukars (a chattering chorus in the early morning) on your trek. A threat to chickens, and killed at any time, are stone martins and weasels. Hunting dogs kill badgers. There are various rodents, bats, hedgehogs, frogs and harmless lizards. It is quite unusual to see a snake, which would be a variety of European adder. There are small scorpions but they are not a great threat. Centipedes sometimes get into boots overnight – it is worth checking in the morning.

Plants, Trees and Flowers

Privation due to less high-yield agricultural methods, especially after the World War II, is remembered throughout Greece, and 'food for free' is still popular with many people in Crete. In the countryside various edible wild greens are gathered in the spring. Snails are also collected in spring (and during Lent), especially after rain.

Crete's geological history and location in the eastern Mediterranean, equidistant from Europe, Asia and Africa, renders the island of great interest to botanists. Below 1000m (3280ft), varying between the south (earlier) and the north coasts, late April and early May are usually the best time for a profusion

Hunters pause at Roussies cistern (Trek 8)

of spring flowers. In the high mountains carpets of crocii, chionodoxa, Cretan tulip, and others, bloom with the retreating snow. Autumn flowers appear in October, with the first rains of the seasonal change. The most commonly seen plants and trees are largely those that taste bad to goats. Except for the resinous pine forests that are (even naturally) thinned out by forest fires, Cretan plants are adapted in various ways to survive the long dry summers. They may be geophytes (earth plants) with sustaining bulbs, corms, or tubers unsuited to well-watered ground, or sclerophylls (hard-leaved) shrubs or trees with long roots and drought-resistant leaves, or thorns. Deep gorges orientated north/south get shade for part of the day, and their sheer walls are a safe haven for many species of chasmophyte (gorge plants).

The limit of the treeline varies: northern slopes about 1450m (4760ft), and southern slopes about 1600m (5250ft). Common mountain trees are Cretan cypress, often contorted by winter winds, but living to a very great age, juniper, evergreen maple, prickly oak and kermis oak, and Cretan pine (similar to Calabrian pine). Mid-level trees include (apart from olive trees) carob with its big black pods, wild pear, deciduous oaks, oriental plane (watercourses, village squares), walnut and the fast-growing pollarded mulberry. At the seashore, juniper and tamarisk are common. Tamarisk is usefully fast growing but despised for the windblown dust (that can land on the dinner table) retained in its foliage. Chestnut groves flourish in places where the type of rock allows a constant water supply.

On the hillsides there are three main types of vegetation:

Maquis Tall, long-lived, woody shrubs classed as trees. This includes prickly oak when it is chronically stunted by browsing goats. Maquis is kept down where mature trees monopolise the available water supply.

Phrygana ('friggan-na') includes heathland plants such as oregano, thyme and spiny spurge (the 'wire-netting' plant) and woody shrubs such as spiny broom, spiny burnet and Jerusalem sage. In late summer shepherds burn areas of *phrygana* to promote regeneration of plants palatable to sheep and goats. If this operation is unlucky, or misjudged, high winds spread the fire. On reaching a ridgetop this type of fire should go out, or at worst 'jump' to elsewhere rather than descend the other side of the ridge. *Phrygana* in flower causes hay fever in the spring. Pharmacies stock remedies for this allergy (called the 'aller-yee-a'). Use your cotton scarf as a mask, particularly when passing Jerusalem sage. (If you take up the work of clearing footpaths, use a builder's mask.) Fortunately goats can nibble the pods of this tough plant, which chokes so many old trails.

Steppe This is comprised of plants that grow on the exposed dry rocky terrain of the south coast escarpment, including white asphodel (spring), maritime squill (autumn) and the weird-looking dragon arum or stink lily. Steppe also includes the long-rooted, nutritious (for sheep) low-profile endemics of the Madares.

Several species adapted to the shadeless, barren terrain, date from geo-historical times indicating that the high mountains were never tree-covered.

In the mountain ranges these three vegetation types grow side-by-side, depending on water supply, orientation and altitude.

USING THIS GUIDE

Grading System
Each walk is graded as follows:
Grade A Short walks, easy underfoot, with hamlets or destinations in sight, for example Walk 1.
Grade B Walks on roads or tracks and popular, well-tramped, easy-to-follow paths, for example Walk 2.
Grade C Walks on less-frequented mountain footpaths, for example Walk 3.
Grade D More demanding day-walks, on remote terrain, for example Walk 6. Any of the backpacking routes, as these are mini-expeditions that need careful planning. Confidence and route-finding experience essential.
Grade E Very remote and rugged mountain routes.

Note 'Remote' means that although final destinations – villages or coastlines – may be in sight in the distance, the terrain is rugged so that getting there safely will take a lot of time and effort.

Walking Times
The time allowance given on some rocky footpath routes may be similar to that listed for well-defined ascent paths. In general, remember that a new route

Anopolis: mules are still needed in the Madares

CALCULATING WALKING TIME

The walking times listed are standardised to an average-time easy-to-calculate formula:

- *per approximate linear km*
  15mins on roads
  20mins on easy-to-follow rough footpaths
  30mins on very demanding rocky terrain
- plus 15mins per 100m of height gained.

Many routes combine sections of all these underfoot conditions. Also, rocky downhill paths may need the same time allowance as linear routes.

always takes longer to walk than one with which you are familiar or that is clearly defined. EOS times on E4 Trail signposts in the mountains are probably matched to the club's strongest walkers who are already familiar with the routes. Where backpacking is mentioned, this refers not to 'gap-year' travellers but to trekkers who are purposely equipped to camp in the mountains.

Monitor your pace on your first couple of walks to check whether you need to reduce or extend the above formula. Firstly, reduce the formula by allowing 10mins per 100m ascent. Some may find the times listed too generous, but it is wise to take your time on such rocky terrain.

On all routes **allow extra time** for any sort of rest stop – picnics, sitting down, taking photographs – an additional 1hr (at least) on most walks. Using Walk 30, Ascent of Kastro, as an example: if there are 10hrs of daylight, you may have only 1.5hrs to spare for preparation and stops. On some other routes you may need to work to a bus or boat timetable.

The kilometre distances are an approximate guide to be read in conjunction with the other data: maps are not sufficiently detailed for very accurate measurement, and many routes include zigzagging footpaths. For a very quick guide to the effort involved on a walk, divide the time allowance figure by kilometre distance. For example, the most well-tramped footpath in Crete, the Gorge of Samaria, works out at 16.5mins per km, while Trek 7a works out at 50mins per km due to the long, steep ascent and care needed on that remote and broken-up old mule track.

In the route notes, the year when a point was last seen by the author, or last reported to the author by other walkers, is sometimes given in brackets. Hopefully, this will add interest to what you see, and should also be useful if you have the impression that things might have changed since that date. Mountain shepherding may be in decline but, conversely, road-building and all sorts of new developments are ongoing.

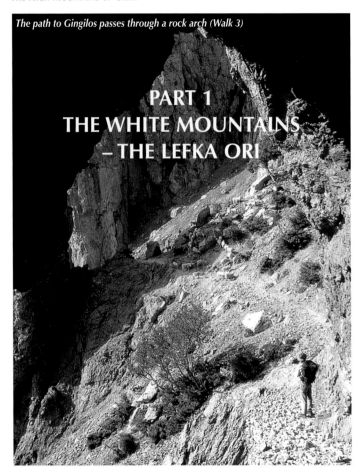

The path to Gingilos passes through a rock arch (Walk 3)

PART 1
THE WHITE MOUNTAINS
– THE LEFKA ORI

There are three quite distinct massifs in this mountain range: west, central and east. The Gorge of Samaria and the Omalos Plain divide west from central, and the Askifou Plain divides central from east. The central massif provides the greatest variety of walking and trekking routes, although routes in all three regions do link up. The Gorge of Samaria National Park is often the main focal point of a walking holiday in or around the central massif.

For information on professional mountain-guiding services contact (multi-lingual) Jean Bienvenu who lives in Chania (see Appendix 3).

ROUTE SUGGESTIONS

On a one-week trip the walk up, or down, the Samaria Gorge can be combined with various other walking routes. Your plan should ideally allow for a contingency day in case of bad weather, when the gorge might be closed. Since there are tourist facilities 'everywhere' along the Sfakiot coast, you could spend several days on a continuous route walking up and down the south coast escarpment, or the gorges, all of which are different.

For example:

- Starting at Imbros (access: Hora Sfakion bus from Chania), walk down the Imbros Gorge to Hora Sfakion and up to Anopolis (bus or walk) for overnight (Walks 24, 46) .
- Next day: Down the Aradena Gorge for overnight on the coast, followed by the coastal walk to Ay. Roumeli (Walks 40, 40a, 49).
- Next day: Up the Samaria Gorge (and be amazed at its size after the others) to Omalos for overnight, followed by down the Ay. Irini Gorge to Souyia, for early bus out in the morning (not Sunday mornings – for that you must continue on to Paleochora, Walks 50, 8, 9, 9a).

This coastline, with its tourist facilities and network of old trails, offers all sorts of choices to walkers who are prepared to travel light. As a result the area has a strong following of repeat visitors who know they will get a good week's walking here.

A very different trip, for those who want to practise their Greek and who like places far from the tourist trail, a semi-backpack, mid-level route when the high mountains are still snow-covered could be:

- From Souyia (access: bus from Chania) up the Ay. Irini Gorge to the Omalos (Walks 9, 8 in reverse), and then to Zourva (Walk 10).
- Then to Drakona (road tramp) via the Theriso road (see Trek 1) and continuing to Kambi, and Melidoni (Walk 14), to Fres and Vafes (Walks 17 or 19).
- Then to Askifou (Walk 21) or Krappis and Lake Kourna (Walk 35).

Meals at Souyia, Omalos, Zourva, Melidoni, Vafes, Krappis, Askifou. Supplies at Souyia and Askifou. Simple supplies at Omalos, Melidoni, Vafes. Accommodation at Souyia, Omalos, Askifou.

Currently, in many foothill villages 'simple meals and beds' would depend on whether a local resident keen to take on fair-priced work can be found. You would certainly take your own sleeping kit and some supplies on this trip and, as a result of the younger generation having left for the towns, some knowledge of Greek would help.

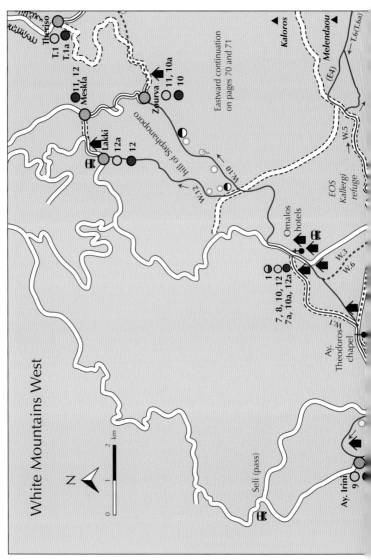

White Mountains West

N

0   1   2 km

Thériso
T.1
T.1a

Meskla
11, 12

11, 12
Lakki
12a
12

Zourva
11, 10a
10

hill of Stephanoporo

W.12

W.10

Kaloros

Melendaou
T.6(T.6a)

(E4)

W.5

Eastward continuation
on pages 70 and 71

EOS
Kallergi
refuge

Omalos
hotels

1
7, 8, 10, 12
7a, 10a, 12a

W.3
W.6

W.1

Ay.
Theodoros
chapel

Seli (pass)

Ay. Irini
9

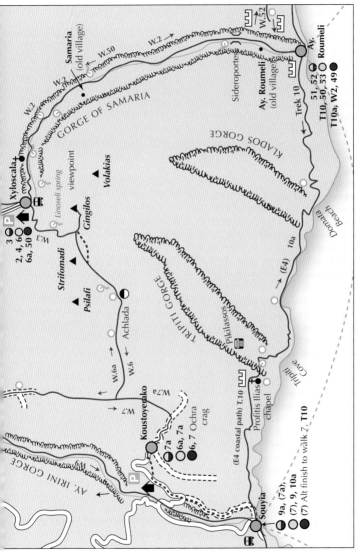

Samaria
(old village)

W.50

W.2

W.2

W.2

W.2

GORGE OF SAMARIA

Sider-
oportes

Ay. Roumeli

Ay.
Roumeli

W.52

Ay. Roumeli
(old village)

Trek 10

51, 52
T10, 50, 53
T10a, W2, 49

Xyloscala

viewpoint

Linoseli spring

Volakias

Gingilos

KLADOS GORGE

Domata
Beach

3

2, 4, 6
9a, 50
6a, 50

W.3

Striomadi

Psilafi

Achlada

W.6a

W.6

(E4) 10a

TRIPITI GORGE

Pikilassos

Tripiti
Cove

Koustoyerako

W.7a

W.7

W.9

AY. IRINI GORGE

7a

6a, 7a

6, 7 Ochra
crag

Profitis Ilias
chapel

(E4 coastal path) T.10

Souyia

9a, (7a)

(7), 9, 10a

(7) Alt finish to walk 7, T10

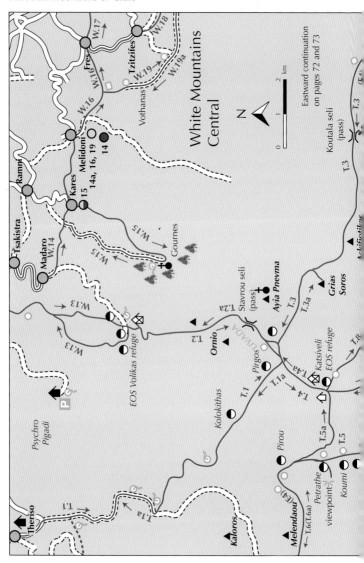

White Mountains
Central

N

Eastward continuation
on pages 72 and 73

0   1   2   km

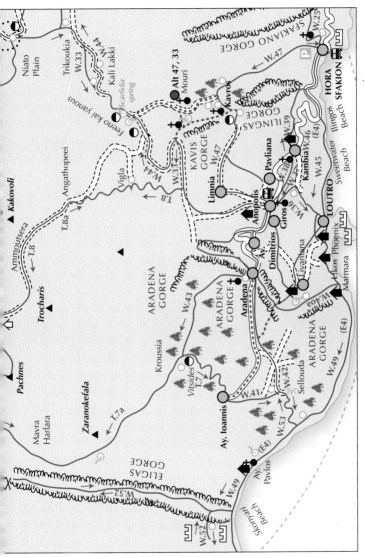

71

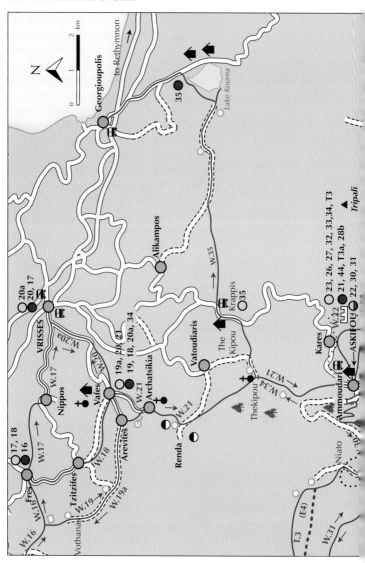

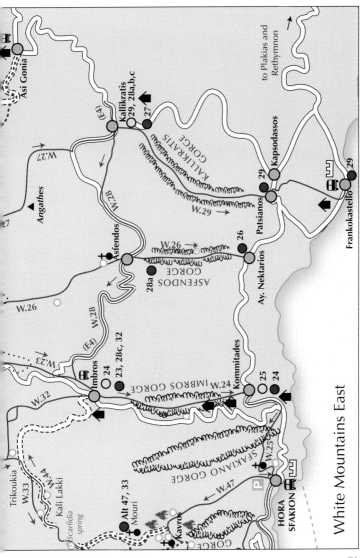

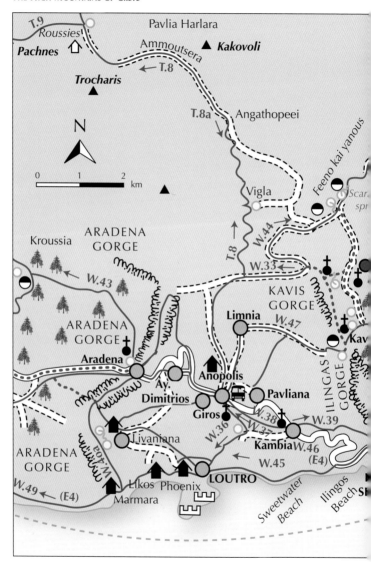

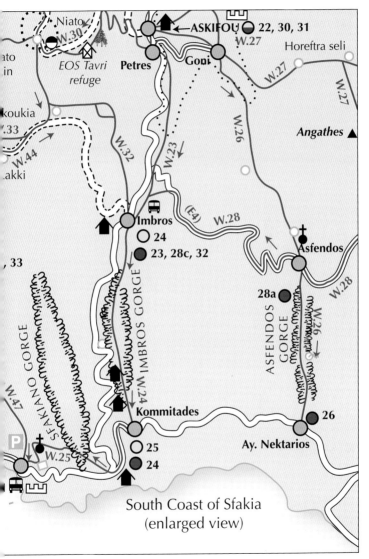

Niato
W.30
ato
in
EOS Tavri
refuge
Petres
koukia
.33
W.44
akki
W.32
W.23
ASKIFOU 22, 30, 31
W.27
Horeftra seli
Goni
W.27
W.27
Angathes ▲
W.26

Imbros
○ 24
● 23, 28c, 32
(E4) W.28
W.28
† Asfendos

, 33

W. IMBROS GORGE
W.24

28a ●

ASFENDOS GORGE
W.26

SFAKIANO GORGE

W.47

Kommitades
○ 25
● 24

26 ●

Ay. Nektarios

South Coast of Sfakia
(enlarged view)

THE OMALOS PLAIN

The Omalos Plain (also called 'plateau') is the largest of several high plains in the White Mountains. On the south side, just beyond the periphery of the plain, is Xyloscala, the busy trailhead for the walk down through the Gorge of Samaria National Park. From Xyloscala other footpaths lead eastwards to the high mountains via Kallergi refuge, or southwestwards to the summit of Gingilos, its massive grey cliff forming part of the northwest wall of the gorge.

At Omalos hamlet ('Omalos hotels') and Xyloscala, various establishments, run by people from Lakki village, specialise in providing quick, sustaining breakfasts for the thousands who walk the gorge each day. Trekkers leaving for the high mountains should note that the only shop, at Xyloscala, does not stock provisions other than snacks. The New Omalos Hotel (at Omalos hamlet) can normally supply meat, eggs, cheese, tomatoes, fruit and bread. Otherwise bring lightweight food supplies up with you.

Omalos 1080m (3543ft) attracts and holds typical mountain weather: rain, mist, winds, frost, and metres of snow in winter. For Cretans who have to work all summer, the hotels, with their home cooking and log fires, make this a popular winter weekend destination, especially when snow transforms a formerly parched summer landscape. At other times of year the cool fresh air is a welcome relief from the heat of coastal resorts and a few days' stay is popular with walking groups. In May people comb the old meadows collecting stamnagathi, the highly regarded edible plant of the Cretan mountains. Growing flat to the ground, its spines have to be removed before it is boiled for about 20mins.

An asphalted ring road serves the plateau and main roads enter it from the north and west. Earthen tracks criss-cross the central area. Two or three long sinkholes drain off snowmelt and rainwater which emerges far below as springs, inland from Chania. Drivers use the tracks tentatively, aware that a new sinkhole might develop at any moment.

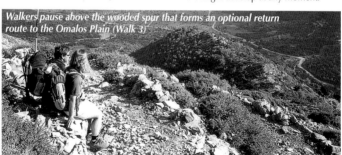

Walkers pause above the wooded spur that forms an optional return route to the Omalos Plain (Walk 3)

WALK 1
Around the Omalos Plain

Grade	A
Start/finish	Omalos hamlet 1080m (3543ft)
Access	KTEL Omalos bus or taxi from Chania
Approx distance	5–6km (3.1–3.7 miles) depending on route
Time allowance	Allow 20mins per km; straight across the plateau is about 2.5km, and return by either rim road is about 3km

On this route walkers can avoid the roads fairly well by using perimeter sheep paths and service tracks. On the plain, patience will be needed with fencing and gates (hence the generous time allowance). The whole area is heavily grazed, but wild flowers survive here and there on the borders of the old meadows or around the sinkholes, one or two of which retain water in the spring. The two-storey, white *taverna* in the hamlet, to the left of the western pass, is a popular destination. Along with refreshments, grills and salad, the *taverna* offers two triple-bed rooms for rent.

A few rare ambelitsia trees, endemic to the Omalos region, grow in the dry watercourse descending from the Strifomadi–Psilafi massif. Ambelitsia wood is used to make the traditional shepherd's crook of Sfakia. Ruined 'summer' houses ring **the** edge of the plateau, as this was (and still is) a transhumance destination for shepherds of Ay. Irini and Lakki. Much needed by the busy hotels, cheese is still made here in the spring – excellent mountain-produced *graviera* that does not reach Chania market.

Leave **Omalos** by walking west, either on the fenced track just north of the hamlet, or on the road just south of it, beyond the last rooming house. These two roads converge at a crossroads behind the hamlet. A massive deluge (2006) has caused a new sinkhole to develop on the left, before this point. To walk straight across the plain, note a dirt track near the end of this disturbed ground – it goes slightly uphill and is fenced on both sides. Walk straight along this. (The white *taverna* is now in view across the plain and this is roughly the direction in which to head.) A wire gate at the end gives access to an enclosure formed around a long sinkhole.

Looking south to Mount Gingilos across the Omalos Plain

Make your way around this to re-join your line of travel. There are one or two more wire gates to negotiate, and various sinkhole features.

Return via the northern rim road or make your way around the southern edge where there are sheep paths near the road. From the south, if you wish to leave the main road, take the dirt track that goes straight across the plateau. It is dead straight and can easily be identified as you walk along the main road from Xyloscala. Keep on this track until you are level with Omalos hamlet where, free of fenced enclosures, you turn right for the main road.

WALK 2

The Gorge of Samaria National Park

See also Walk 50
Grade	B
Start	Xyloscala 1240m (4068ft)
Access	KTEL Omalos bus or taxi from Chania
Finish	Ay. Roumeli
Access to finish	Coastal boat service (see below)
Height loss	1230m (4036ft)

Approx distance	18km (11.2 miles)
Time allowance	Xyloscala to Ay. Nikolaos chapel 1hr 30mins; to Samaria old village 1hr 10mins; to Iron Gates 1hr 10mins; to park boundary 40mins; to Ay. Roumeli waterfront 30mins: total 5hrs
Admission charge	€5 (2007)

This hugely popular walk down the Samaria Gorge has brought much prosperity to western Crete. Perhaps as a result several smaller gorges in Crete have been developed as attractive walking routes. Although the National Park of the Gorge of Samaria has evolved in this way, part of it was designated a nature reserve as long ago as 1929 when biologists determined that the Cretan ibex, or *agrimi* – (the 'kri-kri') – would become extinct if they did not take steps to save it. This ongoing project has its ups and downs but is a fundamental reason the gorge is today a well-organised National Park run according to World Conservation Union standards.

The *agrimi* ('the wild one') is a type of goat, an ibex, about the size of a sheep, with a black stripe down its back. Both sexes and even the newborn have horns, but an old male sporting the huge horns once so prized by hunters may not exist in the wild at present. Some *tavernas* still feature kri-kri horns as wall decorations but these date from the time before this delightful animal was protected from hunting. Only the sight of the massive cliffs and steep mountainsides of the upper gorge can explain how the kri-kri has managed to survive into modern times. The *agrimi* features in Bronze Age illustrations, but since it can be tamed and milked (or eaten), archaeologists rate it as an even older native of Crete – perhaps a Neolithic domestic goat. In the spring when there is plentiful food on the high crags you may not see a kri-kri. But in the autumn, when food is scarce, it should be easier, as some of them – protected by the wardens – frequent the Ay. Nikolaos chapel area and Samaria old village. In spite of conservation efforts there is inter-breeding with domestic goats. Amongst domestic goats nearby and in the lower part of the gorge you may see half-breeds with the characteristic black stripe down their backs (see also 'Wildlife and Hunting' above).

A river fed by mountain springs and snowmelt runs down the gorge, disappearing and reappearing at intervals, typical of limestone terrain. Ay. Roumeli depends on this water supply. A big black pipe, starting in the riverbed at the source of the largest spring, Kefalovrisi (just north of the Iron Gates) conveys this water down to the village storage tank. Temporary timber walkways are positioned at the many river crossings on the walk. For those who prefer to wade (bring sandals) the river is not fast-flowing by the time the gorge opens to the public.

Xyloscala: entrance to the Samaria Gorge

Principal man-made features are the old village of Samaria halfway down – from which the population was resettled in the 1960s – and the old village of Ay. Roumeli, just outside the park boundary at the bottom. New Ay. Roumeli is 1km further on, right on the seashore. Other constructions in or near the gorge, apart from mule tracks, are chapels, ruined Turkish forts and water conduits to ruined sawmills or used for irrigation.

The park makes a significant cultural contribution by inducing town-dwelling Cretans to rediscover the beauty and worth of their own countryside and the pleasures of walking. Locals can choose their day: overcast, cool Sundays are preferred, when whole families can be seen trooping down alongside the tourists. Local teachers may also take their pupils on the walk.

As this part of the south coast is free of roads, tour groups finish by being transferred from Ay. Roumeli to Hora Sfakion, or Souyia, by boat where they are met by the same coaches that took them up to Xyloscala. It is a long round for the bus drivers and an even longer day for the tourists. This standard tour method of hurrying down the gorge, and then leaving it almost immediately, detracts from the experience and does not fully reward the effort involved. Walk outside the 'rush hours' and make a point of staying overnight in Ay. Roumeli if you can.

The main trail is so well tramped that it is easy to follow and needs no signposting. Instead, signboards indicate points of interest. Drinking water, WCs and smokers' stopping places are provided at intervals. Wardens patrol the route and a mule-borne rubbish-collection patrol operates late afternoon, after most walkers have gone. Keep your ticket; it is collected in at the other end.

The National Park is officially open 1 May–31 October, with an entrance fee (€5 in 2007). These dates can vary

Walkers pause to be sure, after hearing the sound of falling rocks

Boat departures from Ay. Roumeli to Hora Sfakion are likely to be at 12.00, 15.45, 17.30 and 19.30 during the main tourist season. A skeleton service operates at other times. The 12.00 and 15.45 departures call at Loutro. For Souyia, departure is likely to be at 16.00 (except for one weekday, likely to be Thursday – check). For ferryboat timetables see Appendix 3. Journey time in either direction is about 45mins, varying with the weather, or a call at Loutro (an extra 30mins), or both. The last KTEL evening bus to Chania (usually packed) waits for the boat. The ticket kiosk with the timetable is at the bottom of Ay. Roumeli main street, on the right. You can always enquire at the Tara restaurant (the landlord speaks English) if anything unusual seems to be happening.

depending on springtime trail preparation work, the level of the water in the river, and autumn weather conditions. The 'Gorge Lazy Way' tour, for those who cannot manage the whole walk, starts earlier in the year. Excursionists arrive by boat at Ay. Roumeli for the 2hr 30min round walk to see the very narrow and impressive 'Iron Gates' part of the gorge.

There are no commercial outlets inside the park. There is no camping. Various guidebooks are on sale at Xyloscala, Omalos and Ay. Roumeli. The park closes at the top at 15.00 to through-walkers but remains open to those (usually with a hired car) who wish to walk a short way down to see the view, before returning to the top again. Organised day tours have left Xyloscala by midday, so an early afternoon start allows you to walk down relatively undisturbed. Otherwise, since the 'rush hour(s)' are early morning up to about 11.00, try to be first at the entrance at 06.00 when the ticket kiosk opens. This early start is well worth it, as this lovely walk is downgraded if too many people are doing it at the same time. A daily average of up to 3000 trippers is quite normal. Fortunately the gorge is so huge, and so rugged, that this foot traffic makes no serious impact. Walkers seem as nothing compared to the ravages of the thaw from the surrounding mountains as the winter ends.

At any time of year, and in spite of all the tourist activity, the gorge remains a wild, rugged and potentially hazardous place. Always be on the alert for falling rocks. Rain followed by wind dislodges them most readily. The park will be closed if such conditions are expected. Tired or injured people, who finish the trip riding one of the few 'rescue' mules from Samaria village (which is expensive) sometimes hurt themselves further by falling, as the pack saddles are extremely uncomfortable. On rare occasions desert-like flash floods occur in Crete, when the parched land cannot absorb the first storms of winter. It is sensible to be aware of this if a storm develops (at any time of year). Unmaintained paths off the main trail are closed to the public (due to accidents in the past) and special permission from the Forestry Directorate of Chania is needed for access to them. ◄

Towards the end of the walk, note the Turkish fort on the western skyline above the valley. The climb to it is not as far as it looks, and for unhurried walkers (wearing boots) it makes an interesting and unconventional way of arriving at **Ay. Roumeli**.

WALK 3
The Ascent of Gingilos

Grade	C
Start/finish	Xyloscala 1240m (4068ft)
Access	KTEL Omalos bus or taxi from Chania
Highest point	Summit of Gingilos 2080m (6824ft)
Height gain/loss	724m (2375ft)
Approx distance	9km (5.5 miles)
Time allowance	Xyloscala to top of first spur 1400m (4593ft) 45mins; spur to Linoseli spring 1500m (4921ft) 45mins; spring to Gingilos saddle 1800m (5905ft) 1hr 10mins; saddle to summit 50mins; ascent total: 3hrs 30mins (trail is clearly defined – some walkers take less time); descent total: summit to spur 1hr 40mins; spur to Xyloscala 30mins; total: 5hrs 30mins
Variation	Spur direct to Omalos hamlet 1hr 40mins

The mountain with the huge grey crag opposite Xyloscala is called Gingilos. This is the most accessible high peak of the White Mountains and the ascent, on a well-beaten footpath, is a deservedly popular walk offering spectacular views from any level. As the return is down the same way, the walk can be curtailed at any stage. On part of the 50min final ascent section minor rock-scrambling ability is needed, but hand- and footholds are easy on the rough rock. As with all Lefka Ori peaks, high winds may affect the summit area and snowdrifts may linger on steeper slopes in the early spring. Take no risks – alter your plans if conditions dictate. Take daysack essentials. For once you will not need to carry much water as Linoseli spring, which supplies Xyloscala, is halfway up the route to the summit.

From Xyloscala viewing terrace, on the west side, Gingilos crag is in front of you. Over to the southeast, Pachnes 2453m (8047ft), the highest peak of the Lefka Ori, rises beyond the east rim of the gorge. Up to the right, to the west, a massive scree slope is bordered by Gingilos crag. Note the patch of spiny burnet at its base, green in the spring and brown in the autumn, which marks the location of Linoseli spring. Note also the saddle on the skyline above the spring. The final pull to the summit is up to the point on the skyline to the left of this.

The ascent footpath starts from the front steps of the restaurant above the viewing terrace. It climbs the flank of the spur

Note On the way down, for Omalos hamlet direct, you can take goat paths down the full length of the spine of this spur and then cross the plateau on service tracks.

in easy-gradient zigzags. After 45mins the spine of this low spur above the Xyloscala road is reached. ◄

The footpath now crosses back towards the gorge and then turns in, heading for an area of rugged pinnacles below the big scree slope. Just before the path loses height to negotiate the pinnacles, note the goat paths (splintered paths) ascending, right, to the top of the ridge.

For Koustoyerako via Strifomadi summit Leave the path here (Walk 6).

For Gingilos After passing through the pinnacles and a spectacular rock arch, the footpath gains height again for Linoseli spring, where there is a concrete tank surrounded by a thicket of spiny burnet, together with two stainless steel troughs and a drinking water tap. The footpath continues from the spring, zigzagging up the firmer side of the scree, alongside crags and boulders.

The saddle, a pleasant place to be on a fine settled day, thinly divides the Samaria and Tripiti gorges. Over to the east, the red-roofed Kallergi mountain refuge has been in view for some time with Melendaou behind, its huge stratified cliff forming the northeast rim of the gorge. ◄

A branch of the E4 Trail is signposted at the north end of the saddle (see Walk 6). This is an unfrequented shepherds' path that undulates across steep crags and scree, forming a Grade D short-cut route to Koustoyerako (Walk 6).

Lammergeiers (bearded vultures) identifiable by their diamond-shaped tails, often soar above at midday. The largest birds in Europe, they roost on inaccessible crags of the Tripiti Gorge, which is now in view. At any time elsewhere in the mountains these huge birds may be seen gliding by on a foraging trip

Southwards, splintered paths continue up from the saddle. On the first section, which is steep, when bare rock takes over from heathland, it is easier to climb up more solid rock a little to the right. A spindly fence indicates the position of a dangerous karst hole in the rocks. The route soon levels out before climbing again and rocks are variously waymarked: in general the route bears left at this stage. The tiny white chapel of Profitis Elias Tripitis is in view far below, to the west, on a crag where the Tripiti Gorge meets the sea near Souyia (Trek 10). Above the rocks the footpath zigzags less steeply, waymarked with vertical timber boards, designed to show above the snow in the spring.

A large cairn marks **Gingilos summit**. A subsidiary rocky summit to the east lies nearer the rim of the gorge. Volakias 2116m (6942ft), the highest peak of the western

massif, is next along the ridge to the south.

To reach Volakias, first descend steeply from Gingilos summit to the small saddle that separates the two peaks. Return on a shepherds' route that contours from there, back to the Gingilos saddle.

Beyond Volakias there is a long, crag-ridden, waterless ridgetop between the Samaria and Klados gorges. From Volakias there is a weather-eroded, unfrequented route down to the coast along the spine of a ridge between the Tripiti and Klados gorges – a Grade E venture that needs an experienced guide. To the west, across the Tripiti Gorge, the Achlada Valley, part of Walk 6 to Koustoyerako, is in view. Looking east, note the ridge leading up to Melendaou (Walk 5 and Trek 6), and then follow the profile of the mountains south from Pachnes to identify Zaranokefala and its summit crag (Trek 7).

Return to Xyloscala the same way you came up.

For Omalos direct (instead of Xyloscala) peel off down the spur above the road. Keep to the spine of this ridge right to

The climb to the 'Gingilos saddle' above Linoseli spring

its end, where you have a bird's-eye view of the plateau. Before reaching this viewpoint, you will pass a ruined shepherds' hut on the left. A very old circular water cistern is also nearby. Note the layout of the plateau's service tracks, because once you are on level ground you will not be able to see the track you want to use. At the viewpoint, cross over to the left for the final descent on a slope that is free of undergrowth. At the bottom, follow sheep paths that link to a dirt road, where you turn right.

WALK 4
Xyloscala to Kallergi Refuge

Grade	A
Start	Xyloscala 1240m (4068ft)
Access	KTEL Omalos bus or taxi from Chania
Finish	Kallergi refuge 1680m (5111ft)
Access to finish	From Trek 6a, or shepherds' road from Omalos (Kallergi vehicle lift service tel: 28210.33199)
Highest point	Kallergi refuge 1680m (5511ft)
Height gain	440m (1443ft)
Approx distance	3km (1.8 miles)
Time allowance	2hrs

The red-roofed Kallergi refuge (tel: 28210.33199), perched high on the northwest rim of the Samaria Gorge, was built for army training during the Greek military dictatorship (1967–74). Thereafter, the Chania EOS took it over and leased it to mountain guide Joseph Schwemburger, who runs it. As an upgraded mountain hut, Kallergi has featured in government courses designed to introduce Crete (and Greece) to young Greek nationals living abroad. Otherwise, from May to October, a steady flow of walking groups and freelance travellers sustains this busy Alpine-style catering enterprise. Facilities include full board and private bunkroom, or a roof-space dormitory. Rainwater collection from the roof does not stretch to inside showers and an eaves-hung water bag substitutes, filled from the additional water supply brought up from Chania. Bottled water and other drinks are expensive. Refreshments and meals are available to passers-by. This is a popular base for the ascents of Melendaou and Gingilos, requiring a two- or three-

E4 Trail: looking down the great scree slope.
The road to Kallergi refuge is seen on the opposite hillside.

night stay, and also a stopping point on the trekking route to Katsiveli and beyond (Trek 6). A shepherds' road (not for taxis) serves the refuge before continuing on under the northern flank of Melendaou.

Leave **Xyloscala** on the east side via the footpath sign-board, which reads 1hr 20mins to Kallergi. Within 40mins join the shepherds' road from the plateau and continue up on this – optional short cuts appear occasionally. A small stone-built corbelled shepherds' shelter with a World War II memorial plaque marks the top. **Kallergi** is in sight, 5mins away. (Keep right – sometimes thick mist envelops the clifftop.)

WALK 5
Kallergi Refuge to Melendaou

Grade	C
Start/finish	Kallergi refuge 1680m (5511ft)
Access	Walk 4 from Xyloscala, or shepherds' road from Omalos
Highest point	Melendaou 2133m (6998ft)
Height gain	483m (1583ft)
Approx distance	16km (10 miles)
Time allowance	Kallergi to Poria 1500m (4921ft) 50mins; Poria to top of ridge 1840m (5902ft) 1hr 10mins; ridge walk to Melendaou saddle 1900m (6233ft) 1 hr; saddle to summit 1hr 15mins; ascent total: 4hrs 15mins; descent total: summit to Kallergi 2hrs 30mins via E4 Trail; total: 6hrs 45mins

Using Kallergi refuge (reservations tel: 28210.33199) as a convenient starting point, Melendaou 2133m (6998ft) – towering to the northeast above the Samaria Gorge – can be reached as a day-walk, allowing non-backpackers a chance of views towards the heart of the range. As it is on the regular schedule of walking groups staying at Kallergi, this route is well tramped and partly waymarked. Kallergi is 50mins walk, on the shepherds' road, to the base of the long ridge leading up to Melendaou. For a circular walk, approach the peak from along the top of this ridge and then return to Kallergi by dropping down (on the waymarked E4 Trail) to the shepherds' road alongside it.

From **Kallergi** walk east on the shepherds' road to Poria, a bracken-filled meadow at the foot of the long ridge. There is a shepherds' hut on the right. Head straight for the steep hillside in front of you, southeast, where waymarks guide you up splintered footpaths to the ridgetop.

Now overlooking the gorge and almost level with Melendaou's huge stratified cliff, start along one of the best ridge walks in Crete. This takes in (or bypasses, to choice) one or two ridgetop peaks. After about 50mins arrive at a saddle below the steep ascent ridge (E4 Trail) leading to **Melendaou** summit. As you climb, look out for red paint waymarks that direct you off the E4 Trail to the summit.

Note The **return route** to Kallergi (E4 Trail poles) descends from this saddle, via a northwesterly traverse followed by a steep path down to the shepherds' road. ▸

From the summit (where there is a trig point) Kaloros 1925m (6315ft) obscures the view down to Chania. A section of the Trek 1 route is in sight, on the way up to Kolokithas. The Potamos Valley (Trek 5) is 140°SE, with the Pachnes massif and Zaranokefala beyond it. Modaki 1224m (4016ft), one of several cone-shaped peaks of the Madares, rises above Katsiveli.

The E4 Trail, once it is beyond the stratified cliff, turns east for Potamos and Katsiveli (Trek 6).

WALK 6
*Xyloscala to Koustoyerako via Strifomadi
or E4 trail variation*

Grade	D
Start	Xyloscala 1240m (4068ft)
Access	KTEL Omalos bus or taxi from Chania
Finish	Koustoyerako 500m (1640ft)
Access to finish	Taxi from Souyia
Highest point	Summit of Strifomadi 1921m (6302ft)
Height gain	501m (1643ft)

Height loss	1421m (4662ft)
Approx distance	14km (8.7 miles)
Time allowance	Xyloscala to goat paths turn-off 1500m (4921ft) 1hr; to Strifomadi summit 1hr 50mins; summit to Achlada Valley 1600m (5249ft) 1hr; Achlada to 1000m (3280ft) 1hr 50mins; to Koustoyerako 1hr; total: 7hrs 10mins
	For Koustoyerako down to Souyia on foot add 2hrs

This is a spectacular mountain route from the Omalos Plain to Koustoyerako and Souyia. Branching off from the Gingilos footpath, it takes in Strifomadi summit before making a long descent to the southwest over hillsides high above the Tripiti Gorge. More centrally placed and just as accessible as Gingilos, Strifomadi offers a better all-round view, but the steep summit approach makes this a walk rarely tackled by organised groups. This walk suits May–November, if the snowdrift under Strifomadi summit is passable. Take daysack essentials and a minimum of 2 litres of water per person.

Alternatively a section of the E4 Trail from Gingilos saddle bypasses the summit route, on a short cut that may suit experienced mountain walkers with a good head for heights, and if the weather is settled. As much of this E4 short cut is loose underfoot it is easiest to walk it from east to west, as it is then mainly uphill. However, since heavy deluges seem now to be commonplace, natural erosion may at any time wreck some part of this small footpath.

Follow Walk 3 to the goat paths turn-off before the pinnacles.

For Strifomadi summit, ascend the ridge. A spindly iron fence borders the top edge of the cliff on the mountainside below the summit. The footpath ascends near the fence until, after gaining most of the height, it traverses right to finish the climb on an easier gradient. If snowdrifts linger, the fence is a useful safety guide. The summit is the highest point above the huge cliff at the head of the Tripiti Gorge.

For the E4 Trail (6a), which crosses this huge cliff well below the summit, continue up to Gingilos saddle (Walk 3). This section of the E4 is a shepherds' or hunters' route across steep crags and scree. It is waymarked with paint and E4 poles. It is not suitable for those who suffer from vertigo, or who are encumbered with heavy packs, or if the weather is unsettled: that is, if there is likely to be thick mist, rain or strong winds.

Losing height from the saddle at first this route then climbs to the top of the thin ridge above the great scree slope. From there it gains more height, undulating across scree, crags, and two sections of bare rock, one a vertical (steep) section, one horizontal. Steel wire handrails fixed across the bare rock have suffered storm damage. The wire across the horizontal rock is no longer in the best position. The highest point of the route is reached on the spine of a wide, shallow spur descending from the Strifomadi summit area. Beyond that, the path loses height to negotiate a re-entrant (several sections are eroded and loose) before climbing again to reach the rim of the west side of the gorge. In the spring a last snowdrift may block the path in this re-entrant. If so there is a steep, but safe escape route up the shallow spur to the summit, which is almost in sight not far beyond the skyline.

To continue the route Beyond the western rim of the gorge – in sight whether you have reached it by walking along the summit ridge or via the E4 short cut – the route continues to the southwest down a bare hillside to trees seen at the foot of a snowmelt watercourse. Beyond, an isolated bare ridge runs east–west above the Achlada valley. (Note that some maps mark Achlada in the Tripiti Gorge, but it is just north of this ridge, in line with Koustoyerako.)

Now clear of the summit crag, turn southwards and make your way downhill fairly near the gorge rim, to avoid a watercourse gully on the right. When you arrive at the E4 pole (which marks the end of the short cut footpath from Gingilos saddle) turn away from the gorge. The path is now much more distinct. Within a few minutes pass a small spring and (very old) small wooden trough. Birds may alert you to its location but note that it may not be running late in the year.

The path continues its descent southwest above the gully that has been in view on the descent, and which develops into a ravine. As you approach the first big crag on the west side of the ravine, look carefully for the continuation of the path. It climbs above this crag to continue high above the ravine. This is the approach to the Achlada Valley and the path follows through, beside cypress trees, to bring you out at the head of the valley. Pass a ruined

Note For those equipped to camp this is a pleasant two-day route.

E4 Trail: heading for Achlada

In 1943 this remote valley was one of the hideouts of the Koustoyerako band of World War II Resistance fighters led by New Zealander Dudley Perkins.

stone hut, then a ruined *mitato* and cistern (poor water). The flat concrete roof of the hut has collapsed under the weight of winter snows, but the former cheese store remains as a useful storm shelter. ◄

Continue for 20mins down the valley, on the E4 way-marked footpath above the watercourse, to a concrete flat-topped cistern (good water) and a roofless stone hut. A fenced water trough near the cistern operates with a ball-valve device. This is a very remote place: check that it is working, as Koustoyerako villagers will need to know if it is not. Cross the riverbed to rejoin the path as it enters the trees. Old charcoal-making sites in the oak forest and a *kalderimi* (paved mule track) that bypasses a drop of large boulders can be seen on the way down.

After about 3km, at an altitude of 1000m (3280ft), the riverbed turns sharply left and south. Here mature pines survived the 1994 Souyia Valley fire. Still very far below, the

valley is glimpsed through the trees. **Note** Walk 7 from Ay.
Theodoros comes in at this turning.

After about 12mins, with the riverbed developing into a
ravine, take a *kalderimi* ascending out of it, left. Follow this
old trail over and down to a fenced concrete cistern, a modern stone-built chapel and a dirt road. Here the mountainside
is cut to bits by roadworks and Koustoyerako is in sight, still
quite far below, under the brow of Ochra crag.

Village vineyards feature on a wide saddle beyond the pine
forest. Descend via the road and sections of footpath,
E4-waymarked, to this saddle with its large concrete water
tank (locked). Continue down the road. (A village-direct
footpath under Ochra crag is now overgrown and disused.)

Koustoyerako has two *kafeneia*, which may or may not
be open. If they can be found, village proprietors are
pleased to open up if visitors arrive. The food menu will
depend on the travelling van delivery, likely to be on a
Wednesday. A Souyia taxi can be called, but expect to wait
because taxis are often busy. There are no rooms because
Koustoyerako villagers channel their enterprise into the
beach resort of Souyia. However, trekking groups sometimes
camp here (enquire).

Koustoyerako to Souyia The footpath down to Livada village
(30mins) starts alongside the *kafeneon* overlooking the
plateia. A delightful path in the spring, this old mule track
negotiates the steep vegetated hillside, losing height through
shady olive groves and across flower-strewn terracing. Turn
left, south, when you reach the main road to walk (for
30mins) through **Livada** (no facilities) and downhill as far as
a T-junction where a dirt road heads due south. Follow this
dirt road for the remaining 1hr walk to **Souyia**. When you
reach a T-junction, turn left, uphill, to find cairns and E4
poles that mark a last footpath section down to the riverbed.

WALK 6A

Koustoyerako to Xyloscala via Strifomadi
or E4 short cut to Gingilos Saddle

Walk 6 in reverse	
Grade	D
Start	Koustoyerako 500m (1640ft)
Access	Taxi from Souyia
Finish	Xyloscala 1240m (4068ft)
Access to finish	KTE!. Omalos bus or taxi from Chania
Highest point	Summit of Strifomadi 1921m (6302ft)
Height gain	1421m (4662ft)
Height loss	501m (1643ft)
Approx distance	14km (8.7 miles)
Time allowance	Koustoyerako to Olisma 1000m (3280ft) 2hrs 30mins; to Achlada cistern 1300m (4265ft) 1hr 30mins; to summit 3hrs; to Xyloscala 2hrs; total: 9hrs. For Souyia to Koustoyerako on foot add 3hrs 15mins

As well as that described in Walk 6, there is an alternative walking route from Souyia up to Koustoyerako. Take minimum 2 litres water per person.

Note
If you happened to tramp this otherwise likely-looking road south from Koustoyerako, and arrived at its end, you would then have to clamber down a very steep hillside to reach the E4 coastal path.

From **Souyia** cross the riverbed on the E4 Trail (see Trek 10a) and ascend the marked footpath to reach the first dirt road of the hillside. Here turn left, and then uphill, right, at the next junction. Walk up this road as far as a stand of beehives (a potentially non-permanent feature), just under the south-facing side of a spur descending the hillside. Now make your way straight up this spur, which is free of the crags that are a feature of the hillside further north near Livada village. By doing this, you will encounter a road at about 500m (1640ft), which contours northwards directly to Koustoyerako. This road serves a radio station that overlooks the coast. ◂

Alternatively, it is easy to reverse the route described in Walk 6. Continue on the dirt road to the T-junction with the main Koustoyerako road. Turn uphill for **Livada**, a linear village perched on a steep hillside. After passing the last outlying hamlet of Livada, which is sited on a spur below the road, keep a careful lookout for roadside cairns that mark the footpath up to Koustoyerako. The path gains height steeply, passing through terraced olive groves.

From Koustoyerako join a waymarked branch of the E4 Trail: leave the *plateia* on an unmade road that ascends (to the left of Ochra crag) to a large concrete cistern and vineyards, and thereafter serves high mountain forest areas. At the cistern, aim for the re-entrant in the mountainside now just above, east, bordered by a crag on the left. Waymarked short-cut footpaths, up through the forest, cut across the road loops. Bear left as the road divides. It ends at a fenced concrete cistern near a modern stone-built chapel. An old mule track bordered with large stones continues the climb up through pine forest to reach a *kalderimi* that descends to the bed of a ravine. Turn up the ravine. At 1000m (3280ft), a locality named **Olisma**, the riverbed is wide and has levelled out. It makes a sharp turn eastwards.

Reverse the route notes for Walk 6 from here, where the route divides: north is Walk 7 in reverse, east is for Walk 6 in reverse.

WALK 7

Omalos to Koustoyerako
via Ay. Theodoros Chapel

Of the two traditional routes between Omalos and Koustoyerako (Walks 6 and 7) this is the least strenuous, as it skirts the western flank of Psilafi, contouring at over 1200m (3937ft), high above the Ay. Irini Gorge and the Souyia Valley. Traversing rough, waterless terrain, this is an unfrequented route offering open views across the valley. A shepherds' road serves part of it. Take daysack essentials, and a minimum of 2 litres of water per person.

Follow Walk 1 across the Omalos Plain to the western exit pass (on the road to Ay. Irini). This asphalted road heads uphill and passes Ay. Theodoros chapel where there are one or two old tombs.

Just beyond the chapel, take the shepherds' road uphill, left. This quickly gains height to a 'shelf' high above the

Grade	D
Start	Omalos hamlet 1080m (3543ft)
Access	KTEL Omalos bus or taxi from Chania
Finish	Koustoyerako 500m (1640ft)
Access	Taxi from Souyia
Highest point	1200m (3937ft)
Height gain	120m (393ft)
Height loss	700m (2296ft)
Approx distance	13km (8.1 miles)
Time allowance	Omalos hamlet to Ay. Theodoros chapel, via northern ring road 1100m (3608ft) 50mins; chapel to last cistern approx 1250m (4101ft) 1hr; cistern to Olisma 1000m (3280ft) 2hrs; to Koustoyerako 1hr 30mins; total: 5hrs 20mins For Koustoyerako down to Souyia on foot add 2hrs

E4 Trail: arriving at Koustoyerako

Souyia Valley. Follow the road south to a small hollow with a concrete water tank and cistern (the last water point on the route). The road has lately been extended, downhill, beyond this place. Southwards, there is a wide descending valley with various sheep paths. Continue the traverse by making

your way down to approximately 1200m (3937ft) to find the best path for the continuing traverse, through sparse woodland. The correct footpath appears as the forest thickens, red-dot waymarked (these might be faded). Your destination is the forested riverbed descending from the Achlada Valley (Walk 6). ▸

After contouring at first, the forest path loses height to 1000m (3280ft) and the spot, **Olisma**, where the wide stony riverbed, with large pine trees, makes a sharp turn from east–west to south.

For Koustoyerako Follow Walk 6 down the riverbed.

For Achlada Turn east and walk up the riverbed on the waymarked E4 Trail. As the trees end, cross over to find the cistern on the northern bank.

If you contoured well above the crags of the Ay. Irini Gorge and yet kept within the treeline, you would eventually reach the riverbed even if you missed the footpath.

WALK 7A

*Koustoyerako to Omalos
via Ay. Theodoros Chapel*

Walk 7 in reverse	
Grade	D
Start	Koustoyerako 500m (1640ft)
Access	Taxi from Souyia
Finish	Omalos hamlet 1080m (3543ft)
Access to finish	KTEL Omalos bus or taxi from Chania
Highest point	1200m (3937ft)
Height gain	700m (2296ft)
Height loss	120m (393ft)
Approx distance	13km (8.1 miles)
Time allowance	7hrs

To get to the trailhead follow instructions for Walk 6a.

When you reach the locality called Olisma – the right-angled turn in the riverbed at 1000m (3280ft) – look carefully on the left for the footpath (cairns/red dots) that continues up through woodland, but in a northerly direction, heading for the west-facing flank of the massif you are now on. **Note** Following the riverbed, the E4 Trail takes you east, up to the Achlada Valley.

Take a minimum of 2 litres of water per person.

WALK 8
Omalos to Ay. Irini Gorge

Grade	B
Start	Omalos hamlet 1080m (3443ft)
Access	KTEL Omalos bus or taxi from Chania
Finish	Ay. Irini Gorge north trailhead 600m (1968ft)
Access to finish	KTEL Souyia bus or taxi from Souyia or Chania
Highest point	1110m (3641ft)
Height gain	30m (98ft)
Height loss	510m (1673ft)
Approx distance	8km (5 miles)
Time allowance	Omalos hamlet to Ay. Theodoros chapel via northern ring road 1100m (3608ft) 1hr; to Ay. Irini Gorge trailhead 2hrs 10mins; total: 3hrs 10mins

An asphalted road serves the pass on the western rim of the plateau, passing the chapel of Ay. Theodoros. After contouring west for 8km it joins the Chania–Souyia road at Seli, a narrow neck of land that is the only 'bridge' between, broadly speaking, the porous sedimentary rock of the White Mountains and the impervious metamorphic rock of the Selino region. Huge valleys descend north–south either side of this watershed. The Ay. Irini Gorge splits the southern valley as a deep gash just under the western flank of Psilafi. Opening out 5km from the shore, its riverbed reaches the sea at Souyia, a beach resort served by KTEL bus and ferryboat. Unlike the new road, the old mule track from Omalos to Ay. Irini takes a direct route down to the gorge and onwards to Souyia. This is an easier route to Souyia than Walks 6 or 7.

Follow Walk 1, and then Walk 7, to **Ay. Theodoros chapel** on the main road.

Four minutes along the road from the chapel a seating area and balustrade mark the start of the E4 Trail waymarked footpath – an old mule track. After about 500m reach a steep scree crossing amongst sparse trees. Here the *kalderimi* zig-zagged downhill and so, with this part now buried due to roadworks, cross the scree on the newly formed path that picks up the old trail further down. This steep hillside is just above a branch ravine of the Ay. Irini Gorge, down which the Feigou robbers' path is routed (see Walk 9); it is not an easy short cut since it is unfrequented and steep. However a circular walk from the balustrade parking area is now fairly popular, descending the Feigou ravine, returning via the upper part of the gorge.

Beyond the scree, a fine section of *kalderimi* with a high retaining wall leads down to a green spurge-covered valley. Cross this to reach a flat concrete cistern (good water) and then continue up in a northwesterly direction out of the valley. Follow another section of *kalderimi* that clings to a crag, right, but as the grey limestone runs out, so does this paved track. You are now in the valley of Ay. Irini Gorge and the Seli Pass is on the skyline, up on your right. Turn south down the spur on a footpath descending to a pine forest. Here another short section of well-built *kalderimi* leads down to a couple of houses, the river, and the bridge to the main Chania–Souyia road.

The entrance to the **Ay. Irini Gorge Nature Reserve** is found just on the left and is signed. This is also a KTEL bus stop: Souyia to Chania buses pass this stop about 30 minutes after departing from Souyia. Otherwise, walk north up the road to a *taverna* (telephone) or continue down the gorge to Souyia (an additional 4hrs; see Walk 9).

WALK 9

Ay. Irini Gorge to Souyia

Grade	B
Start	On the Souyia road just south of Ay. Irini village 600m (1968ft)
Access	KTEL bus or taxi from Chania or Souyia (see below)
Finish	Souyia (sea level)
Access to finish	KTEL Souyia bus or taxi (see below) or coastal boat service between Ay. Roumeli and Paleochora
Height loss	600m (1968ft)
Approx distance	8km (5 miles)
Time allowance	To Koustoyerako bridge 3hrs; to Souyia by road 45mins; to Souyia by riverbed footpaths 1hr; total: 4hrs

This short but varied gorge bordering the western flank of the White Mountains is a nature reserve of the Forest Directorate of Chania. There is a small admission charge. The trail is easy to follow. WCs and water taps do not operate early in the year; in spring, near the top, a river flows for some distance. Areas of humidity and shade sustain a variety of plants, and gigantic ancient plane trees grace a large clearing halfway down. This gorge is offered to tourists as a day tour excursion, but it is less visited than Imbros and Samaria because the Chania–Souyia road is narrow, long and winding – although it is a good scenic ride.

Signboards mark the Feigou hideout where outlaws lived during the Turkish occupation. They used the big chapel-shaped boulder beside the trail as their 'church'.

The walk starts from the Chania–Souyia main road just south of Ay. Irini village, a spot well known to taxi and bus drivers. **From Chania** Some taxi drivers may not want this job – find another driver. **From Souyia** Taxi drivers are used to the road but they are often busy – book in advance. There is a daily KTEL bus service.

Walk down to the refreshments kiosk and WCs in the woodland. From there the well-tramped, made-up footpath is easy to follow. ◄

A car and tour bus park, and a *taverna* or two, mark the end of the gorge. Continue along the road beside the riverbed. A more pleasant option for the walk to Koustoyerako bridge is to turn off down an unsurfaced slip road on the right, and cross the riverbed to pick up an older track on the opposite bank. At the bridge turn right for the main road to Souyia. Otherwise make your way down the riverbed on goat paths. The KTEL afternoon bus to Chania usually departs 15.30.

Starting down the Ay. Irini Gorge

Souyia, with its mountainous hinterland, is a scenically attractive beach resort of Selino province. It draws many repeat visitors, including young families, although locally the black-stoned beach is not seen as 'bucket and spade' because – like that of Ay. Roumeli – it shelves away fairly rapidly. In addition to the walk down, or up, the Ay. Irini Gorge, there are rugged coastal walks in both directions, including boat–taxi transfers in the tourist season. Souyia has several rooming houses, shops and restaurants. There is an ATM cash dispenser. Souyia is on the south coast ferry-boat schedule between Ay. Roumeli and Paleochora.

WALK 9A
Souyia to Lissos and Paleochora (E4 Trail)

Grade	C
Start	Souyia
Finish	Paleochora
Access	Both villages served by KTEL bus from Chania, and coastal ferryboat schedule
Height gain/loss	Undulating coastal route: about 300m (984ft) gain/loss
Approx distance	13km (8.1 miles)
Time allowance	4hrs 45mins

This route is not in the White Mountains district but, as previously mentioned, it is possible to continue to Paleochora from where there is a much more frequent KTEL bus service to Chania. This is a popular section of the E4 Trail, particularly with excursionists from Paleochora who take the morning ferryboat to Souyia then walk back. The waymarked footpath goes up a small gorge before climbing over a headland to reach the exceptionally beautiful Lissos Valley. Lissos is free of roads and has several ancient remains since, apart from the sheltered inlet, there is a permanent freshwater spring. However, Lissos has probably been saved from development because it is a serious habitat for midges. If you plan to camp here bring an insect-proof tent. Unfortunately, this otherwise excellent walk is let down by its last section which is a 4km road-tramp along the shore east of Paleochora.

This can be a hot walk and there is no water to be found beyond Lissos – fill up at the spring if necessary.

Walk west along the **Souyia** seafront to the small harbour and ferryboat jetty. Pass behind the harbour to get onto a well-tramped footpath leading up the Kakos Potamos Gorge. It eventually climbs out of the gorge, to the left, and crosses over the headland above **Lissos**. Consequently there are fine views of the valley before you descend to it. Bear right to find the spring near a hut in shady woodland. ◄

For Paleochora cross the riverbed from the spring, and after bearing a little to the left climb the hill. Cross a road and again keep straight on uphill on a footpath through the *phrygana*. At the top of the hill keep straight on along a narrow track that heads back towards the coast. The path is well waymarked.

WALK 10
Omalos to Zourva

Grade	D
Start	Omalos hamlet 1080m (3543ft)
Access	KTEL Omalos bus or taxi from Chania
Finish	Zourva 600m (1968ft)
Access to finish	Taxi from Chania or Fournes
Highest point	1100m (3608ft)
Height gain/loss	Steeply undulating route: overall height loss 500m (1640ft)
Approx distance	9km (5.5 miles)
Time allowance	Omalos hamlet to Forestry Service cistern 800m (2624ft) 1hr 5mins; cistern to Vothanas 1000m (3280ft) 1hr 15mins; Vothanas to Sterna 800m (2624ft) 30mins; Sterna to inspection chamber 600m (1968ft) 45mins; to ridgetop 750m (2460ft) 45mins; to Zourva 50mins; total: 5hrs 10mins

Initially losing height rapidly from the Omalos plateau, this route then traverses three ridges of the northern foothills above Lakki. An unfrequented walk on shepherds' footpaths, it crosses only one road and has Amalia's *taverna* at Zourva as its destination. **Note** There is another Vothanas above Vafes (Walk 19).

Starting from **Omalos hamlet**, walk north on the main road and up to the plateau rim. ▸

Turn off right, towards a big concrete water tank, then clamber down onto a section of mule track running below and parallel to the road. In a few minutes this turns east as a footpath down a valley. Follow this footpath, passing areas of old terracing. The valley finally ends at a cypress-tree-filled cleft, which brings you out over a short, but steep, descent to a shepherds' road in a narrow valley. Turn left down this road for 200m to an old-style Forestry Service cistern.

For Lakki Continue down the road (Walk 12).

For Zourva Leave the road at the cistern to ascend the next ridge east, on a footpath. (The footpath hardly shows but, knowing it is there, examine the ridge and note a dip in the skyline with a large rock and trees. The path climbs to this spot before gaining the top of the ridge from there.)

Cross the riverbed and bear right to find the path, which ascends steeply at first before turning left and heading up towards the large rock, or crag. Ascend the crag and then continue up, with woodland on your left. At the top – from where there are views of neighbouring valleys and ravines – turn right up the spine of the ridge for a short distance to reach a main path traversing eastwards to the next descending spur.

For Sterna cistern direct Contour around to the left and make your way eastwards, across the hillside, down towards a stand of mature trees to find the cistern.

To visit Vothanas 'secret valley', climb over this spur for the short descent over old terracing (no cistern). Beyond the east rim of the valley a pipe conveying water to Meskla can be seen clinging to the far side of a deep gorge.

However, halfway along Vothanas, bear left through shady trees to the north rim. Make your way downhill, right, to mature oak or pear trees on the descending spur, a place called Sterna (*sterna* is a Greek word for cistern). Beside a big walnut tree, a very old barrel-vaulted cistern (good water) is sited above the terracing which infills a small re-entrant. A

Note A last section of the old 'Mousourou Road' by a telegraph pole over on the left.

Spurge-covered foothills on the way to Zourva

Escape route to Lakki (of sorts)
The footpath down the west side of this valley climbs around the end of the spur before descending through a very overgrown stretch to a confluence of gorges below Lakki. From there it is 20mins up to the village (Walk 12).

broken concrete animal trough is imprinted (in Greek) with the name Kandidakis, a Lakkiot family, long since emigrated.

Continue on the main route Beyond the cistern, pass a ruined stone hut and a shrine, and continue a short way down the ridge to where two bracken-filled gullies descend steeply to the valley from the gorge. Pause here to note a shepherds' hut, almost directly opposite on the skyline of the next green ridge. The final stage of the footpath to Zourva leads down from that hut.

Over old terracing, bracken and spurge, now descend the right-hand gully to the valley below, where the path leads to an (unlocked) inspection chamber of a water supply pipe. Take good care not to contaminate this village water supply. ◄

For Zourva Follow the path from the inspection chamber as it crosses the tree-lined riverbed for the ascent of the next ridge. It is easiest to climb the right-hand spur, now just above. Arrive at the hut and cistern (or seepage well) on the ridgetop. Zourva is in sight, on the next ridge looking east and, in the valley now just below, a shepherds' path heads for it. After entering forest, this footpath crosses a watercourse before joining a vehicle track in the woodland and the olive groves below the village. Turn right here and head for a large sheep shed. Behind the shed find the footpath that leads up left to the main road, where you turn right for the *taverna* and the village. Taxis can be called. Apart from her busy lunch-hour trade Amalia and her family have many years' experience of walkers' needs: a roaring stove on a wet day, an evening meal and so on (tel: 28210.67470 or 33258).

WALK 10A
Zourva to Omalos

Walk 10 in reverse	
Grade	D
Start	Zourva 600m (1968ft)
Access	Taxi from Chania
Finish	Omalos hamlet 1080m (3443ft)
Access to finish	KTEL Omalos bus or taxi from Chania
Height gain	Steeply undulating route; overall height gain 500m (1640ft)
Approx distance	9km (5.5 miles)
Time allowance	7hrs

From the *taverna* walk downhill past the war memorial, then turn sharp left onto a gated footpath that descends to olive groves and a large shed. Take the track from the front of the shed for a minute or two, and then enter the forest by bearing left up a footpath.

From there reverse Walk 10.

WALK 11
Zourva to Meskla

Grade:	A
Start	Zourva 600m (1968ft)
Access	Walk 10, or taxi from Chania
Finish	Meskla 300m (984ft)
Access to finish	Taxi from Chania
Height loss	300m (984ft)
Approx distance	3km (1.8 miles)
Time allowance	50mins

There are pleasant routes down to Meskla via the network of roads serving the olive groves of the valley on the eastern side of the Zourva ridge. The route described here is the shortest, but for a longer walk cross the valley to roads descending the far side.

Walk down the road from the *taverna* and take a footpath short cut from the chapel. Alternatively, follow the road downhill until you overlook the next valley to the east. From this spot, just beyond the first left-hand bend, descend right on an unmade olive grove service road. After contouring round a re-entrant, keep left, along under the Zourva spur. Arrive at a Y-junction. The left-hand option heads uphill, but bear right, downhill, and thereafter keep left. Rejoin the village main road. Leave it again on a narrow, concreted lane that descends steeply on the left to join the village main street.

To call a taxi, the supermarket (further downhill) has a telephone (or enquire at the house just above it). **Meskla** is on the KTEL weekday village schedule.

WALK 12
Omalos to Lakki and Meskla

Grade	C
Start	Omalos hamlet 1080m (3443ft)
Access	KTEL Omalos bus or taxi from Chania
Finish	Lakki 500m (1640ft)
Access to finish	KTEL Omalos bus or taxi from Chania
Highest point	1110m (3641ft)
Height loss	610m (2001ft)
Approx distance	9km (5.5 miles)
Time allowance	Omalos hamlet to Stephanoporo hill 800m (2624ft) 1hr 15mins; to below Lakki 1hr 15mins; up to Lakki 20mins; total: 2hrs 50mins

This is an old transhumance trail and a direct footpath between Lakki village and the grazing pastures of the Omalos Plain. Wear long trousers as lately it has become overgrown through disuse. In 2003 the section directly below the village was cleared.

Follow Walk 10 as far as the Forestry Service cistern, then continue along the shepherds' road to an isolated spur from where the road makes a sharp turn uphill. This spur can be identified on contour maps because of its distinctive shape: a thin saddle, or pass, at 800m, linking to an oblong hill, orientated almost north–south, and just south of Konstantiou peak (809m/2654ft). ▶

Another old-style Forestry Service cistern is now just below, at the head of a descending valley, whilst at the top of the shepherds' road, west, the Lakki–Omalos main road is in sight at a place called Fokyes.

Fokyes is several kilometres by road from both Omalos and Lakki. The footpath routes may be in a disused state but they are much more direct.

Make your way down the valley, overgrown with Jerusalem sage; the path is on the right-hand side at first and then continues down the centre. At the bottom continue

This is the hill of **Stephanoporo**, where World War II Special Operations Executive (SOE) agent Dudley Perkins and others were fatally ambushed in 1944.

around the corner, and head northeast towards a dry water-course bordered with cypress trees. Cross the watercourse to pick up the footpath that now descends alongside the riverbed, crossing it at intervals. The houses of Lakki come into view as the riverbed turns north. The descent ends at a tree-filled confluence of ravines below the village. Ascend to the village past ancient olive trees. Bear right, across a watercourse, for the correct path.

Lakki has a small shop, *kafeneia*, *tavernas*, rooms and a church clock. It is on the KTEL Omalos–Chania bus route.

For Meskla Walk north on the main road for about 500m, around a left-hand bend, and then turn down, right, onto a service road that descends through olive groves. Just before this road junction there is a short-cut footpath that bypasses part of the road.

WALK 12A

Lakki to Omalos

Walk 12 in reverse	
Grade	C
Start	Lakki 500m (1640ft)
Access	KTEL Omalos bus or taxi from Chania
Finish	Omalos hamlet 1080m (3443ft)
Access to finish	KTEL Omalos bus or taxi from Chania
Highest point	1110m (3641ft)
Height gain	610m (2001ft)
Approx distance:	9km (5.5 miles)
Time allowance	4hrs 25mins

Leave **Lakki** via the concreted lane just under the terrace of Niko's *taverna* and then turn sharp left, downhill, just before a small concrete slaughterhouse. The path down this damp, sheltered and thickly vegetated re-entrant crosses a small stream, passes ancient olive trees and brings you down to a tree-filled confluence of ravines. From here keep straight on, and up the ravine which is orientated north–south, following the footpath as it crosses to either side to avoid deeper parts

of the ravine. When the trees in this watercourse finally end bear right and cross over to get to the foot of the next valley.

From there reverse the notes for Walk 12. This valley is overgrown with Jerusalem sage but the shepherds' road at the top can be seen just above a concrete cistern – make your way up to it.

On the footpath from Lakki to Omalos

THE NORTHERN FOOTHILLS

The foothills of the White Mountains, in the districts of Kydonia and Apokorona, appear as a confusing mass of green spurge-covered ridges, spurs, valleys, gorges and ravines. Rainfall is much higher here than on the south side of the range. In spring, areas of lush vegetation contrast sharply with the snow-capped mountains above. Old terraces are carpeted with wild flowers, and steep hillsides are densely covered with shrubs in bloom interspersed with pockets of surprisingly varied woodland. At the treeline, dark green cypresses adorn rocky hillsides, and higher still steep bare mountainsides form some of the roughest and least-visited terrain of the entire range.

During the Battle of Crete, May 1941, when Allied and Greek army rearguard defenders at Alikanos deadlocked the German advance eastwards, a battalion of élite Mountain Division (Alpine) troops apparently found their way across this 'steep, broken and trackless' (and waterless) level on a very tough three-day march to get forward of the battle area.

The old trails of Apokorona province, with its good water supply and easily cut sandstone, are dotted with the modest ruins and relics of a sensitive pastoral culture remembered to this day. Vineyards, olive groves and keeping sheep concern villagers here. Some of the village-linking footpaths mentioned (in much better condition decades ago) are among those that were used by George Psycoundakis on his journeys between Askifou and the Omalos ('the Cretan Runner' in the book of the same name – see Appendix 2 – a member of the World War II Resistance.)

Ongoing depopulation has rendered many old trails overgrown, even within a decade, and it may be years before these footpaths are reclaimed for recreational walking. Scratchy plants are never pleasant, but with long clothing, and the patience to take it slowly, many old routes are still negotiable. Cut out a branch or two along the way if you have time as this helps to keep routes open. In general, when route-finding in densely vegetated areas, remember that heavy snowfalls in winter may have caused trees to fall across old paths.

The villages of the foothills are on the KTEL village schedule (see Public Transport). In time amenities may improve since retired townspeople have taken up renovating their inherited properties in the countryside.

KAMBI

Attractively sited on a fertile shelf above a large cultivated upland valley behind Chania, Kambi at 600m (1968ft) is the highest village of the foothills. For trekkers, one of the main north–south routes over the mountains (via Volikas EOS refuge) starts here. A continuous low-level traverse all the way to Askifou

The northern foothills from Kambi

also starts here (unless you don't mind long road-tramps, in which case you could begin at Zourva or Drakona).

Kambi is a quiet place, depopulated and far from the tourist trail. Bring your own food supplies. The *kafeneon* opens mornings and evenings, depending on demand. Although it is possible (town bus to Nerokourou) to walk from Nerokourou village on the southern outskirts of Chania, up the escarpment on a footpath to a Venetian chapel and overland to Katohori (the starting point for a walk down the Dictano Gorge), there is at present no walkers' route from the bridge at Katohori up to Kambi since the old mule track is fenced off. Locals, if they pass by, are generous in giving lifts up the road.

The path above Nerokourou on the way to Keramia (Kambi);
Chania, Akrotiri and Souda Bay in the background

WALK 13
Kambi to Volikas Refuge

Grade	C
Start/finish	Kambi 600m (1968ft)
Access	KTEL Kambi bus or taxi from Chania
Highest point	Volikas EOS refuge 1300m (4265ft)
Height gain/loss	700m (2296ft)
Approx distance	14km (8.7 miles)
Time allowance	Ascent from Kambi to Volikas EOS refuge 1480m (4855ft) 3hrs 30mins; descent via Volikas ravine 2hrs; via west ravine 2hrs 45mins; total: 5hrs 30mins or 6hrs 15mins

The two ravines from Kambi church

This circular mountain walk can be done at any time of year in settled weather, providing the snowline is above 1500m (4921ft). The walk, to the limit of the treeline and with Volikas EOS refuge as its objective, is a particular delight in the spring when wild pear trees are in blossom and the snow has recently melted in the high meadows.

Volikas is one of several mountain refuges in Greece dating from the 1950s when all materials had to be brought up by mule. Solidly built, with steel doors and shutters, these buildings have weathered decades of winter storms. Contact the EOS in Chania to arrange an overnight stay. Otherwise, passers-by can use the spring, and a utility shed alongside is left unlocked. A shepherds' road from Madaro passes below the refuge. However, part of the old mule track from Kambi remains intact because it is routed up a forested ravine.

Just south of Kambi is an area of low hills. Above that, note (visible from the *plateia*) two forested ravines, here called 'east' and 'west'. Volikas may be seen (through binoculars) just above the treeline at the top of the east ravine. The highest peak on the skyline is Spathi 2048m (6719ft), a 4hr 30min round trip from Volikas refuge (Trek 2), and to the left of it is Ay. Pnevma, its long approach ridge accessed from Kares or Melidoni. This walk to the refuge ascends the east ravine. An option for an attractive circular walk is to cross over from the refuge and descend the west ravine.

From **Kambi** *plateia*, pass in front of the church on the asphalt road heading south straight for the mountains, and after 5mins arrive at a Y-junction. There are road signs here for Madaro and Ramni (to the left) and to the right, Plativoli, Geroprinos, Psychro Pygadhi (a weekend-stay *taverna* high on the forested hillsides west of Kambi) and for your route 'Monopatti (footpath) Kambi – Volikas'. After a minute or so, turn left at the next junction, onto a track skirting a vineyard, and continue south to a sheep shed. Here turn up left on a waymarked footpath and go right, passing through a wire gate to get onto the hillside. Splintered paths climb to a shepherds' road immediately above. Follow this, heading southeast, across the low hills to the gully formed by the west ravine.

Just across the gully, leave the road on splintered footpaths that climb the hillside. Various footpaths then head uphill towards the east, or Volikas, ravine – the best is waymarked with a few red dots, and there are various cairns. In the ravine, cypress trees shade the old trail, which is built up in places.

When it opens out, continue straight on up through the next cleft. As this opens out, **Volikas refuge** is in sight on the hill above, due south. Cross the shepherds' road when you come to it – eastwards on the road would lead you down to Madaro (no facilities), but the road is long and winding. The path climbs the last stretch to the refuge by first traversing to the left.

From the refuge terrace, face the crag. About 400m to the left, note a patch of green creeper in the crag. This marks the spring – a small but steady drip from the rock face collects into a large concrete cistern. Cross the hillside below a line of rocks to get to it.

Behind you under the hillside is another old stone corbelled hut, once used by Kambi villagers to hide World War II Allied Army escapees after the Battle of Crete. The Volikas spring is the nearest functioning water supply.

Descent Retrace your steps for the easiest return to Kambi, or head for the neighbouring west ravine for a more interesting round trip. Take the footpath traversing west from the refuge into a small rocky gully. Climb the west rim of this to get onto a descending footpath. After about 200m note a large complex of old *mitata*, looking like a pile of rocks, on the hillside below to the northwest. Bearing left, descend a shallow gully orientated north–south, and then head for the *mitata*. ◄

Walk through the *mitata* complex and make your way down a steep gully to a flat-floored valley. On the west side enter trees and bear left over a large rock to pick up the path again. It now descends to the top of the west ravine. The footpath down the ravine crosses from side to side, but finishes up on the west side. Emerging above the low hills area, make your way almost straight down to the shepherds' road. Turn left and west to retrace your steps to Kambi.

Descending the west ravine

WALK 14
Kambi to Melidoni

Grade	B/C
Start	Kambi 600m (1968ft)
Access	KTEL Kambi bus or taxi from Chania
Finish	Melidoni 400m (1312ft)
Access to finish	Taxi from Vrisses (KTEL bus 7am and midday, weekdays); Kares has a twice-weekly KTEL bus service – enquire at Chania bus station
Height loss	Undulating route: overall height loss 200m (656ft)
Approx distance	10km (6.2 miles)
Time allowance	Kambi to Kares 2hrs 40mins; Kares to Melidoni 2hrs; total: 4hrs 10mins

Far from the tourist trail, this walk links four hill villages: Kambi, Madaro, Kares and Melidoni. Apart from a few short sections on roads, the route follows shepherds' footpaths over a series of low ridges in an almost forgotten pocket of rural Apokorona. Long clothing will be welcome in some sections. There are intermittent red-dot waymarks.

Note The Kares to Melidoni section, which passes through woodland and scrub, is now very overgrown (awaiting improvements). It is not impenetrable but it needs patience. A pruning saw and leather gloves are worth taking on routes like this.

From **Kambi** *plateia*, pass in front of the church on the asphalt road heading south straight for the mountains. After 5mins bear left at a junction with several signboards – turn left for Madaro ('Mathe-ar-ro'). If you do not mind clambering over shepherds' brushwood leave the asphalt road after 5mins, to the left, on a track to some sheep sheds (2mins). Here turn down to the right to pick up a walled section of the old mule track. It makes a pleasant short cut across this small valley.

Rejoin the asphalt road and walk uphill as far as a single storey house. From here the Madaro road loops around an open valley to pass the hamlet of Tsakistra, but there is a short cut through the olive groves: turn down to the right, and keeping straight on for 2mins, arrive at a clearing. Turn sharp left, through a gate, and after another 2mins bear right on to a cobbled mule track (cleared 2007). This ends at an

old shrine, and rejoins the asphalt road just opposite a road to Ramni. Turn right, heading south, for the unavoidable 10min walk on the main road to **Madaro**.

Shepherds live here and their dogs will probably bark noisily at your arrival. The road ends at a turning circle, as Madaro's cluster of houses is on the end of a spur. The summit ridge of Mount Ida is in view, far to the east. Turn down right on a concrete-surfaced track (the shepherds' road to high pastures), passing the village church (water tap). Either continue on the road as it passes around the valley or, just beyond the church, leave it alongside a stone wall, on an overgrown footpath that leads down to a dry riverbed. From the opposite bank a passable but disused section of paved *kalderimi* ascends a forested knoll to join the shepherds' road, which has skirted the valley. Follow the road up to the crest of the ridge. About 100m further on, turn down off it on footpath alongside a fence. The road continues up the mountainside to grazing areas near Volikas refuge and also contours around to the seepage wells on the next ridge east.

Follow this path heading east up to the next ridgetop, the first of four ridges to be crossed, on the way to Kares. The

On the path from Madaro to Kares in April

117

path has easy gradients since it was made to suit pack animals. Rejoin the road at the ridge top ('gate' beside the main gate). Although your next objective is the re-entrant below, to the right, first follow the road, left, to the ancient seepage wells and huge oak tree. From there sheep paths direct you back to the re-entrant.

On the ascent of the next ridge, pass a tree with a flat rock set in its lower branches: a nice shady seat for one person. The next ridge after that is much higher, but the (splintered) path maintains an easy gradient on the climb to the crest.

Detour If you walk northwards along this high ridge it is possible to look west, down into the deep valley you have just crossed, to see a small isolated cave at the bottom of the crag below the seepage wells. Old photographs, descriptions and the proximity of the water supply indicate that this cave, with its fire-blackened roof, was most certainly one of the hideouts, outlying from Kyriakosellia village, used by SOE Intelligence agents during the years 1942–44.

On the path, an old round stone shepherds' shelter lies just beyond the crest of the ridge, and from there continue down into the next re-entrant. Just over the top of the next lower ridge another huge deciduous oak has a fig tree growing in a fork. Across the valley a large stone-walled, tree-filled enclosure is the next objective – pass alongside its top wall. In 1992 a devastating bush fire raged through this region, but the trees inside the enclosure escaped. Follow the *kalderimi* as it descends this final ridge and ends. From there ascend to a track that soon joins a shepherds' road (leading up to Gournes, the deep valley under Spathi, Walk 15). Cross this road to pick up the continuation of the old mule track, which now makes a short descent to **Kares**.

Road access to Kares is long and winding, so that Kares *plateia* with its huge plane trees and ancient water source is definitely 'sleepy'. On the far side, opposite the spring, a small *kafeneon* opens in the late afternoon and at other hours to suit the locals: passers-by are welcome to picnic here if it is closed. No food is on sale, as there is no demand for it; villagers use the twice-weekly bus service to buy what they need down in Neo Horio. Kares' vineyards are on the next ridge looking east (also the way to Melidoni).

From Kares war memorial – to local patriots 'fallen heroically in battle' including as ever, so many in early 20th-century Balkan conflicts – cross the dry riverbed on the road up to the church. The churchyard has a large canopy and a WC (the *kafeneon* proprietor looks after the churchyard). With the churchyard on your right, keep straight on up an old mule track that ends beside a house on an ascending service track. Turn right here, and then almost immediately turn left at the next junction. This leads to a T-junction.

For Gournes (Walk 15) turn uphill, right.

For Melidoni keep left. Follow a straight section of track uphill (north), to arrive at a steel-tube gate. Beyond are Kares' olive groves and vineyards, but just before the gate climb above the road to rejoin the mule track. Follow it for 1min to the crest of the ridge, where there is a Y-junction of paths: turn left.

A deep ravine lies between the Kares and Melidoni ridges, now in view to the east. Pause here to examine the profile of Melidoni ridge for an advance understanding of the next stage. Over on the far left, to the northeast, a lone vertical cypress tree punctuates the skyline. Note the high-level hillside terracing in front of it. The footpath, heading for this feature, makes a gradual ascent to it from the ravine bed now just below. It is not as far as it looks.

Keep north on the walled mule track that soon turns and descends to the ravine bed. Apokorona shepherds may block old paths with piles of branches. These direct sheep here and there, and are not intended to stop people walking through (very few pass as it is). Clamber over the branches. Heavy winter snowfalls of 2003 and 2004 caused trees to fall across the ravine bed.

The footpath (cleared 2004) leaves the ravine on a long, straight traverse, and then ascends over old terracing to a thin, rocky, descending spur. This spot is quite high above the ravine. Note a large weather-eroded outcrop of grey rock just across the re-entrant. The footpath passes above this. Turn up sharp right and then head straight across old terracing, choked with Jerusalem sage, to a shady shelf in the re-entrant. The Akrotiri peninsula is in sight, far to the northwest. Beyond the big rock the footpath bears right, up to a crag in sparse trees, on this last part of the ascent to the hillside terracing. Cross to the low crag on the far side of the terracing. Climb it and bear right to pick up the footpath down the ridge. This meets a vineyard/olive grove service road. Continue down to a road junction. Turn left, to head northwest, and – keeping straight on past a big cypress tree – walk down to a large fenced flat concrete cistern. Turn right for Melidoni *plateia*, down a village street bordered with terrace-retaining walls.

Melidoni has two or three *kafeneia*, one of which should be able to rustle up a hot meal. There will be some items on sale such as gas cylinders, biscuits and tinned food. Taxis can be called.

WALK 14A
Melidoni to Kambi

Walk 14 in reverse

Grade	B/C
Start	Melidoni 400m (1312ft)
Access	Taxi from Vrisses
Finish	Kambi 600m (1968ft)
Access to finish	KTEL Kambi bus or taxi from Chania
Height gain	Undulating route: overall height gain 200m (656ft)
Approx distance	10km (6.2 miles)
Time allowance	4hrs 40mins

Leave Melidoni *plateia* heading south, up the road with the terrace-retaining walls. At a T-junction where there is a large fenced flat concrete cistern, turn left (east). In 10mins reach a Y-junction with the big cypress tree. Keep right, and then turn up right at the next junction.

From there reverse the notes for Walk 14. The route is overgrown but passable, and red-dot waymarked in places.

WALK 15
Kares to Gournes

Grade	C
Start/finish	Kares (Apokorona) 550m (1804ft)
Access	Via Walk 14, or taxi from Neo Horio, or KTEL twice-weekly bus (Chania bus station) or hired car
Highest point	Gournes Ay. Pavlos chapel 1020m (3446ft)
Height gain/loss	470m (1541ft)
Approx distance	8km (5 miles)
Time allowance	Kares to Gournes via mule track 2hr 35mins; Gournes to Kares via shepherds' road 1hr; total: 3hrs 35mins

The huge amphitheatre-shaped valley of Gournes is found northeast of Spathi summit and 1000m below it. Spectacular rock formations on the hillsides and rich woodland of mature cypresses combine to make this the most impressive of all the 'hidden' valleys of the northern foothills.

It was here, in January 1943, that SOE intelligence agent Patrick Leigh Fermor, and two associates, left the corbelled hut in which they were sheltering and hid from a German patrol by climbing a 'large snow-laden cypress tree'. George Pyscoundakis relates how he escaped at this moment by traversing the rugged, snow-covered mountainsides west of Gournes, eventually to descend at Kambi. In those days Gournes was reached from Kares – and also from Kyriakosellia (near Ramni) – on a direct mule track, a section of which still remains. Since there is good grazing at Gournes, a shepherds' road now serves the valley.

If Walk 14 is far from the tourist trail, this circular walk to Gournes is even more so. Bring your own supplies as there is no shop at Kares. A newly discovered cave system in the mountainside high above Gournes also attracts a few visitors (information from Chania EOS).

The watercourse draining from Gournes develops into a wide and steep-sided ravine. However, there is a break in this at the level of Kares, and the village is sited where the watercourse is shallow. The old mule track goes up the east side of the ravine, whilst the new shepherds' road is routed on a spur and hillslopes of the west side (see Walk 14 Kambi to Kares section: that footpath crosses the shepherds' road just a few minutes walk from Kares *plateia*). For a circular walk it is easiest to ascend via the mule track, and return by walking downhill on the new road.

With the village war memorial on your left, leave **Kares** by crossing the riverbed and walking straight uphill on the concreted road to the church. As you reach the churchyard's retaining wall keep straight on up the disused mule track that runs beside it. This ends at an ascending road, beside a house. Turn right and then almost immediately left to reach a T-junction. Left is for Melidoni (Walk 14) and uphill, right, is for Gournes. This road serves a white house at the top of the hill but before you get there, note (left) a track leading to a new house. The start of the mule track (red arrow and red-dot waymarked 2004) is found on the right-hand side of this track. Follow this up to open ground (about 620m/2034ft) from where you can see the Gournes ravine, Tsakistra church due north and, just across the valley, the short downhill section of mule track on which you will return to Kares *plateia*. Spathi summit is 180° degrees south. The hillsides of the huge spur descending from Ay. Pnevma are now above you. The paved mule track continues as a footpath leading uphill to a small meadow with a cistern (690m/2264ft). Bear right here, following alongside a stone wall.

Continue up the hillside (there are old terraces to the right of the trail) to reach another meadow in an area of woodland 820m (2690ft). There are two meadows in this copse. Since the old mule track is engulfed by undergrowth here, the waymarked path continues from the left-hand corner of the first meadow – behind a tree. Clear of the woodland it gains height across the *phrygana*-covered hillside. but just a few minutes after leaving the meadow look carefully for a Y-junction of footpaths – bear right for **Gournes**.

A part-paved section in sparse woodland under a crag now traverses the hillside and leads up to a T-junction of paths – bear left, and after another short distance uphill arrive at a second T-junction, with one or two stone marker cairns. Left (east) is a shepherds' path that crosses to the spur above Melidoni, and right (west) is the footpath which continues the uphill traverse towards the ravine. This soon evolves as a much more obvious continuation of the old

trail. The mountainside steepens as you near Gournes ravine, and the cypress-wooded terrain becomes rocky so that a built section mule track appears again. This leads up to a level area where there is a ruined corbelled hut on the right 950m (3117ft). The path crosses this before taking up a few zigzags to reach a natural 'shelf' in the mountainside, forming a pleasantly level traverse high above the ravine. There are fine views from here, and big slabs of rock provide seats.

The path loses height to enter the Gournes Valley near a shepherds' concrete hut. Join the shepherds' road here as it serves Ay. Pavlos chapel and various workstations. On the eastern side of the valley an unmade road climbs the Ay. Pnevma spur towards a complex of corbelled stone huts. However, return to **Kares** by following the shepherds' road downhill as far as the saddle on the spur above Kares, where the mule track noted at the start leads down to the *plateia*.

On the mule track high above Gournes ravine in May

WALK 16
Melidoni to Fres

Grade	B/C
Start	Melidoni 400m (1312ft)
Access	Taxi from Vrisses
Finish	Fres 200m (656ft)
Access to finish	Taxi from Vrisses
Height loss	200m (656ft)
Approx distance	5km (3 miles)
Time allowance	2hrs

Melidoni has vineyards and olive groves, but is also a shepherding village with a road to high pastures under Ay. Pnevma 2254m (7395ft), the next mountain east of Spathi. This walk follows the shepherds' road at first, but then peels off down the fairly rugged footpaths of the Fres ravine. As foothill scenery goes this is not the prettiest of walks, but it is a way of avoiding the main road, and also extends the day-walk from Kambi.

From **Melidoni** *plateia* follow Walk 14a to the big cypress tree. Keep to the left and continue east to a low pass on the next ridge, 1.5km from Melidoni.

(Melidoni's mature pine forest was destroyed by fire in 1992, but this fine tree survived the inferno. Two ancient seepage wells blend in so well just beside the tree that you could easily miss them.)

In view from this pass is a large, open valley at the foot of the ravine descending from hillsides under Ay. Pnevma. Outcrops of unsightly black rock occur in places. On the far side, beyond the olive groves, a spurge-covered ridge borders the east side of the ravine. A large concrete water storage tank is also on the opposite bank, further up the valley. The route to Fres starts down the dry riverbed of the ravine. ◄

Note Walk 19, to Vothanas, leaves from behind the big water storage cistern on the opposite bank.

Leave the pass going east, downhill, and follow the road as it loops right around the olive grove and back towards the riverbed. (Short cuts are fenced off.) Leave the road on any suitable route down to the riverbed.

Various sheep paths descend beside the riverbed. When it starts to develop as a gorge, bear left, above the west bank. Stay on this path until, as the gorge ends, it descends steeply to a road-head beside a chapel built on top of a freestanding rock. Take the road (there may be a gate) and bear left for **Fres** *plateia*, which is entered through an arched passageway. Fres has several *kafeneia* and shops. Taxis can be called from Vrisses.

WALK 17

Fres to Vrisses

Grade	A
Start	Fres 200m (656ft)
Access	Taxi from Vrisses
Finish	Vrisses 100m (328ft)
Access to finish	KTEL main road bus sercvice
Height loss	100m (328ft)
Approx distance	5km (3 miles)
Time allowance	1hr 30mins

From the church in **Fres** *plateia* walk northwards down the street to a crossroads with a three-arched shrine. Turn right (east) and keep straight on past the cemetery ('necro-taf-eeon') to the end of the road. Turn downhill: the old walled muletrack is now overgrown – make your way down through the olive groves to the right of it to join an asphalt road that loops around a small valley. Beside the crushed remains of an old burnt-out bus, turn up a village lane to join the main road from Fres to Vrisses, where you turn left, passing the war memorial.

A 2km short cut between Fres and Nippos improves this walk, which is otherwise on the main road.

Vrisses is now 3km away on the asphalt road – turn left, north, at the next T-junction. As you arrive in Vrisses' main street, turn right for the KTEL bus stop (*kafeneon*), shops and restaurants.

Vrisses is a busy place that has attracted residents from the foothill villages. KTEL buses for Chania, Rethymnon,

125

Heraklion and Sfakia stop here. Village supermarkets are open all week, as are restaurants and souvenir shops. Rooms are available. Two rivers converge here: plentiful water and foliage attract mosquitoes. Supermarkets sell mosquito coils if you need them.

WALK 18
Fres to Vafes via Tzitzifes

Grade	A
Start	Fres 200m (656ft)
Access	Taxi from Vrisses
Finish	Vafes 250m (656ft)
Access to finish	Taxi from Vrisses
Highest point	300m (984ft)
Height gain	100m (328ft)
Height loss	50m (164ft)
Approx distance	5km (3 miles)
Time allowance	1hr 30mins

During the Nazi Occupation 1941–44, SOE intelligence agents were assisted by the Vandoulakis family in this hamlet. The old-style walled house and courtyard where they used to meet still stands.

Leave Fres *plateia* on the main road heading southeast for Tzitzifes, 2km distant. Arrive at **Tzitzifes** and pass first one cheese-making dairy and then another (in what appears to be a block of flats). Almost opposite, take a surfaced road uphill towards the village church.

This is the shepherds' road to Vothanas grazing area, from where there is a link to Vafes.

From the church keep straight on, down a service track. This crosses overland, passing woodland and old terracing, in the direction of Vafes. You may see just a few sections of the old mule track route. Keep going and you will eventually join a back road to Vafes. Turn right, uphill, to reach a road junction. Bear right for 'upper Vafes' hamlet. ◄

Vafes main village is now seen below, clustered on an isolated hill. Many of these old houses are restored as holiday homes, or houses-for-rent by the village co-operative. The road to the main village now passes below the old schoolhouse, in its grove of shady pine trees.

Vafes *plateia* has two *kafeneia*, one of which sells basic supplies, including bread. There is also a special foods gift shop, and a special quality restaurant, Kourtsa, open at 19.00 Wednesday–Sunday (reservations tel: 08250.51201 or 0977.800387).

WALK 19
Melidoni to Vafes via Vothanas

Grade	C
Start	Melidoni 400m (1312ft)
Access	Walk 14 or school bus from Chania (enquire) or taxi from Vrisses or Ay. Pandes (taxis in this area are often engaged in nearby beach resorts of Kalives and Georgioupoli; consult locals for most likely service)
Finish	Vafes 250m (820ft)
Access to finish	Ongoing Walks 20a, 21, or taxi from Vrisses
Highest point	760m (2493ft)
Height gain	360m (1181ft)
Height loss	510m (1673ft)
Approx distance	12km (7.5 miles)
Time allowance	Melidoni to large cistern 50mins; cistern to roadhead 760m (2493ft) 1hr 45mins; roadhead to Vothanas 600m (1968ft) 40mins; Vothanas to Vafes 1hr; total: 4hrs 15mins

On a west-to-east traverse of the foothills this walk extends the route from Melidoni and allows you to stay in the mountains above the 600m (1969ft) level. The first section crosses an unfrequented, rugged area of mountainside between two different shepherding districts.

Note This unfrequented route is covered (but not marked) on the Anavasi map 'Pachnes'. (On Walk 10 there is another place called Vothanas.)

Follow Walk 16 to the pass 1.5km eastwards from Melidoni from where you can see hillsides to the east, on the other side of Fres ravine. The ravine develops, downhill to the left, after the watercourse has crossed a fairly level area (with

Vothanas

olive groves), but upstream the riverbed can be seen coming from a small gorge. The route to Vothanas (a large flat-floored valley, or doline) passes behind the ridge that borders the watercourse, fairly near the top of that gorge. To get there, follow Walk 16 to the riverbed and make your way across to the large concrete water cistern.

The terrain that has to be crossed between this cistern and the nearest shepherds' road is extremely rugged in places. Patience is required, but an old path does exist because there is a natural, deep water hole in the rock en route up to the shepherds' road. The road then links to Vothanas and Arevites ('Arry-veet-ez') hamlet (for Vafes), crossing terrain so covered with large rocks and thorn thickets that it otherwise would be impassable to walkers.

The first stage is to climb to a saddle on the ridge behind and above the big concrete tank and then turn south, around the hillside, to make your way down and round to the valley that lies on the other side, where the going underfoot is easier. The unfrequented footpath to the shepherds' road passes more or less up the centre of this valley. A very remote white chapel is seen on the mountainside high above the valley, and the shepherds' road from Vothanas ends (2002) at a spot that is almost directly below that chapel.

The valley footpath passes ruined stone huts in one place. Not far above these look out for the natural well, to your left. Set on a big rock, the low wall surrounding it makes it look like a fairly typical old cistern. To draw up water your very longest line will be needed (see General Information, Skills and Equipment). The roadhead is now just a short distance above the cistern. From there it is a straightforward tramp down to **Vothanas**, a mountain plain of about 1km² with areas of grass, woodland, thistles and Jerusalem sage. There are one or two modern shepherds' huts on the periphery, and a huge old cistern in the centre beside a disused cheese dairy. Either walk the road or cross the plain on more direct paths.

Note the Tzitzifes shepherds' road coming in from the north, but for Arevites keep east. Arevites is sited on top of an isolated spur.

For Askifou If you wish to continue at high level and keep straight on for Askifou, join Walk 21 by leaving the road before you arrive at Arevites: peel off down a disused track to the right. This crosses a spurge-covered valley to join the road from Archatsikia on the next spur east.

For Arevites A surfaced road links Arevites with Vafes (see Walk 21). Alternatively you could take an overgrown old path that is routed down the spine of the Arevites spur. To get onto this, follow the main road as it leaves the village. Note a double-width gate on your left, under the hillside. Go through this to pick up the footpath. After reaching a large old barrel-vaulted cistern the route bears right and leads down, through undergrowth, to join the main road beside a telegraph pole. There are one or two further short cuts between the road loops. But as there are crags between 'upper' and 'lower' **Vafes** there is no direct short cut footpath to the *plateia* – follow the main road down past the old schoolhouse.

WALK 19A
Vafes to Melidoni via Vothanas

Walk 19 in reverse	
Start	Vafes 250m (820ft)
Access	Walks 20, 34, or taxi from Vrisses
Finish	Melidoni 600m (1968ft)
Access to finish	Taxi from Vrisses or Ay. Pandes
Highest point	760m (2493ft)
Height gain	510m (1673ft)
Height loss	360m (1181ft)
Approx distance	12km (7.5 miles)
Time allowance	Vafes to Vothanas 1hr 35mins; Vothanas to roadhead 1hr; roadhead to large cistern 1hr 30mins; cistern to Melidoni 1hr; total: 5hrs 5mins

Take the road to Arevites by following the **Vafes** main street west, uphill towards an outlying part of the village ('upper Vafes') and the old schoolhouse. Continue on above the schoolhouse. There are two footpath short cuts: the first cuts out a loop in the road, but the second – which heads up to the spine of the spur – is not so easy to find since it is over-grown and only a small cairn by a telegraph pole marks the spot where you leave the road. Beyond **Arevites** the road continues as a track which gains height and then heads west for Vothonou and beyond, where it ends (2002) just as the mountainside steepens.

From here, reverse Walk 19: a white chapel is seen high on the steep mountainside and you now overlook a valley descending northwards. To the west, the valley system around Melidoni is in sight. A shepherds' path leaves from the road end (2002), where the hillside is less steep. Follow this downhill to the 'water hole' cistern and onwards down the valley to reach a flat area. Ruined stone walls indicate that this valley was once an important grazing area, presumably sustained by the natural water source. The terrain between this place and the Fres ravine riverbed is very rough. Either turn east for the rim of the gorge at this point, and then (patiently) make your way along the hillside above it, or keep north to contour around the hill in front of you, before turning east. Your destination is a big concrete water tank beside the Fres riverbed.

From there either walk down to Fres, or west to **Melidoni** (Walk 16).

WALK 20
Vafes to Vrisses

Grade	A
Start	Vafes 250m (820ft)
Access	Taxi from Vrisses
Finish	Vrisses 100m (328ft)
Access to finish	KTEL main road bus service
Height loss	150m (492ft)
Approx distance	4km (2.5 miles)
Time allowance	1hr 10mins

Walk downhill on the **Vafes** main road, and then bear right, heading for the church and cemetery. Just beyond the church, a huge circular water storage cistern and associated works supplies the fast-expanding village of Vrisses. The Vafes–Vrisses old mule track descends alongside the northeast wall of the cemetery and joins the main road at the foot of the hill.

Either turn right on the main road and follow this heading north to a bridge over the riverbed, east. Cross this for a back-road route to **Vrisses**, which brings you to the main street beside an impressive white marble memorial marking the 19th-century Struggle for Independence from Turkish rule. Turn left across the bridge for the bus stop (a *kafeneon*).

Alternatively, when the mule track from Vafes reaches the main road, cross the road to pick it up again as it continues down through the olive groves. Keep straight on (cross a service road), as it eventually joins the main Vrisses–Vafes road, where you turn left (north).

WALK 20A

Vrisses to Vafes

Walk 20 in reverse	
Grade	A
Start	Vrisses 100m (328ft)
Access	KTEL main road bus service
Finish	Vafes 250m (820ft)
Access to finish	Taxi from Vrisses
Height gain	150m (492ft)
Approx distance	4km (2.5 miles)
Time allowance	1hr 30mins

Leave Vrisses on a narrow street behind the Struggle for Independence memorial and walk south past orchards and olive groves. Near a small waterworks station, bear right. Cross a bridge and turn left on to the main road to Vafes. Follow the road as it gains height and rounds the steep, wooded hill in front of you, looking out for the start of the old mule track which leaves the road, steeply left. Keep left at a junction as this climbs the hill to Vafes church.

Either keep straight on from the church on a track alongside a stone wall. This leads to a small road junction. Keep straight on here to join the main road just before **Vafes** *plateia*.

Alternatively, taking the main road, the village is about 1km uphill from the church.

Vafes to Askifou Plain

Grade	C
Start	Vafes 250m (820ft)
Access	Taxi from Vrisses
Finish	Askifou–Ammoudari 790m (2591ft)
Access to finish	KTEL Sfakia bus or taxi from Chania or Vrisses
Highest point	900m (2952ft)
Height gain	650m (2132ft)
Height loss	110m (360ft)
Approx distance	10km (6.2 miles); circular walk 7km (4.3 miles)
Time allowance	Vafes to Achatsikia 400m (1312ft) 50mins; to Renda 540m (1771ft) 1hr 10mins; to TheKipou 800m (2624ft) 1hr 35mins; to rim of plain 940m (3083ft) 1hr 10mins; to Ammoudari 790m (2591ft) 50mins; total: 5hrs 50mins Circular walk 2hrs

In his introduction to George Psycoundakis' World War II memoir *The Cretan Runner*, Patrick Leigh Fermor describes their first meeting in a thicket above Vafes. Looking up at the steep shrub- and spurge-covered crags above the village, you might wonder where this hideout could have been. However, further up the mountainside, out of sight of Vafes, are two old shepherding *metochia*, or hamlets, Archatsikia and Arevites. Arevites is sited on a spur to the west (above 'upper Vafes' hamlet) and Archatsikia is on the hillside directly above Vafes main village. An overgrown footpath down the spine of a spur below Arevites links to upper Vafes. Since it passes an old cistern and a small stone shelter built into the boundary wall of an olive grove (such as described in SOE agent Xan Fielding's memoirs *Hide and Seek*) it is fair to assume this was the hideout. The walking route west to Askifou, however, goes via Archatsikia.

If you have at any time travelled from Vrisses to Sfakia on the KTEL bus you may have seen, looking westwards as it approaches Krappis, the little white chapel of Ay. Pnevma perched on top of an isolated hill. The footpath route Vafes–Askifou has to keep above a complex series of ravines, and passes behind this chapel before ascending the mountainous rim of the Askifou Plain.

From **Vafes** *plateia* look south. The surfaced road zigzagging uphill immediately across from the *kafeneia* serves Archatsikia ('Ar-shat-see-k'ya'). Take this road by bearing left at the road junction beside the Kourtsa restaurant. The hillside levels out above the crags and shady woodland of deciduous oaks comes as a pleasant surprise, because it cannot be seen from the village. As the trees end, open views to the east include a little white chapel, Profitis Ilias, on top of a steep spur (road access to this chapel, although not in sight, is from Embrosneros).

Continue up the road and on through the hamlet of **Archatsikia**. The road, now a track, still climbing, passes a small olive grove where there is a track junction.

For a circular walk back to Vafes via Arevites Turn right here, and, passing through the olive grove, join an unused overgrown track that leads down to a valley (water tap and sheep troughs) and then up to join the Vothanas–Arevites road, from where you can return down to Vafes (see Walk 19).

For Askifou via Renda Continue uphill to where the road ends at a U-bend. An overgrown footpath now takes over: starting from the low stone wall now in front of you it contours south along the retaining walls of old terracing. It gains some height, rounding the hillside, and then heads, through thickets of Jerusalem sage, for a bracken-filled fenced enclosure. You are crossing to a different shepherding district and there will be brushwood across the trail in one place. Make your way to the top right-hand corner of the bracken-filled enclosure to reach the fertile high-level 'hidden' valley of **Renda**, which is served by a road from Vatoudiaris. Across the valley an old *mitata* complex (cistern) together with a large modern sheep shed is sited on a low hill. Look beyond this towards the Askifou foothills, to the southeast, and note a forested ascending gully – the path to Ay. Pnevma chapel and TheKipou ('Theh-KEE-pou') is routed up this.

Heading east, follow the Renda road as it loses height to round a spur above a steep ravine. This thin spur is almost entirely demolished by the bulldozed road. Gain height again, passing sheep sheds, and at the crest of the hill leave the road by keeping straight on, on a footpath that heads for the forested gully. (The road descends to Vatoudiaris – rooftops can be seen).

Ascend the forested gully to reach a small open valley with old terracing. The path continues up the gully on the left-hand side of the valley. This leads through a cypress-tree-filled cleft to a small flat-floored hollow. Just before this hollow, however, carefully look left to spot the best continuing footpath. It contours around a small crag and then heads up through sparse woodland to join the track that serves both TheKipou and Ay. Pnevma chapel (no cistern). At this road, turn right for **TheKipou**, a clearing in the forest with a ruined shepherds' hut. The cistern here has passable water, but there is no shelter. Leave TheKipou on the shepherds' road heading east (en route to Vatoudiaris). Beyond the trees, Krappis and the Vrisses–Askifou main road are in sight on the far side of the valley and Askifou's steep mountainous rim is now directly above you.

For Krappis (*taverna* and bus stop) Walk down the road to a flat area with a sheep shed from where footpaths cross overland to Krappis.

For Askifou Ascend the steep hillside alongside a watercourse – as you leave the trees beyond TheKipou, look out for red-painted arrows at the roadside. These mark the best place for the start of the ascent. The path gains height and then crosses the lower section of the watercourse gully to continue the ascent on its east side. When the terrain gets easier, the path crosses over to the west side again.

At the top you have two choices:

Continue south, along a small, wooded valley (cistern) of Askifou's mountainous rim. Beyond the cistern a short track joins the Niato–Askifou shepherds' road – a good escape route in bad weather.

Alternatively, to avoid this long road-tramp down to the plain, turn left, just after you enter the valley, to follow a footpath that gains height eastwards. It evolves as a section of paved mule track which bears right to cross the mountain-top before leading down to a road-end where there is a concrete-topped cistern and an old sheepfold. Walk straight down this road to join the Askifou main road near a modern red-roofed church and a *taverna*. Turn right for **Ammoudari** and the bus stop, or left for **Kares**.

Note Only the Anopolis–Chania bus serves Kares plateia. Other KTEL buses stop (on request) at the main road junction with the Kares road.

THE ASKIFOU PLAIN

The Askifou Plain, at an altitude of 700m (2300ft), is lower than the Omalos. Villages on the busy main road to the south coast are inhabited all year round, even though they may be snowed in for several days in winter. Askifou's most distinguishing feature is a Turkish fort sited on the highest knoll, one of several built after the failed 1866 Revolution during the Struggle for Independence from Turkish rule. Seepage wells on the valley floor enable the cultivation of

cereals, potatoes and vines, crops that reflect the changing seasons in a patchwork of meadows. In spring carpets of wild flowers add blazes of colour.

Three of the four villages of the plain are situated along the road skirting the western side. Since Askifou is on the busy Samaria Gorge tour bus round trip, the main village, Ammoudari, now has a short bypass road. Ammoudari's former main road (now the village 'high street') has what passes for a *plateia*, marked by a whitebeam tree and monuments to local heroes. This remains the main KTEL bus stop, called 'Askifou'. Certain KTEL buses may use the bypass, so tell the conductor that you want to alight at Ammoudari – you may be let off at either end of the bypass. Ammoudari has rooms, *tavernas* and *kafeneia*. A few minutes from the *plateia*, along the road to the south, the village of Petres has a supermarket (08.00–20.00 daily), stocking everything a trekker needs. Currently (2007) there are small bakeries at Ammoudari and Kares, and *kafeneia* in every village except Goni ('Gon-nee').

This is a Sfakiot mountain community and the main agricultural occupation is shepherding. Two cheese dairies,

*A shady section
in the Imbros Gorge (Walk 24)*

136

The Askifou Plain in May (Walk 30)

which operate from April to June, supply outlets in Chania. At Kares one or two private collections of weaponry, equipment and bric-à-brac, jettisoned by Allied forces retreating after the 1941 Battle of Crete, await proper housing. Ask for the 'museo'.

Several good walks extend from Askifou, although most of them are not circular. The frequent KTEL Chania–Sfakia bus service is useful for access to trailheads.

To the west, Kastro 2218m (8446ft) rises beyond the plateau rim. After the Gingilos group and Melendaou, Kastro is the next most accessible high peak of the Lefka Ori. From the Niato Plain at the foot of Kastro paths lead south to Anopolis, or Imbros, and E4 Trail poles mark one end of a challenging east–west mountain traverse via the north flank of the Kastro massif. Just behind Goni village, eastwards across the plain, a distinct divide in the mountainous rim marks the old mule track to Asi Gonia. Asfendos and Kallikratis can also be reached from Goni. A few remains of a pre-1940s road can still be followed as a walkers' short cut to Hora Sfakion via the Imbros Gorge. There is also Walk 34, to Vafes, and lastly, by taking the bus to Krappis, you could follow Askifou's old transhumance trail down to Lake Kourna and Georgioupoli.

WALK 22
Around the Plain

Grade	A
Start/finish	Ammoudari–Askifou 790m (2592ft)
Access	KTEL Sfakia bus or taxi from Hora Sfakion or Vrisses
Highest point	Turkish fort approx 100m (328ft) above plain (optional)
Approx distance	5km (3 miles)
Time allowance	1hr 45mins

This circular tour of the plain may need patience with fencing and gates. It is a good infill walk if you have time to spare before returning to Chania.

Askifou: Goni village

From Ammoudari *plateia* walk south on the main road past the cemetery and a roadside enclosure memorial to historic battles against the Turks. Turn left down the asphalt road to Goni, but at the first bend keep straight on through a hamlet

of mainly local holiday homes, and then bear left down a track to a white shrine. Turn left for Goni, which is in view, sited on a rocky knoll.

At **Goni** (to skirt the knoll) turn sharp right for the road end. Follow an old village lane (beside a house marked '20') through to the surfaced road on the other side of the knoll. There is a well-preserved threshing floor at this point. Turn left along the road. Beyond the houses, keep straight on towards the rear of the hill with the fort. This path evolves as an old mule track and there are shepherds' gates. Follow it up to the saddle north of the hill. A track serves the hilltop with its ruined fort (the 'Gou-leh'– a Turkish word) and barracks. From the top note the way to Kares ('Ka-rezz'), and also the central track back to Ammoudari. From **Kares**, direct paths to Ammoudari tend to be blocked-off so it is probably easier to walk back to **Ammoudari** on the central track.

WALK 23
Askifou to Imbros

Grade	A
Start	Ammoudari–Askifou 790m (2591ft)
Access	KTEL Sfakia bus or taxi from Hora Sfakion or Vrisses
Finish	Imbros 800m (2625ft)
Access to finish	KTEL Sfakia bus or taxi from Hora Sfakion, Vrisses or Askifou
Highest point	900m (2952ft)
Height gain	110m (360ft)
Height loss	100m (328ft)
Approx distance	5km (3 miles)
Time allowance	1hr 20mins

Follow Walk 22 as far as the white shrine.

A fenced establishment on part of the rocky knoll, left, keeps dogs and partridges. Together with the hotel above the main road at this point it apparently forms a hunters' holiday centre. From the shrine, keep south on a track. It joins the main road at a T-junction with the road to Akones, Asfendos and Kallikratis. Like many other road signs in Sfakia (see

This is a walkers' short cut to Imbros along the route of the old road.

139

Sfakiot men are keen on owning guns ('If anyone threatens Crete we are not waiting for Athens to tell us what to do'), and road signs are used for target practice. Tourists are never involved and guns, as though by common agreement, are kept in low profile during the tourist season. However, it is the (so far irrepressible) local custom to fire guns into the air at ceremonies such as weddings and christenings, and at effigies of Judas Iscariot on Easter bonfires. If you attend any of these be alert to the fact that bullets accelerate downwards at great force after their initial kinetic energy is spent, the whole process taking about 60 seconds. Choose your position carefully.

box), the former Askifou road sign has been so shot up it may not have been replaced.

Keep straight on, downhill from the pass, on a short cut offered by one of the last remaining sections of the pre-1940s road. Pass through a wire gate and turn right for the main road through the village.

Imbros (800m/2625ft) is claimed to be the highest village in Crete, although it is not inhabited in winter since the community has another village, Skaloti, on the south coast. In summer Imbros benefits from the cool breezes funnelled up the Imbros Gorge, making it a popular lunch spot for Samaria day tour coach drivers who have time to spare on their journey to Hora Sfakion. The KTEL Sfakia schedule provides easy access to the Imbros Gorge trailhead and there is a steady demand for refreshments, breakfasts, and so on. There are two holiday flats for rent – enquire at the Three Brothers Katsanavakis restaurant. There is a WC block opposite this *taverna*. Due to the popularity of the Imbros Gorge there is also a supermarket.

WALK 24

The Imbros Gorge

Grade	B
Start	Imbros 800m (2625ft)
Access	KTEL Sfakia bus or taxi from Hora Sfakion
Finish	Kommitades 200m (760ft)
Access to finish	Taxi from Hora Sfakion
Height loss	600m (1968ft)
Approx distance	5km (3 miles)
Time allowance	2hrs 25mins

This gorge is so accessible from the main road that it now provides an organised walking route suitable for bus tour groups. Tickets (about €2) are sold at a kiosk at the top, where footpaths enter the gorge. A warden's hut, with WCs, is halfway down, beside a Venetian well (the only water supply in the gorge). The warden sells canned drinks, which are raised up from the well. A mule or donkey is available for emergencies and for refuse collection.

This 5km route is the most popular gorge walk after Samaria, and also the alternative tour option if Samaria is closed. Unlike gorges further west, which have perpendicular cliffs, the Imbros has steep vegetated spurs. Several areas of deep shade along the way make this a possible midsummer walk although – since there are no springs – there are no water points: take your own supply. Two refreshments outlets are sited just before the end of the gorge and, on the main road nearby, Kommitades has several *tavernas*.

Access by KTEL bus Three *tavernas* along the road south of the village claim to be on starting points for the walk. Unless these stops offer a less crowded start, Imbros village proper (Three Brothers *taverna*) is probably best.

On foot from Askifou Continue south to Imbros' roadside *plateia* with its *tavernas*, bus stop and WC block.

Starting from the *plateia*, bear left down a dirt track to the dry streambed of the valley where splintered footpaths head south, straight for the gorge. Features in the gorge include a few still-intact paved sections of old road, the warden's hut, two or three very narrow shady clefts with smooth-sided

On the mule track down to Asfendos (Walk 26)

walls and, lower down, a huge rock arch. After about 2hrs 15mins, with the main road in sight below, pass the two refreshments outlets and leave the gorgebed westwards via a walled mule track heading for the *tavernas* of **Kommitades** on the main road.

Note At busy periods there may be a mini-bus service for transfers back to Imbros or Hora Sfakion (enquire).

WALK 25
Kommitades to Hora Sfakion

Grade:	A
Start	Kommitades 200m (760ft)
Access	Taxi from Hora Sfakion
Finish	Hora Sfakion
Access to finish	KTEL Sfakia bus service
Height loss	200m (656ft)
Approx distance	4km (2.5 miles)
Time allowance	1hr 15mins

Walk west from **Kommitades** for about 1.5km to join the Askifou–Imbros–Hora Sfakion main road. A large isolated *taverna* marks this junction and bus (request) stop. At about 15.45 the daily Chania–Anopolis bus should be making its way down the hill. If you see it at the top you will have quite a few minutes to get to the bus stop in time. (There are also other daily buses on the KTEL Chania–Sfakia schedule).

The coastal village of Hora Sfakion is called 'Sfakia' locally.

Continue down the road as far as the bed of the Sfakiano Gorge with its gravel extraction works. Leave it on the unsurfaced track, on the west side, and head straight overland to a white Byzantine-style chapel in the distance.

This is (or was) '**upper Hora Sfakion**', a ghost village long since bypassed through changed circumstances. In the path of the 1941 evacuation of the defeated Allied Army, inhabitants here must have struggled to fill soldiers' water bottles from their own meagre household rainwater-collecting cisterns. The modern water supply comes from an abundant underground source.

From the chapel (closed – it is structurally unsound, probably due to earth tremors) cross the road and follow a lane downhill alongside an old ruined house.

Still to be seen here are the remains of earthen (clay mix) roofs, the local roofing material until concrete became available in the 1950s. These roofs needed re-laying annually to be effective. Even so, in wet places like Askifou, they leaked after prolonged rain – a discomfort still remembered by those who experienced it.

Cross the next road, and continue straight down on an old lane. Bear right at all lane junctions. This takes you down to the main road. After the left-hand bend, leave the road on another steep descent leading to a flight of steps. This is followed by further short-cut sections that lead straight down to the car park, bus stop, and boat ticket kiosk – and the harbour waterfront.

WALK 26
The Asfendos Gorge from Askifou

Grade	B
Start	Ammoudari–Askifou 790m (2591ft)
Access	KTEL Sfakia bus to Askifou
Finish	Ay. Nektarios 120m (396ft)
Access to finish	Taxi from Hora Sfakion
Highest point	1000m (3280ft)
Height gain	300m (984ft)
Height loss	880m (2887ft)
Approx distance	11km (7 miles)
Time allowance	Ammoudari to Goni 35mins; to pass 1000m (3280ft) 1hr 30mins; to Asfendos 800m (2624ft) 40mins; to Ay. Nektarios 120m (393ft) 2hrs; total: 4hrs 45mins

Asfendos is a summer-only village in a quiet valley above the Asfendos Gorge, the next large gorge east from Imbros. The gorge develops below the valley as the escarpment steepens, and ends just above Ay. Nektarios on the south coast road. It is a relatively unfrequented gorge because Ay. Nektarios is about 6km from the Hora Sfakion main road bus route, and busy Sfakia taxis may be unavailable. When planning this walk, check bus times in advance at Hora Sfakion or Chania. The 17.30 Sfakia–Rethymnon service passes on its scenic route east, or a relief bus (for Samaria returnees) may be brought into service, from Frankokastello.

Before modern-day tourism, village communities escaped from the south coast heat by transferring *en masse* up to their 'summer villages' in the mountains. Asfendos was one of these, as were Kallikratis, Imbros, Kali Lakki and Mouri (high above Hora Sfakion). Understandably, elderly people of Sfakia remember those days with some nostalgia.

Starting from Ammoudari *plateia*, walk 100m north and then turn down right on a concrete-surfaced track. Cross the bypass road and follow the track straight across the plain as far as the third right-hand junction. Take this to join the asphalt road to Goni.

Arriving at **Goni**, bear left around Goni hill: the asphalt road ends at an old threshing circle. Keep straight on here,

past a grove of mature prickly oaks, to join the main track up the valley, which heads south up to a pass in the hills that surround the plain. Keep on the road as it passes a large concrete sheep shed and fenced enclosure. Just beyond this, look down to the left to see a section of an older road. Clamber down on to this. Before long it ends (with the new road above, continuing south); just before it ends, note a waymarked footpath heading uphill to the southeast. This leads to a valley with a cistern (good water) and a stone-built section of *kalderimi* that leads up to and over a pass. You now overlook the Asfendos Valley. Passing two cisterns along the way, follow a shepherds' road and short-cut footpaths down to the village. It has several old stone houses and a church, but no *kafeneon*.

On the path down to Asfendos: the road to Imbros is seen in the background

For Kallikratis Walk east on the road (which comes from Imbros).

For the Asfendos Gorge Start downhill on a track just to the right of the valley watercourse. This route evolves as a footpath that is easy to follow down into the gorge. Below the

narrow section, between great cliffs, where the trail is concreted over, the old mule track breaks up and the footpath
zigzags down a *phrygana*-covered hillside to a shepherds'
hut. From there it crosses and recrosses the streambed until
it finally sticks to the west side. An old chapel is seen, perch-
ing on an east-side crag. Arrive at a path junction at the end
of the gorge, and keep left for the final descent to **Ay.
Nektarios**, where there is a *kafeneon*.

WALK 27
Askifou–Goni to Kallikratis

Grade	D
Start	Ammoudari–Askifou 790m (2591ft)
Access	KTEL Sfakia bus service
Finish	Kallikratis 750m (2460ft)
Access to finish	Walks 28a, b, c and 29
Highest point	Summit of Angathes 1511m (4921ft)
Height gain	811m (2660ft)
Height loss	510m (1673ft)
Approx distance	10km (6.2 miles)
Time allowance	Ammoundari to Goni 700m (2296ft) 35mins; Goni to Horeftra pass 1300m (4265ft) 4hrs 20mins; Horeftra to Angathes summit 1511m (4921ft) 1hr 20mins; Angathes (north side) to Kallikratis 1hr 20mins; total: 7hrs 35mins

The three mountain shepherding communities of Anopolis, Askifou and Asi Gonia
were once linked by mule track, some sections of which still remain. This high
mountain walk to Kallikratis starts off on the mule track between Goni and Asi
Gonia which climbs to Horeftra pass, on the watershed of this lower, but very
rugged, eastern block of the Lefka Ori.

Kallikratis is sited in an isolated fertile valley high in the mountains on the
border of Sfakia and the Rethymnon hills. The village has had a road link to
Imbros for many years but a more recent road climbs the steep escarpment above
Kapsodasos, linking Kallikratis and Asi Gonia directly to the south coast.
Fortunately these roads leave the Kallikratis Gorge as a pleasant walking route.

In 1943 the community suffered a devastating Nazi reprisal for supporting a Resistance hideout (which may well have been at Spileo Lakkos, to which there is now a shepherds' road). The memorial to this tragic event is just beyond the white two-storey *taverna*. There are also *kafeneia*. It may be possible to arrange overnight accommodation indoors somewhere, although sleeping kit may be needed. This is a pleasant valley with orchards and gardens. The village may develop further now that road access is much improved. Until lately Frankokastello (on the coast) has been a more obvious place in which to invest capital but shepherds, walkers and car tourers exploring the back roads provide the *kafeneia* with midday trade.

Follow Walks 22 or 26 to Goni.

From the old threshing circle continue on for 4mins to the grove of mature kermis oaks. On the left there is a ruined wall and line of young walnut trees and a faint footpath that leads to the bordering thicket. A wire-netting gate allows access to a plateau-perimeter mule track. Turn right and, after 4mins, pass through another gate. At the gate turn immediately uphill heading east and you are now launched on the old road to Asi Gonia ('As-see-gon-ya').

Splintered paths ascend through prickly oak and maple woodland to a first small valley with a barrel-vaulted cistern. Passing straight up this valley, continue to the 950m (3117ft) level where there is an old *mitato* and cistern served by a shepherds' road coming in from the north. This starts from the main Sfakia road some distance north of Askifou. Do not think of it as an easy escape from stony tracks as it is a very long road-tramp back to Askifou, and there is no bus stop. Also, this mule track route Goni–Asi Gonia is the only easy way over the very steep east rim of the plain.

A distinct footpath continues east, up the scree of the shallow gully above the cistern. Just before the pass at the top there is a small, flat plain (no cistern). On entering this valley, bear right. The footpath ascends a short distance through low rocks to a meadow where there is a walled paddock, a deep barrel-vaulted cistern and a ruined *mitato*. One room may still be weatherproof. ▸

For Asi Gonia Follow the path eastwards over the pass down to another small plain with a cistern – the last water on the route. From here on the path is attractive at first, but

This place, the pass on the watershed, is called **Horeftra**. In clear conditions Tripali 1498m (4915ft) is within easy reach as a round detour over various rocky ridges.

147

The Kallikratis Valley from the north; the Kallkratis Gorge is on the right, the west side

eventually the rock changes and ongoing steep and loose-surfaced paths make the final descent very trying.

For Kallikratis Settled visibility is necessary as this follows goat paths across ridges and hollows that all look the same and, therefore, you need to be able to see your destination. Start from Horeftra with 2 litres of water – Kallikratis is further than you may think.

Take the footpath on the south side of the paddock. It curves around to cross a small rocky valley and ascends a first low ridge. From this first viewpoint (and as if you were still at the pass) identify Angathes 1511m (4921ft) by taking a bearing off the summit. The shepherds' path to Kallikratis crosses a pass just north of the summit.

Find the best route across this area by taking it slowly and arrive at a distinct basin just below the peak. Ascend to the pass above the east rim – or to the summit with its flat boulderfield and trig point. Of all the varied elements that make up the 360° view, the great sweep of rock on the north flank of Kastro (Trek 3) is the most striking.

In common with the other high tops of this region, the slopes of Angathes are very rugged. As mentioned, the best onward route descends southeast from a point north of the summit. Still high above **Kallikratis**, join a service road in the valley below, and follow this down to the village. There is a direct short-cut footpath near the end of this road.

For the south coast via the **Kallikratis Gorge**, see Walk 29.

WALKS 28A, B, C
Connecting Walks from Kallikratis

a Kallikratis to Asfendos

Highest point	900m (2952ft)
Height gain	110m (360ft)
Height loss	100m (328ft)
Approx distance	4km (2.5 miles)
Time allowance	1hr 15mins

An undulating route on the main road between Imbros and Kallikratis.

b Asfendos to Goni–Askifou

Highest point	1000m (3280ft)
Height gain	200m (656ft)
Height loss	300m (984ft)
Approx distance	6.5km (4 miles)
Time allowance	2hrs 20mins

c Asfendos to Imbros (E4 Trail)

Highest point	1000m (3280ft)
Height gain	200m (656ft)
Height loss	200m (656ft)
Approx distance	5km (3 miles)
Time allowance	2hrs

From Kallikratis to Asfendos

The main E4 Trail passes through Kallikratis on its way east across the Rethymnon hills to the Amari Valley and Mount Ida. However, to return to Sfakia district, either tramp the road (going west to Imbros), or join it after taking a short cut across the valley following footpaths heading northwestwards from the two-storey *taverna*.

From Asfendos to Askifou

Turn northwestwards up the valley, keeping the church on your left, and reverse Walk 26 to Goni.

For Imbros Avoid a large zigzag in the road by ascending westwards on a steep short cut to the top bend in the road. The road passes the huge disc of Akones NATO listening station (said to be the largest in the Mediterranean), which is on a hilltop site not visible from the Askifou–Imbros main road. As you pass under Akones hill, look carefully for a cairned footpath that, leaving the road, traverses the hillside below it and heads west for a watercourse which is directly above the Imbros Valley. An eroded path keeps to the south side of the watercourse and leads down to the ruined hamlet on the east side of the valley. Alternatively, and easier underfoot, just before the last part of the descent on the road, take a track that leads down to houses at the north end of the valley.

For the Asfendos Gorge See Walk 26.

WALK 29
The Kallikratis Gorge

Grade	B
Start	Kallikratis 800m (2624ft)
Access	Lift from Askifou or Imbros, or via Walks 25 or 26
Finish	Patsianos 150m (492ft)
Access to finish	Taxi from Hora Sfakion or Frankokastello
Height loss	650m (2132ft)
Approx distance	6km (4 miles)
Time allowance	2hrs 20mins

As a relatively undemanding route from Kallikratis down to the south coast road at Patsianos ('Pats'yan-oss'), this pretty tree-lined gorge is often combined with the Asfendos Gorge to make a circular walk.

Follow the Kallikratis–Patsianos road going south, past the two-storey *taverna* and war memorial. It curves west around the valley to the outlying hamlet of **Kataporia**, and to the gorge, before heading uphill on a very long route over and down to Kapsodassos. The gorge footpath, off the road, is easy to find. It starts down through sparse maple forest. In a narrow section bordered by great cliffs, the mule track surface was once concreted. Further down, where the gorge opens out, it is paved in places and negotiates a large rockfall. From **Patsianos** turn east to Kapsodassos for the north–south overland track (1hr) to **Frankokastello**, a small beach resort with a 14th-century ruined Venetian fort.

An infrequent bus service to Hora Sfakion leaves from beside a large *taverna* opposite the fort.

WALK 30
Askifou–Ammoudari to Niato (E4 Trail)

Grade	B
Start/finish	Ammoudari–Askifou 790m (2591ft)
Access	KTEL Sfakia bus or taxi from Vrisses or Hora Sfakion
Highest point	Niato 1220m (4002ft)
Height gain	430m (1410ft)
Approx distance	8km (5 miles)
Time allowance	Ammoudari to plateau rim 1100m (3608ft) 1hr 10mins; to Niato E4 Trail signpost 1220m (4002ft) 50mins; ascent total 2hrs; descent total: 1hr; total: 3hrs
	Extension: Circuit to E4 trailhead and last cistern 1hr 30mins

The Niato Plain, at the foot of Mt Kastro, is a grazing pasture of about 2km². Compared to Askifou, Niato is small, but that gives it its particular character as a hospitable valley and place to camp perhaps before you climb Kastro, or tackle the E4 Trail east–west traverse (Walk 30, Trek 3). Reached via a section of the old Askifou–Anopolis mule track, which zigzags up to the plateau rim through shady oak woods, Niato makes an attractive walking destination in itself via this circular route.

From **Ammoudari** *plateia* walk uphill, west, on a village road that passes a large cheese dairy (the shepherds' road to Niato). At the next bend a signboard and balustrade marks the E4 Trail. Keep straight on up this footpath to a track that serves a sheep shed. Leave this, alongside a fenced compound, on a waymarked short cut up through oak forest. This re-joins the Niato road at a drainage conduit.

Stones bordering the mule track blend in but a timber balustrade marks the continuation of the trail: find it just beyond the conduit. The trail zigzags uphill through prickly oak woodland. After about 30mins arrive at a small meadow bordered with maple trees. Askifou's Ay. Pnevma chapel is seen at the top, over on the right. Continue up to the left at first, and then double back to reach the top in another 15mins. ▸

Walk westwards for 5mins (marked with an E4 Trail pole) and descend to a small valley with a track, a new hut and a concrete water tank. Turn right to rejoin the shepherds' road from Askifou (E4 Trail pole) and then turn left for **Niato**.

Alternatively – for less of a walk along the road – bear left up this valley for 3mins to a cistern with a pump and an old cheese-making dairy (shelter). Continue south on the track for 5mins and then turn right, westwards, up a small valley. The refuge is now ahead, up on the right – this footpath joins the refuge access road.

The refuge has no outside covered shelter or available water, but its terrace has a wall to shelter by. A cypress tree holds a nice draughty sleeping platform (just the spot on a summer's night). Mount Ida's summit ridge is seen far to the east and, through binoculars, so are two or three E4 Trail poles high on the spine of Kastro's north ridge.

When you reach **Niato**, pause to examine the view. Across the plateau at 280°W note the distinct re-entrant in this east-facing flank of Kastro – the easiest route to the summit is up, and down, that wide gully. After it skirts the plateau, note the shepherds' road continuing northwestwards over a small pass. The trailhead of the E4 main Trail (Trek 3) is just beyond that pass. Close to, on the valley floor note a flat concrete cistern on the right amongst clumps of spiny burnet. A tree marks a small vothia, or sinkhole, adjacent that provides shelter for a brew up if a cold wind is blowing. Alternatively, for campers, the east side perimeter track leads to a new concrete cistern. On the hillside just beyond there is a dis-used corbelled stone hut – the only roofed shelter at Niato (but check for soundness).

Now follow the road round to an E4 Trail signpost with encouraging, but optimistic, timings (presumably for tough EOS walkers who are already familiar with the routes). ▸

Do not miss the novelty of walking across this flat-floored plain (just a few minutes without stones!) to reach the northwestern pass. Just beyond the E4 Trail trailhead (marked with poles) the track ends at a cistern and then

Cypress trees provide welcome shade for this bird's-eye view of Askifou, now far below, whilst contrasting with tree-dotted hills nearby the starkly barren twin peaks of Kastro rise to the west above the rim of Niato. South, the seldom-used red-roofed Tavri EOS refuge (locked) is sited on a hilltop.

For **Imbros or Anopolis** Turn to the south (see Walks 32 and 33).

continues northwestwards as a footpath to another cistern under a lone, tall kermis oak. From here the rocky footpath, now under Kastro's north flank, continues to an area of huge flat boulders, low enough in altitude to suit ancient cypress trees. It is worth getting this far just to see them. Beyond is what the shepherds call 'a very wild place' that includes a labyrinth of huge boulders bordering a massive depression. Companions are needed if you wish to explore this entirely unfrequented part of the mountain.

Return to **Niato** the same way.

WALK 31
The Ascent of Kastro

Grade	D
Start/finish	Askifou–Ammoudari 790m (2591ft)
Access	KTEL Sfakia bus or taxi from Vrisses or Hora Sfakion
Highest point	Summit of Kastro 2219m (7280ft)
Height gain/loss	1429m (4689ft)
Approx distance	16km (10 miles)
Time allowance	Ammoudari to Niato 1220m (4002ft) 2hrs; ascent/descent circuit from Niato 5hrs 30mins; Niato to Ammoudari 1hr; total: 8hrs 30mins

Ascents of Gingilos and Melendaou, near the Omalos plateau and Kallergi refuge, are very popular with recreational walkers. However, although Kastro is also a fairly accessible peak, it is seldom climbed. On all sides, Kastro forms very challenging walking terrain; even the easiest path to the summit is not well tramped.

Allow a minimum of 9hrs for this circular walk from Ammoudari (normally suitable from June to November) and plan an early departure to make the most of daylight hours because, for the best views westwards, you should arrive on the summit before the midday sun moves round. Plan a choice of dates – you want settled weather for this walk if possible. If daylight hours are short, as in the late autumn when conditions may otherwise be ideal, consider an overnight camp at Niato, or the EOS refuge. You can always hide unnecessary items in the rocks until you return from the summit, but be careful to note the spot, and protect your food from goats.

Just because summit routes are largely in view from Niato, do not assume the ascent is going to be a 'doddle'; it is further than it looks. The belt of crags that must be climbed just above the vegetated scree at the start of the route (and elsewhere at that level) forms a barrier to normal foot traffic, and above it you are somewhat cut off. The crags will have to be carefully negotiated on the descent: reserve energy for doing this competently. The going gets easier the higher you get, but a strong wind often affects the summit. Take daysack essentials including a survival or 'bivi' bag. Unless melting snow prevails there is no water – start with a minimum of 2 litres of water from Niato.

Follow Walk 30 and, from the entrance to **Niato**, study Kastro's east-facing flank. Apart from the re-entrant also note the spurs descending to the plain either side of it – there are alternative routes (shepherds' paths) up or down these. Cross Niato heading straight for the vegetated scree slope below the re-entrant, passing through the sparse perimeter tree belt to pick up the best footpath to the crags. Climb up through the boulders of the crag – if you have found the easiest route you should see signs of others having done this. Bear left at

On the ascent of Kastro (September): looking down at Niato from above the first line of crags

The Madares: looking west from the summit of Kastro, April

the crag top and cross over to a position more directly below the route of the dry watercourse in the re-entrant. Ascend to about 1900m (6176ft) and then bear right, to the northwest, for the final 30mins to the **summit**.

A wide panorama of the peaks of the central massif extends to the west across the grim-looking depression of crags and sinkholes called the Pavlia Harlara. To the south, far down below, a white two-storey building at Kambia (Anopolis) is just in sight, a fact well known to those who used to frequent that particular *kafeneon* (now closed). To the east, Mount Ida's summit ridge rises beyond the hills of Rethymnon.

'Footpath' maps feature different routes on the eastern spurs of Kastro above Niato. Unless you have lots of daylight to spare, avoid these demanding rocky routes in favour of a return down the re-entrant.

WALK 32
Askifou to Imbros via Trikoukia

Grade	B/C
Start	Ammoudari–Askifou 790m (2591ft)
Access	KTEL Sfakia bus or taxi from Hora Sfakion or Vrisses
Finish	Imbros 800m (3046ft)
Access to finish	KTEL Sfakia bus or taxi from Hora Sfakion, Vrisses or Askifou
Height gain	430m (1410ft)
Height loss	370m (1213ft)
Approx distance	10km (6.2 miles)
Time allowance	Ammoudari to Niato 2hrs; Niato to Trikoukia 1160m (3805ft) 30mins; Trikoukia to Imbros (via ridgetop) 1hr 45mins; total: 4hrs 15mins

The mountains often attract cool breezes when the coast is very hot. This easily reached round walk on shepherds' paths in the mountains above Askifou and Imbros makes a welcome change from gorge and coastal walks.

Follow Walk 30 to **Niato**'s E4 Trail signpost.

Turn left, south, on a red gravel track that evolves as a footpath through freestanding rocks. Follow this up to a low pass and then down to **Trikoukia**, another flat-floored plain. Bear right to find a cistern and a concrete hut (locked). Here, a road from Imbros (a long tramp) comes in from the south.

For Anopolis See Walk 33.

For Imbros on footpaths Turn east along the north side of the fenced enclosure and follow it round to find the path, which heads east up a shallow gully. Note an old *mitato* hut over on your left (shelter). Its front room, which has crafted roof vaulting, is structurally unsound but its cheese store is intact.

The footpath continues east and, passing through some big rocks, enters the next flat-floored plain. Bear right up to a low pass.

From here two routes lead down to Imbros
(a) straight down from the pass, or
(b) along the north–south ridge just above, for the best views.

For descent (a) Follow the footpath immediately downhill to a cistern, then bear right past what looks like a very old tree-circled threshing circle. Keep downhill on the path to where the re-entrant evolves as a small gully. The path traverses to the right here, southeast, leading down to the valley below, where wild pear trees provide shade near a deep barrel-vaulted cistern (dead animal = bad water).

For descent (b) Turn south up the ridge. The Akones NATO listening station is in view to the east. The path passes above a hollow, to the right, where there is a weatherproof old *mitato*, but no water. Continue south near the edge of the ridge until it ends above a small valley. Descend to the valley and turn east on a footpath leading down a shallow gully – this brings you down to join descent (a) near some large oak trees.

To continue Leave this valley, in which oak trees grow, heading south on a distinct footpath. A ruined hut features on the far side of the next small plain. Bear to the right and follow the footpath down to a shepherds' road. Follow the road down to a left-hand bend at the head of a ravine. Note the old mule track on the south side of the ravine – either leave the road here for the mule track (which may be in shade) or continue down on the road – walking time for the descent is the same. As you approach **Imbros** village, bear right for the red-roofed church, which is on the main road, and then turn left for the *plateia* and bus stop. ◄

For Askifou Reverse Walk 22 (1hr 30mins).
For Hora Sfakion See Walks 23 and 24 (4hrs).

Note If the last Hora Sfakion–Chania KTEL bus is packed with Samaria gorge returnees, there may be a second relief bus – enquire at the taverna.

WALK 33

*Askifou to Anopolis (or Hora Sfakion)
via Kali Lakki and Mouri*

Grade	C/D
Start	Ammoudari–Askifou 790m (2591ft)
Access	KTEL Sfakia bus or taxi from Hora Sfakion or Vrisses
Finish	Anopolis 600m (1968ft) or Hora Sfakion
Access to finish	KTEL Sfakia–Anopolis bus or taxi from Hora Sfakion
Height gain	430m (1410ft) to Niato, then undulating route to Anopolis with basic height loss of 630m (2066ft), or 1230m (4035ft) via Mouri to Hora Sfakion
Approx distance	21km (13 miles) via road to Anopolis
Time allowance	Ammoudari to Trikoukia 1160m (3809ft) 2hrs 30mins; Trikoukia to Scarfidia spring 1350m (3723ft) 2hrs; Scarfidia to Anopolis 2hrs 20mins; total: 6hrs 50mins Alternative routes via Mouri: Scarfidia to Kavros 1hr; Kavros to Anopolis 2hrs 30 mins; Kavros to Hora Sfakion 3hrs

This walk offers several choices as it encounters the old high-level mule-track network between Imbros, Askifou, Anopolis and Hora Sfakion. If you are equipped to camp on a continuous trek you could plan to spend a couple of days exploring these routes (no facilities), all of which are within the treeline, with marvellous views down to the south coast.

A shepherds' road links Imbros (via Trikoukia) with the old 'summer' hamlet of Kali Lakki, where one or two houses have been restored. Beyond Trikoukia, roadworks have obliterated a lower section of the old mule track. Fortunately, the mule track continues above the new road, so that an attractive section still remains although this eventually joins a shepherds' road to Anopolis. Thereafter you have the choice of getting to Anopolis by tramping on this road, or of going via Mouri, the site of the old summer hamlet of the Hora Sfakion community, on a route that crosses the Kavis (Ilingas) Gorge. At Mouri there is also the option of walking straight down to Hora Sfakion. Whichever route you choose, the last part of the walk will be mostly downhill and there are fine views along the way.

Follow Walks 30 and 32 to **Niato** and **Trikoukia**.

From Trikoukia cistern continue southwest on the shepherds' road to Kali Lakki. ◄

To the south the valley evolves as the Sfakiano Gorge. There are shepherds' paths down into that gorge from Kali Lakki, but not from here.

After about 10mins look carefully for roadside cairns and red paint that marks where the new road sliced through the mule track, the lower sections of which are now buried. Alternatively, you can walk to Kali Lakki along the road and then join the mule track from there. Otherwise, the mule track is found about 3m above the road – clamber up to get onto it. It is easier to follow as you approach the ridgetop and from there it takes up an undulating, contouring route through sparse woodland. Fairly mature trees grow on the path in places, as this mule track has been disused for many years. However, for walkers, there are cairns and red-dot waymarks. From a fairly long, straight traverse, the ruined hamlet of **Kali Lakki** on the hillside below is glimpsed through the trees. Beyond, the path loses height to a forested spur where there is a small spurge-covered meadow bordered by a low stone wall. ◄

For Kali Lakki, and the road back to Trikoukia, turn sharp left, down a forested gully.

Alternatively, if you have walked the road to Kali Lakki, pause as you round a last bend and the hamlet (which is mostly ruined) comes into view. In the far corner of the valley (a large re-entrant) note a stand of light green maple trees at the top of a forested gully. Join the mule track by climbing for 15mins up that gully to reach the meadow as described above. Kali Laki is not linked to Scarfidia by road because this helps shepherds to protect their animals from thieves.

The mule track continues from the southwest corner of the meadow. Looking westwards across the next valley, you can see it zigzagging up the opposite spur – look carefully, as it blends into the terrain. The path crosses the flattish top of that spur and then heads downhill, across scree in places, to join the Anopolis shepherds' road (roadhead) at a *mitato* and spring called **Scarfidia** ('Scar-fee-the-ah'). The spring emerges over a shallow pool of bright green waterweed. Follow the road west from Scarfidia, and turn left when you arrive at a T-junction. Walk downhill to where the road makes a big right-hand loop around the valley. On the other side, south, note a subsidiary road off this, heading uphill. This leads to access roads serving two different spurs: the right-hand option is for Mouri. You now have a choice: to

Anopolis on this main shepherds' road or to Mouri, from where there are three more route options.

For Anopolis, via the shepherds' road Avoid the loop by taking a short-cut footpath down to a workstation and spring called Feeno Kai Yanous. Continue west on the road. It passes high above the Kavis Gorge. Disused sections of old mule track are seen here and there, below the road. The next important feature is a junction with an ascending road: this is the shepherds' road to the Madares (see Trek 8).

After that, views open up as the road continues west, well clear of the gorge, before descending open mountainside in a series of long loops. There is one particularly useful short cut down to a valley with a cistern, but otherwise the terrain is too rocky to make short cuts worth the trouble. Remains of the mule track are seen here and there, but it is hardly useable.

Finally, **Limnia** hamlet (Anopolis comprises several hamlets) is seen through the pines from the last straight descent, which ends at a bend near the foot of a steep ravine. The old mule track to the Madares is routed up this ravine (Trek 8). Tramp the road, or take a worthwhile short cut; follow the path straight from the ravine. It passes through the pineforest; 25mins to a fenced enclosure and sheep shed where you rejoin the road for the last 12mins to **Anopolis** *plateia*.

For Mouri Mouri's route choices are included here, en route from Askifou, because they are easiest and most pleasant to walk in the downhill direction. However, these walks can also be approached from Hora Sfakion (Walk 47) or from Anopolis (especially if you can arrange a lift to Mouri). From the Feeno Kai Yanoos road loop, take the road that serves the Mouri spur. The straight-on option leads down another spur. It is possible, from the end of that spur, to make your way downhill to the bed of a tributary ravine and then climb up the other side to Mouri, which is in sight on the skyline. However, the road to Mouri is probably more interesting, allowing you a view of the site as you approach it from above.

An EU LEADER-funded restored white house, over on the left, is the first building of the village and the old direct mule track (short cut) can be found to the left of this. Alternatively, if you continue downhill on the road you will soon pass another LEADER-funded stone house (purpose not apparent) with a fenced terrace and old-style covered cistern. However, when the road reaches the first level area of the spur, note that it makes a left-hand loop.

For the path down to Timios Stavros chapel (see route notes below) leave the road here, bearing right for the gorge rim and the correct ravine for the descent: you should see a cairn or two, and on the left side, the remains of an ancient mule track heading down the ravine.

For Mouri, continue past the ruins of old houses, to the impressively large church which, like Kavros chapel, is nowadays kept locked. From the church follow the road down (cistern at the roadside) to the next level (which is in sight), where you can take a short cut to avoid a big loop and then keep on down to the lowest flat level of the spur (not in sight from the church) to reach the ruins of Kavros hamlet. Over on the right, to the southwest, note a small white chapel (cistern 1min northwest from the chapel). The footpath to Anopolis leaves from this chapel.

You now have the choice of three ongoing routes: (a) to Anopolis via the Kavis Gorge **(b)** back to Mouri via the bed of the Kavis Gorge **(c)** to Hora Sfakion on a long descent, continuing down the spur.

(a) Anopolis via the Kavis Gorge Southwest of the chapel a red-dot waymarked footpath leads, in 5mins, to a passage down through the crag that overlooks a steeply descending spur (flocks of sheep also use this route). The spur is on the east side of the upper reaches of the Kavis (Ilingas) Gorge and a road is seen climbing the opposite side. Follow the path down the spine of the spur to where it levels out and then bear right, downhill on paths through the Jerusalem sage, to the gorgebed where there is a battered concrete-topped cistern – a victim of the flash flood of year 2000. You now have the choice of continuing to Anopolis on the road or of returning to Mouri via the gorgebed.

For Anopolis Cross the riverbed to join the unsightly new road that climbs out of the gorge and then heads for Limnia hamlet. It is a long tramp but there are good views along the way. Turn sharp left at **Limnia** church for **Anopolis** *plateia*. Alternatively, there is an overland short cut to Kambia, via **Pavliana** hamlet: after you have climbed out of the gorge and reached the first level area, note fenced enclosures and a workstation on the right. Just beyond this place, look carefully on the hillside for the remains of a mule track that was cut by this new road. On the left side, it is marked with a blue-dot waymark on a rock. (Note the waymark could be partly obscured by Jerusalem sage – cut out this shrub if you have time).

The mule track can be seen climbing the hill opposite – it is a short cut to the shepherds' road to Scarfidia, but, long disused, it is very rough underfoot. Going south, the old trail heads for the concrete water tank above Pavliana, from where a road leads down to the Anopolis main road. There is a locked gate below the water tank.

Alternatively, remains of the Pavliana mule track network can be found in the gully on the east side of the

Making traditional cheese pies in Askifou

163

Pavliana spur. There are wire gates but it is still passable down to the main road.

(b) For Mouri (or Anopolis) via Timios Stavros chapel The gorge bed is passable in both directions although, southwards, to Ilingas and the main road, is not easy since it needs some rock-scrambling ability. Northwards, the gorgebed is easy to walk as far as the ancient, and partly restored, **Timios Stavros chapel**, sited right in the gorgebed near a source of fresh water: a spring emerges inside a large cave in an adjacent east side crag. A small brass panel marks this place as a hideout for fugitives during the 14th-century period of Venetian rule.

For Anopolis From the chapel a footpath up the 'easy' west side of the gorge brings you to a roadhead. After a couple of kilometres this road joins the main shepherds' road down to Anopolis (at a junction where the useful downhill short cut can be found).

For Mouri From near the cave there is a steep but relatively short route up to Mouri. To find it, take about 120 paces southwards from the cave. This brings you to the moss-covered ruins of a very old building in the woodland. The unfrequented footpath, marked with cairns in places, climbs the wooded spur from this spot. Halfway up it loses a little height, down to the right, to reach a gully (a watercourse). Make your way up this 'easy' gully and at the top bear right to get onto the remains of an old mule track which must once have linked to the spring. At the top you arrive very near the road descending from Feeno Kai Yanoos and just a little above the level of the ruined village and church.

(c) Hora Sfakion from Kavros (Mouri) This route follows the old trail linking Hora Sfakion with its 'summer village' of Mouri. This is a steady descent of 950m (3116ft) down a large, forested spur between the complex systems of the Kavis (Ilingas) and Sfakiano gorges. Since the footpath is indistinct in places, the disused old telephone line between Hora Sfakion and Mouri – which follows it almost exactly – forms a useful guideline to follow, even in thick mist.

From the chapel at Kavros, cross over northeast to pick up the *kalderimi* that heads downhill to the southeast. It lies between walled enclosures at the end of the road. After the last walled enclosure, which is floored with sand, the old trail enters dense cypress forest. After a few metres arrive at a Y-junction of paths – keep right and gain height. After about 100m the path bends sharp right to follow the telephone line. Stay with the telephone line: it has a short right-hand turning lower down. Cairns may also mark the route here and there and the hillside is not steep at this point.

Arrive at a small plain in the forest where there is a concrete-topped cistern. Turn south from the cistern, steeply downhill beside a shallow gully, and then bear southeast, slightly away from the telephone line, to continue the descent where the underfoot is easier (nearer the spine of the spur). A large lone shady cypress tree marks the 500m (1640ft) level. The spur has levelled out here and the telephone line crosses over to follow the route of the old mule track where the underfoot was less rough – take this route or just make your way down the centre of the spur before descending to the right, west, to reach a shepherds' workstation which is easily seen from above.

This is at the end of the shepherds' road that climbs the hill above Hora Sfakion. Walk down the road, past junctions with two tracks on the right, as far as a concrete-topped cistern also on the right-hand side of the road. Follow the telephone line again by doubling back to the left here, to pick up a footpath that heads for a ravine – one of those which, lower down, are directly behind **Hora Sfakion**. What is left of the mule track leads down the east side of the ravine, to cross a track, and then, as a footpath, continues down alongside a stone-walled enclosure, to a ruined hamlet sited on a spur high above the village.

There is a chapel on the end of this spur and the mule track continues from there, zigzagging down to the next level, before crossing over to the left to take up a long traverse of the hillside above the village. When you reach the main road take a village footpath lane almost opposite, the start of which is incorporated in a building complex called 'Notos Suites'.

WALK 34
Askifou to Vafes

Walk 21 in reverse

Grade	C
Start	Kares or Ammoudari–Askifou 790m (2591ft)
Access	KTEL Sfakia bus or taxi from Hora Sfakion or Vrisses
Finish	Vafes 250m (820ft)
Access to finish	Walks 19a, 20, or taxi from Vrisses
Highest point	940m (3083ft)
Height gain	150m (492ft)
Height loss	690m (2262ft)
Approx distance	10km (6.2 miles)
Time allowance	Ammoudari to rim of plain 940m (3083ft) 1hr 15mins; to TheKipou 800m (3046ft) 1hr; to Achatsikia 400m (1312ft) 1hr 45mins; to Vafes 30mins; total: 4hrs 30mins

Heading north from **Ammoudari** *plateia* on the main road to Kares, and just before the red-roofed church turn up left on a surfaced shepherds' road. At a junction, keep left on this road. It gains height before ending beside a flat-topped concrete cistern and an old sheepfold. The road to Niato is seen high on the hillside above.

Continue on a footpath from the sheepfold. It heads up towards the right side of the valley to join a section of paved mule track. This leads northwest, and then descends as a footpath to a valley – one of several in the mountainous rim of the plateau. ◄

To return to Askifou
Bear left down the valley, passing mature oak trees and an old cistern, to reach a slip road from the Askifou–Niato shepherds' road.

For Vafes Bear right as you reach the valley, northwards, on the footpath that now tackles the steep descent to the TheKipou–Vatoudiaris shepherds' road. When a rocky watercourse gully develops, the path crosses to the east side. Make your way down to the road and then turn left, west, for **TheKipou**. Passing the cistern, follow the road to the chapel for a few minutes, looking left, for a sheep-herding path that leaves the roadside and heads straight down through woodland. As this valley steepens, note that the path traverses out of it by traversing a crag to the left. This brings you to another gully. Continue down this to an open area of old terracing.

Cross over to the left, and make your way down a prickly oak-tree-filled gully to join another shepherds' road, from Vatoudiaris to Renda.

Turn left, west, for Renda and Vafes. The road loses height past a sheep shed before climbing again to round a thin spur. On top of this spur a large sheep shed is built adjacent to a complex of old stone huts (cistern). This is **Renda**. There are several workstations in this 'hidden' fertile valley.

Renda has two fenced crop-growing fields. There is a wire gate in the far northwest corner of the first field; the path to Archatsikia (and Vafes) starts from that gate. Go though and follow alongside the fence until you overlook a bracken-filled fenced enclosure. Outside the fence, old terracing on the hillsides is overgrown with Jerusalem sage and spiny broom. The correct path, nowadays used by sheep at least, starts its contouring route – around a re-entrant to the next spur – from the level of the fence at the bottom of the enclosure. Make your way down to that fence. A few metres below it pick up the path and follow it, around old terracing, to the next spur. Clamber over a 'gate' of brushwood. Beyond the spur the path loses some height, before taking up a contouring route again. Arrive at a stone-built wall and an unmade road (at the roadhead). This leads down to **Archatsikia** and **Vafes**. ◄

If you want to stay in the mountains, walking west to Vothanas and Melidoni, turn off left when you reach the first olive grove (see Walk 18a)

WALK 35
Krappis to Lake Kourna

Grade	B
Start	Krappis 500m (1640ft)
Access	KTEL Sfakia bus or taxi from Vrisses or Askifou
Finish	Lake Kourna village 50m (164ft)
Access to finish	Taxi from Georgioupoli
Highest point	540m (1771ft)
Height gain	40m (131ft)
Height loss	480m (1574ft)
Approx distance	10km (6.2 miles)
Time allowance	Krappis to east end of Dafnokorfes Valley 2hrs 30mins; ruined hamlet 350m (1148ft) to Lake Kourna 1hr 30mins; total: 4hrs

Lake Kourna, a deep freshwater lake 1km wide, comes as quite a surprise – especially if you have just got used to arid mountains. Hidden away inland from the Georgioupoli main road and surrounded on three sides by steep or precipitous crags, the lake is fed by springs emerging underwater at its southwestern corner. The water is used for agricultural irrigation, so is suitable for swimming.

This walk links with Askifou by following the Askifou shepherds' traditional droving route down to winter pastures around Georgioupoli. Nowadays mountain sheep are billeted in sheds over the winter, but all the older shepherding people of Crete remember what fun the transhumance operation used to be, with whole families travelling together. Krappis is a fertile valley with a small red-roofed church, about one third of the way down the Askifou–Vrisses road. A large *taverna* marks the bus stop. Since it is very isolated, Krappis is an ideal location for weddings and christenings when Sfakiots fire off their weaponry. Opposite Krappis *taverna* note the memorial to historic battles with the Turks in the defile just above (now full of scree), that was once the 'entrance' to the wild and remote region of Sfakia.

A footpath leaves the northeast rim of the Krappis Valley to join a road along the valley under Dafnokorfes. From there another footpath descends steeply to the lake, where there are rooms and *tavernas*, but no bus. The nearest reliable bus stop is at Georgioupoli on the busy main north coast road. Georgioupoli taxis may not be readily available at busy times. However, on a trip from Askifou to eastern Crete (travelling light) an overnight stop at Lake Kourna (good swimming) might suit well.

Starting from the church at Krappis, pass a house and bear right on the footpath which runs the length of the perimeter fence of the cultivated meadows. Turn left around the end of this enclosure, and cross, heading northeast, to pick up an ascending wide, stony track that bears left for the rim of the valley. The Dafnokorfes Valley, with its road from Alikampos ('Alee-kam-bos') is now in view. Taking care on this very rugged terrain, follow the path going right, northeast, as it crosses a low hill or two on the way down to the road. Walk east (a water tap can be found at a large ugly roadside sheep shed). At the end of the valley, an older track, branching right, serves a disused stone-built hamlet with adjacent terracing and a well (poor water). This must have been an important stop-off place on the old transhumance trail.

You cannot yet see Lake Kourna – continue on the new road for a couple of minutes. Below is a large amphitheatre-shaped descending valley, with **Lake Kourna** at its foot. Down this valley, in the centre, low hills at an intermediate level conceal a ruined hamlet. The footpath from the road heads down to this and the descent to the lake continues from there.

Detour If you have time before making the descent, take a 20min detour to a nice picnic or camping spot beyond the old hamlet. From the well, keep on round the terraced area to pick up a footpath heading east through trees. It traverses the mountainside to a final descending spur with a ruined stone hut on its east-facing side. Probably the best view ever of Lake Kourna and beyond is from this hut, perched on a crag. The ruin overlooks what was the final descent section of the old mule track, a long straight traverse of the adjacent hillside, but it is now broken up and overgrown with spiny broom and Jerusalem sage. Under a huge oak tree, just before you reach the hut, note a cistern (good water) covered with logs.

Take the footpath that goes steeply down and then contour around the mid-level hills to the ruined hamlet. This is about halfway down to the lake. Below the hamlet (where cheese was once made) bear left to pass across a crag (one move needs care) and then descend over scree and along stony footpaths to join the road above the lake. Turn left and keep straight on for Georgioupoli or, after crossing the bridge over the exit river, turn right for Lake Kourna shore.

ANOPOLIS

Sited above the precipitous south coast escarpment, on a wide shelf backed by steeply rising peaks of the Lefka Ori, Anopolis village is made up of several hamlets. Its south-facing olive grove flourishes at this altitude (600m/1968ft), although mountain shepherding is the main traditional occupation. The tough lifestyle that goes with this, in a harsh, dry, formerly inaccessible region of crags and stones, has done much to mould the independent Sfakiot character, well known throughout Greece. Personal self-esteem and a sense of community remain strong, despite the influences of tourism. You will not encounter obsequious manners here, where fairness and skill with money are equally respected.

Anopolis central, with its population of young families, has a *plateia* with the 'Platanos' *kafeneon*, rooms (the landlady speaks English) and a small but well-stocked shop (www.anopoli-stakia.com). Alternatively, Kostas' *kafeneon* (the KTEL bus terminus) on the corner just west of the *plateia* is the first choice for refreshments of walkers arriving from Ay. Roumeli and Aradena. Anopolis, and Ay. Ioannis further west, are on south–north mule tracks over the mountains. A shepherds' road-cum-mule track connects with Askifou, and various footpaths lead down to the coast.

The Anopolis bus to Chania, which departs from the *plateia* about 06.30, serves trailheads at Hora Sfakion,

The mule track to Loutro from Ay. Ekaterini chapel (Walk 36)

The Anopolis Valley in May: the ravine of Trek 8 is seen on the right

Imbros, Askifou, Krappis and Vrisses and arrives at Chania by 09.15 (this may suit flight departures). Returning, it departs Chania at 14.00, Vrisses at 14.40 and Hora Sfakion at 16.00, arriving in Anopolis about 16.45 (every day except Christmas Day and Orthodox Easter Sunday and Monday).

Kambia, the last hamlet in the east (or the first if you arrive from Hora Sfakion) has a modest rooming house and restaurant, and a small bakery. To alight here ask the driver for the 'Panorama' (proprietor Anastasios Athitaki) at Kambia or he may pass straight through, assuming you are going to the *plateia* which is 2km further on. There are (or were) two more *kafeneia* up the road from the Panorama. The first was The Elvetia, now closed; it can be identified (for Walk 38) as the place with

two two-storey buildings opposite one another on the main road.

Kambia's view out over the sea is enhanced by the brilliance of the light resulting from the juxtaposition of escarpment, sea and sky, making this an attractive spot to car tourers and others arriving by bus or on foot. Kambia is built around a small fertile plain at the cliff edge. The fields are now disused, but as a point of interest, in the days of subsistence farming (well within living memory) an area like this – along with sheep, goats, hens and bee-keeping – could sustain two or three extended families. Start from Kambia for the easiest walking route down the escarpment to Loutro, rather than from Anopolis *plateia* (Walk 37).

171

WALK 36
Anopolis to Loutro

Grade	B
Start	Anopolis plateia 600m (1968ft)
Access	KTEL Anopolis bus or taxi from Hora Sfakion
Finish	Loutro waterfront
Access to finish	Coastal boat service from Hora Sfakion or Ay. Roumeli, or boat taxi
Highest point	687m (2253ft)
Height gain	90m (295ft)
Height loss	687m (2252ft)
Approx distance	4km (2.5 miles)
Time allowance	Anopolis plateia to Ay. Ekaterini chapel 687m (2252ft) 30mins ; chapel to Loutro 1hr 30mins (joining Walk 37 on descent); total: 2hrs

The little white chapel of Ay. Ekaterini, and the site of ancient Anopolis, a Dorian and then Roman town, tops the ridge enclosing the south side of the valley. The old mule track between Anopolis and Loutro passes below the chapel, and then zigzags straight down the steep escarpment to Loutro.

From the monument to Daskaloyannis (a notable early revolutionary against the Turks) in **Anopolis** *plateia* take the village street heading south out of the square and follow it through to the road up the ridge. When this turns south, note the boundary wall of ancient Anopolis up on the right. Just before the crest of the ridge, detour for 5mins on a footpath up to the chapel for a stupendous view of mountains, valley and coast.

The **Loutro** peninsula is seen directly below, with its harbour and ruined Turkish fort on the hill above the village. Far to the east Mt Kedros can be seen bordering Messara Bay with Paximada Island and, to the south, Gavdos and Gavdopoula islands are 48km out across the Libyan Sea (Libyan shores cannot be seen, even from Gavdos). To the

west, bounded by a wall of huge blocks, the remains of ancient streets, modest houses, and a cistern or two, cover a surprisingly large area of the ridge top. Inhabitants of ancient Anopolis cannot have minded the arduous daily descent to the fertile valley or the chill of living in such a draughty place – unless this was a summer-only settlement. Whatever the lifestyle, the mule track routes that still link the ancient sites of Anopolis, Aradena and Phoenix are surely very old.

Return down to the main trail. An old shrine at the clifftop marks the start of the mule track down to Loutro.

The Loutro peninsula from Ay. Ekaterini chapel

173

WALK 37
Kambia to Loutro

Grade	B
Start	Kambia hamlet 580m (1902ft), Anopolis
Access	KTEL Sfakia–Anopolis bus or taxi from Hora Sfakion
Finish	Loutro waterfront
Access to finish	Coastal boat service or on foot
Height loss	580m (1902ft)
Approx distance	3km (1.8 miles)
Time allowance	1hr 20mins

From Anopolis *plateia* the path climbs the ridge, but from Kambia –where the ridge has run out – the route down is quicker.

Walk south off the main road through **Kambia** hamlet to the church and cemetery, which is near the edge of the escarpment. The old mule track link to the downhill path of Walk 36 is now fenced off. Therefore, until this route is reopened, follow the shepherds' car track from beside the church. This leads down to a cistern on the right-hand side of the road: the footpath from Ayia Ekaterini chapel joins the road at this point.

Due to Loutro's status as an Area of Outstanding Natural Beauty (AONB), the road soon ends at a sheep shed. However, beyond the cistern the footpath to Loutro branches off the road just after the next left-hand bend. This path can be seen heading downhill towards a thin, steeply descending spur. When you arrive at the steep spur, there is another path junction: keep left for Loutro direct, or bear right down into a gully (where there is a carob tree with low branches) for a traverse that, after 10mins, offers another route choice: turn left downhill for **Loutro** via the Turkish fort, a large rectangular ruin on the hill above the village, or keep straight on to join a mule track up to **Livaniana** (Walk 48) or a road that serves Phoenix and Likos bays.

The mule track divides; bear right for the longer way down to Loutro, or for Likos

WALK 38
Kambia to Anopolis or Ay. Ekaterini

Grade	B
Start	Kambia hamlet 580m (1902ft), Anopolis
Access	KTEL Sfakia–Anopolis bus or taxi from Hora Sfakion
Finish	Anopolis plateia 600m (1968ft)
Access to finish	KTEL Anopolis bus or taxi from Hora Sfakion
Height gain/loss	20m (65ft)
Approx distance	2km (1.2 miles)
Time allowance	40mins

On the main road through **Kambia**, note two two-storey buildings opposite one another, either side of the road,

The modern main road has replaced much of the valley's network of hamlet-connecting mule tracks, including the 'old road' extension of the pre-1940s road through Askifou, Imbros and Hora Sfakion. In terms of modern recreational use a cobbled road all the way from Vrisses to Anopolis and Ay. Ioannis is an intriguing thought. Much of the route can still be followed (Walks 23, 24, 25 and 46). In Anopolis all but a few surviving sections of old tracks are fenced off and overgrown at present. However, since it can be a useful short cut between Kambia and central Anopolis, a 2km mule track running the length of the valley under the escarpment ridge remains open.

once a *kafeneon*/rooming house, now closed. With the south-facing flank wall of the west-side house on your right, take the concrete approach road to the house behind. Just before the house, peel off alongside a fence to join a walled mule track where you turn right. Keep straight on – there will be a couple of wire gates. The walled section joins a service track and, just before this bears round to the right, re-join the old mule track as it heads uphill, to the left. (At the top of this short hill another footpath peels off down to the right to join the main road).

Ay. Ekaterini chapel

Although the mule track has lost its original surface here, keep straight on westwards.

The whole of the Anopolis Valley, with its large olive grove, is now in view. The mountains rise steeply to the north. After crossing an old terrace the path loses height: pass through a wire gate and continue straight on through **Riza** hamlet to reach the road of the Ayia Ekaterini ridge. Turn up left for the chapel, or turn right downhill for **Anopolis** *plateia*.

WALK 39
Kambia to Hora Sfakion

Walk 46 in reverse	
Grade	B/C
Start	Kambia hamlet 580m (1902ft), Anopolis
Access	KTEL Sfakia–Anopolis bus or taxi from Hora Sfakion
Finish	Hora Sfakion
Access	KTEL Sfakia bus or coastal boat service
Height loss	600m (1968ft)
Approx distance	4km (2.5 miles)
Time allowance	Kambia to Ilingas Gorge 1hr 10mins; to Hora Sfakion by road 30mins; total: 1hr 40mins (add 10mins for bus stop or waterfront)

Keep on the main road downhill out of **Kambia**, and after rounding the corner (Sweetwater Beach is directly below this part of the road) join the mule track route at a deep right-hand bend directly above a steep valley. Leave the road here and make your way straight down the valley on footpaths, and on a track. The track ends at a small water-works.

Continue downhill on a footpath that leads to the bed of a ravine. A few traces of paved mule track are seen here and there but the flash flood did much damage, forming several 'steps' in the ravine, one of which is about 2m (6ft) high. Walkers have piled up rocks to make this step easier. At the bottom the ravine forms a T-junction with the Ilingas Gorge (known as the Kavis Gorge further inland). Turn right to join

A severe flash flood in the winter of 2000 caused much damage to some sections of this trail so that minor rock-scrambling ability is needed in the ravine section.

the main road at a concrete bridge above Ilingas *taverna* and beach, and then left for **Hora Sfakion**.

Alternatively, when you arrive at the gorgebed, climb up the opposite bank – much damaged by the flash flood – to join a remaining section of *kalderimi* that can be seen clinging to the east side of the gorge. Before the main road was built, this old road between Hora Sfakion and Anopolis took the easiest way across the mountainside. Nowadays a new shepherds' road (see Walk 46) zigzagging uphill, and road-widening works on the main road, have destroyed its final descent to the village.

On the western approach to **Hora Sfakion**, just beyond the first right-hand bend in the road, an old lane leads down to the waterfront, its entrance steps now incorporated in a new building complex. For the KTEL bus stop and boat ticket kiosk continue on the main road. Turn down right, to the car park, which is overlooked by a small chapel.

WALK 40
Anopolis to Aradena

Grade	B
Start/finish	Anopolis plateia 600m (1968ft)
Access	KTEL Anopolis bus or taxi from Hora Sfakion
Highest point	620m (2043ft)
Height gain	Negligible
Approx distance	6km (4 miles)
Time allowance	Anopolis to Aradena Gorge rim (or to bridge) 40mins; kalderimi 15mins down, 20mins up, to Bailey bridge via church 20mins; bridge to Anopolis 45mins; total: 2hrs 20mins

From Anopolis the main road continues west to Aradena and Ay. Ioannis, where it ends. Aradena village ('A'raTH-then-ah'), its ruined houses perched on the west side of the Aradena Gorge near a water-collecting hollow, draws many visitors. During the period of extreme privation after World War II, an escalating vendetta – triggered by two boys disputing the ownership of a goat's bell in 1947 – obliged the community to disperse and settle elsewhere. Their descendants did not return as the village was so cut off.

In the mid-1980s the gorge was spanned by a Bailey bridge, a gift to the Ay. Ioannis community from four brothers of that village who had prospered in the oil industry of Piraeus. Until then the *kalderimi* which zigzags up and down both sides of the gorge served both villages – there was no other road. Aradena was preserved as the best 'museum of a village' Sfakia has to offer, rather to the bemusement of locals for whom the old houses are a reminder of the 'bad old days' of hard physical toil. One or two examples of the Sfakiot vernacular in Aradena have qualified for EU-funded restoration works.

More examples of the traditional house types of Sfakia can be seen (usually as ruins) in the various hamlets of Anopolis, particularly Giros ('Yee-ross'), and in old Ay. Roumeli, Livaniana, upper Hora Sfakion, and Askifou. Room width was restricted to the length of available tree trunks for beams. Stone-built *kamara* arches were often used as a solution, making two rooms side-by-side and also, deep, shady front porches. First-floor living rooms typically had window openings that encouraged cross-ventilation, a practical design feature usually forgotten in today's rooming houses. Single-room houses with high ceilings had galleries at each end – one as a bedroom, the other for the weaving loom beside a window. Until about 1920 women made cloth and the family's clothes, rugs and other items, using raw cotton, sheeps' wool and goats' hair. Most houses had a conical-shaped oven for baking bread and a large basin for treading grapes.

As ever, olive oil was a very important product: for food, oil lamps, soap, and a host of other uses. Villages had communal olive presses. The Aradena press, seen from the footpath between the bridge and the church, is ruined. A restored press, of this 1880s design, can be seen in the old village of Samaria (Samaria Gorge). Olives were softened by boiling before being crushed under heavy mill-stones, turned by donkey around a circular platform. The resulting mush was then sandwiched inside woven jute or goats'-hair envelopes, piled up, again softened with boiling water, and finally pressed under a plate forced down by a turning screw mounted between vertical iron pillars. For flour, stone-paved circular threshing floors were used for threshing and winnowing harvested grain. A ruined windmill, dated about 1830, is seen on the hillside south of Loutro's Turkish fort.

The modern bridge offers fascinating bird's-eye views of the gorge. Although the old *kalderimi* looks quite an undertaking, the scale is deceptive and the round walk of *kalderimi*, Byzantine church and bridge is popular with car tourers. The bridge is sometimes used for the sport of bungee jumping.

From **Anopolis** *plateia,* walk westwards past Kostas' *kafeneon* for 10mins along the road to **Ay. Dimitrios**, the most westerly hamlet of Anopolis.

The bridge over the Aradena Gorge and the refreshments kiosk

With the church on your right and large kermis oak trees on your left, leave the main road and walk behind the older houses of this hamlet. Turn uphill at the end. A shepherds' track now follows the line of the old paved mule track. Follow this beyond an animal shed and then turn off left to pick up the mule track again as it passes beside a large lone olive tree. Turn west here to re-join the main road.

At the road you have a choice: either turn left for the bridge, or, for the gorge *kalderimi*, leave the main road on the footpath that now continues west, direct for the gorge. From the top it takes about 15mins to the bottom, and 20mins up the other side. Walk straight on past ruined houses, turn left by a chapel, and walk up through old lanes past the Byzantine church, to get to the bridge where there is a car park and a refreshments kiosk.

WALK 40A
The Aradena Gorge

Grade	C
Start	Aradena Gorge rim 580m (1902ft), east or west side
Access	Walk 40 or taxi from Hora Sfakion
Finish	Marmara Beach
Access to finish	E4 coastal footpath to Loutro (Walk 49)
Highest point	Aradena 580m (1902ft)
Height loss	590m (1935ft)
Approx distance	5km (3.1 miles)
Time allowance	Aradena kalderimi to main 'step' rockfall 30mins; rockfall section 20mins; base of rockfall to Livaniana path 10mins; to Marmara Beach 3hrs; total: 4–4½hrs (several rockfalls to negotiate)

The Aradena Gorge is absolutely spectacular, its massive walls adorned with a variety of plants, but it is not a popular tourist bus north–south walk. Aradena is fairly remote and at the bottom of the gorge, at Marmara Beach, there is no access road – just the coastal footpath. (Likos, the next beach on the way to Loutro, is served by a road that branches off just east of the Aradena bridge, going via Livaniana.) In the gorge, some distance down from the bridge, a massive step formed by huge boulders used to be passable only by means of two iron ladder pitches and a hand rope. This kit is still in place, but as a way of bypassing it a new modern-style footpath has been built into the crag high above the rockfall. However, perhaps built to a minimum specification it has already suffered badly from natural erosion.

Take the **Aradena** *kalderimi* (from either side of the gorge) to the gorgebed, and turn downhill to pass under the bridge. The path down the gorge is marked with red dots and cairns here and there. Note the new *kalderimi* path on the west side of the gorge when you arrive at the big rockfall.

About 10mins down the gorge from the rockfall a small footpath from Livaniana comes in from the left. From there, follow Walk 48. If you see a dead goat or two this is

The Aradena Gorge mule track

due to the sudden noise made by vehicles when they cross the bridge. Animals grazing on the cliffs may jump off in fright. Domestic goats quite often miss their footing in any of these Sfakiot gorges.

WALK 41

Aradena to Ay. Ioannis and Sellouda

Grade	B
Start/finish	Aradena bridge 600m (1968ft)
Access	Walk 40 from Anopolis or taxi from Hora Sfakion
Highest point	Ay. Ioannis 800m (2624ft)
Height gain/loss	200m (656ft)
Approx distance	11km (7 miles)
Time allowance	Aradena to Ay. Ioannis (road walk) 1hr 20mins; Ay. Ioannis to Sellouda 595m (1952ft) 45mins; Sellouda to Aradena 1hr 5mins; total: 3hrs 10mins

Before road access Ay. Ioannis was another interesting old village built in Sfakiot vernacular style. Approached on 4km of cobbled mule track, its wall-enclosed houses were separated by paved lanes. Almost all of this has now gone. The old schoolhouse was operated as a *kafeneon* but is now closed. An 'honesty box' drinks dispenser may be in service during the summer. Otherwise the nearest refreshments outlets are the kiosk at the Aradena bridge, the *taverna* on the coast at Ay. Pavlos, and the *plateia* in Anopolis.

For the coast and Ay. Roumeli, a footpath leads down from the village to a spot called Sellouda, the only passable place through the cliffs (Walk 41). Alternative 'secret' routes in these forested crags do, or once did, exist. Some maps misguidedly promote this idea, disregarding the ravages of natural erosion and depopulation on unmaintained paths.

From the **Aradena** bridge the asphalt main road continues 4km up to **Ay. Ioannis**. (You may be able to arrange a lift from Anopolis and then walk back via Sellouda and Aradena.)

For Sellouda Leave Ay. Ioannis near the chapel outside the village entrance gate on a footpath descending to the southeast. Keep on the footpath for 2km, downhill through the pine forest, to a small valley with a cistern and sheepfold served by a shepherds' road. Continue southwards for 10mins beyond this valley to **Sellouda** (which is approached – final section – on a walled mule track) for the clifftop view, or, for **Aradena**, take the road east and then keep straight on overland to a large sheep shed below the Ay. Ioannis road. At the shed enclosure either turn up sharp left to join the road or continue on, through gates, on a broken-up surviving section of old mule track.

This circuit takes in three Byzantine churches, each with 14th-century frescoes. In Aradena the church of Mikhail Arkhangelos, with its unusual dome, is easily spotted from across the gorge. In Ay. Ioannis the churches of Ay. Ioannis and Panayia are found just below the road before the village entrance gate. However since the frescoes are very valuable each church has to be kept locked. Enquire first at The Platanos, Anopolis *plateia* (Poppy, the landlady, speaks fluent English), for latest information as to who holds the keys.

WALK 42

Aradena to Ay. Roumeli via Sellouda

Walk 53 in reverse

Grade	B
Start	Aradena 600m (1968ft)
Access	Walk 40 from Anopolis or taxi from Hora Sfakion
Finish	Ay. Roumeli
Access to finish	Coastal boat service
Height loss	600m (1968ft)
Approx distance	11.5km (7 miles)
Time allowance	Aradena to Sellouda 1hr 5mins; Sellouda to Ay. Pavlos 1hr 30mins; to Ay. Roumeli 1hr 15mins; total: 3hrs 50mins
	Starting from Anopolis add 40mins; total: 4hrs 35mins

Walkers enjoying the view from Sellouda

Follow Walk 40 to **Aradena** and continue westwards up the Ay. Ioannis road. Just beyond the fence of the second sheep shed below the road, make your way down to pick up the footpath from that shed (or walk through the sheep-shed area, closing the gates as you go). The path is a broken-up section of the old mule track – follow this as it gains height to join a shepherds' track which heads towards pine forest. Sellouda is in the direction of about 240°SW. At the third left-hand junction of the track, note a single-storey white-washed stone hut in the woods – this marks the correct turn-off. Follow the road to its end where waymarks on the left mark a walled mule track that leads to **Sellouda**.

From here, reverse Walk 53.

WALK 43
The Aradena Forest and Kroussia

Grade	B/C
Start/finish	Anopolis plateia 600m (1968ft)
Access	KTEL Anopolis bus or taxi from Hora Sfakion
Highest point	Kroussia 1220m (4002ft)
Height gain/loss	To forest floor 100m (328ft); to Kroussia 1420m (4658ft)
Approx distance	Various; for the route below 18km (11.2 miles)
Time allowance	Anopolis plateia to top of Aradena main kalderimi, west side 600m (1968ft) 1hr 20mins; to Aradena forest 680m (2230ft) 25mins; to Kroussia 1220m (4002ft) 3hrs 25mins; to Ay. Ioannis 800m (2624ft) via ravine 1hr 20mins; to Aradena bridge 1hr; to Anopolis 40mins; total: 8hrs 10mins

North of Aradena, on the west side of the gorge, there is a large pine forest. A day's walking in this quiet, shady woodland can make a welcome change from being out in the 'boiling sun'. The trees have long taken over what was once a cultivated hillside, judging by the remains of old terracing that can be seen on the forest floor and in the small ravines. For shepherds the focal point, 4km uphill from the second *kalderimi* of the gorge, was Kroussia, a small grazing area on the mule track route to Zaranokefala and Potamos (see Trek 7). However, since flocks of sheep no longer clear the trails, footpaths in the forest are now indistinct. It would be easy to find your way up to Kroussia if the hillside was bare, but as it stands the dense forest, and the labyrinth of faint paths, certainly provide route-finding challenges – this may entertain those with a GPS and the Anavasi map. You cannot get lost for long because, using the gorge for direction, you can always find your way back to the Aradena bridge. Even so, since the forest is unfrequented, companions are needed. Remember also that pine forests are much at risk from forest fires. Lightning strikes are apparent in this forest, but fortunately only small areas are damaged so far.

Take 2 litres of water per person in case you reach Kroussia (open cisterns, poor water) from where there is a long descent down to Ay. Ioannis (see Trek 7).

From **Anopolis**, follow Walk 40 to the **Aradena bridge**. On the east side of the gorge, just before the bridge, there is raised 'viewing terrace'. From here, note a big crag rising above the forest at 350°NW. Note the long forested spur in front of it; one of the paths to Kroussia leads straight up this spur, bearing left just before the crag. The other path (which has some cairns) climbs the 'streambed' south of the spur.

The 1:25,000 Anavasi map 'Sfakia' is useful here because contours show the spur and the 'streambed' running down from Kroussia to the gorge. If you find these routes, note that both lead to up a clearing where there is a large walled enclosure. From there, keep straight on for Kroussia – through a shallow gully beyond the clearing, and bearing left when you come to the next Y-junction of paths.

On the barren hillside north of the ruined house at the top of the main kalderimi (west side) there is a steel-fenced enclosure. ◀

To continue, make your way up to this from behind the ruined house. Unlocked gates (in a separate fence) allow you to walk up the west side of the enclosure. Turn right at the top and after about 50m climb up from there to reach the forest.

You now have a choice of routes:

Either make your way along paths parallel to the gorge rim – and in that way head for the relevant spur if you are aiming for **Kroussia**;

Or turn left, down a sheep trail to join a path, an old mule track, coming up from the few houses on the western side of **Aradena** village. (It follows that you can return to Aradena that way, or alternatively use that route to enter the

This obviously special enclosure is interesting; it has been in place for at least 20 years and shows the extraordinary variety of vegetation that would blanket the hillside if it were not grazed by sheep and goats.

forest.) Since there are no particular landmarks in the forest (apart from the big crag) these route hints are offered as a starting point for your explorations.

Note Relevant to walking in the forest, the Aradena Gorge has three built *kalderimia:* the main one near the bridge, the second one about 1km north of this (although its west side has succumbed to natural erosion) and the third one about 500m further north again. (This hillside was clearly very busy at one time.) Between the first and second *kalderimia* there is a fairly difficult 'waterfall' section of smooth rounded rocks, but between the other two the gorgebed is fairly easy underfoot. There is road access (east side) to the second *kalderimi* – a dirt road that branches off from the main bend on the Anopolis–Aradena road about 1km west of Ay. Dimitri hamlet. The third *kalderimi* is accessed from the T-junction on the Madares road (before it reaches the foot of the 'Trek 8 ravine'.) This is the route (not walked by author) to the cave system, Drakolimni, photographs of which are seen on the wall of Kostas' taverna, Anopolis *plateia*.

WALK 44
Anopolis to Askifou via Kali Lakki

Walk 33 in reverse

Grade	C/D
Start	Anopolis plateia 600m (1968ft)
Access	KTEL Anopolis bus or taxi from Hora Sfakion
Finish	Ammoudari–Askifou 790m (2591ft)
Access to finish	KTEL Sfakia bus or taxi from Hora Sfakion, Vrisses (or Askifou)
Height gain	Undulating route between 600m (1968ft) and 1220m (4002ft); basic Height gain 630m (2066ft)
Approx distance	21km (13 miles)
Time allowance	Anopolis plateia to Feeno Kai Yanoos mitato 1120m (3674ft) 4hrs; to Scarfidia 1240m (4068ft) 35mins; to Trikoukia (mule track route) 1220m (4002ft) 2hrs; to Niato 1260m (4133ft) 35mins; to Ammoudari–Askifou 1hr; total: 8hrs 10mins

Part of the old high-level mule track between Anopolis and Askifou still remains, although nowadays shepherds' roads approach it from either end. This walk is easier starting from Askifou because the long road-tramp at the end is then downhill. However, if starting from Anopolis suits your itinerary, directions to the trailhead follow.

From **Anopolis** *plateia* follow Trek 8 to the foot of the mountains and the mule track ravine.

Take the road: after an initial long straight uphill section it gains more height in wide loops before heading northeast towards the upper reaches of the Kavis Gorge. A major T-junction (with a noticeably rougher road) marks the turn-off for the Madares (of Trek 8). Keep straight on here to pass a shepherds' workstation and spring, called Feeno Kai Yanous.

For Mouri Beyond this, as the road loops around a large bend, there is a right-hand junction – the turn-off for Mouri – and also another spur – but keep right for Mouri (see Walk 33 for walking routes from Mouri).

For Scarfidia Continue on the road (or take a short-cut path uphill from the workstation to miss the bend) as far as the next T-junction. Turn right here, and walk downhill to the road-end at Scarfidia spring and *mitato*. Red paint marks the start of the footpath-cum-mule track to Trikoukia and/or Kali Lakki: turn north, uphill, bearing to the right, to pick up this route, which becomes more distinct as you near the crest of the hill (the first ridge, or spur, to be crossed on the way east). The little spurge-covered meadow in the forest above Kali Lakki (a ruined 'summer' hamlet) is on top of the next ridge east from here. From that point you can either make your way down to **Kali Lakki** and its road link to Trikoukia, or continue on the mule track. Follow Walk 33 in reverse from the meadow.

THE SOUTH COAST OF SFAKIA

For walkers, the gem of western Crete is the region of Sfakia ('Ss'fak-ya') with its spectacular mountain scenery and gorge-punctuated coastline largely free of roads from Hora Sfakion to Souyia. Coastal villages, and therefore several trailheads, are served (spring to autumn) by regular ferryboat schedules.

Another delight is the climate; the south coast is often sunny – or at least dry – when the north coast is overcast or wet. Rocky coves with white- or black-stone beaches offer good bathing from the coastal walks that link the villages, with their harbours, and the various gorges. Waterfront restaurants are free of the unsightly picture-menus of north-coast resorts and much of the accommodation is not pre-booked by tour operators, allowing for a flexible itinerary.

There are various small bays along the coast, some of which have tavernas. Proprietors bring supplies around by boat. If conditions suit they may offer (obviously 'own risk') boat-ride transfers to and from a nearby resort.

HORA SFAKION

'Village of Sfakia' is tedious to say – locals (and the bus crew) call it 'Sfakia'. This is a former fishing village at the end of the road down the steep south coast escarpment. Nowadays it is part of the Samaria Gorge round trip; ferryboats from Ay. Roumeli land passengers here by the thousand for their bus journeys

back to other resorts. Much of this operation circulates east of the promenade, by a large car and bus park, leaving the rest of the village to carry on almost as normal.

Sfakia has supermarkets, shops selling souvenirs, books, maps, clothes and beach kits, a bakery, restaurants and lots of accommodation. Sfakia also has noise: late-night dining, refrigerator motors, water pumps, barking dogs and so on. Rooming houses more distant from the waterfront will be quieter. The community has shelved the idea of public WCs – given the numbers of potential users – and instead the coffee bars and restaurants are supposed to offer this service. The harbour beach below the promenade and the town beach on the west side of the village are both good for swimming. Regular boat trips to Gavdos Island, 30km offshore, are offered during the tourist season.

After the Battle of Crete thousands of Allied soldiers were evacuated under heavy bombardment from Hora Sfakion, and the nearby beaches of Imbros and Ilingas, by the Royal Navy on 28–31 May 1941. A memorial to this event, flying the flags of Greece, Great Britain, New Zealand and Australia, is sited on the main ferryboat pier. Old shells may still be seen, used as house embellishments in Loutro and Anopolis. The evacuation was organised from a cave in one of the ravines behind Hora Sfakion. There is a big cave (with a disused

Hora Sfakion from the east: the road to Anopolis and the 'mule track' ravine is seen in the background

chapel inside) just above the road to Anopolis. This cave is too exposed to have been used for that purpose, but if you have time to spare, climb up to it for an alternative view of the whole modern set-up below – or take the mule track up the adjacent spur, east, to an old ruined hamlet in a small pinewood (see Walk 47).

There are good views also from the village waterworks in the 13th-century Venetian castle, just above the bus park. A bus to Chania departs 07.00 daily (and at other times) providing walkers with access to trailheads inland at Imbros or Askifou.

LOUTRO

The sheltered natural harbours of Loutro and nearby Phoenix Bay, which has springs, have often been mentioned in the history of Mediterranean seafaring. Loutro (or Phoenix) has been a Roman port, a Venetian harbour, a community of seafaring merchants, a Sfakiot pirates' lair, and a Turkish stronghold.

Today, in total contrast, Loutro is a mildly upmarket tourist resort and a designated EU Area of Outstanding Natural Beauty (AONB). Fortunately, thanks to the difficulty of making road access to Loutro, oil-tanker moorings were established at Kali Limenes in central Crete rather than here. This was relatively recently, although before today's tourism levels were even guessed at. AONB status protects the exceptionally attractive

Loutro harbour: the coastal footpath to Hora Sfakion and the Anopolis mule track are seen on the left

view of Loutro when seen from an approach by sea. A road from Anopolis via Livaniania to Likos and Phoenix bays to the west is (2007) the nearest road-head.

There is safe swimming from the harbour beach, with an outlying islet providing a focal point for strong swimmers. Sunbeds can be hired. There are supermarkets, restaurants, lots of accommodation, and shops selling souvenirs, books, clothes, and beach kits. There is an Internet café. A boat-taxi supplements the regular boat schedule and various trips are offered to nearby bays. The ferryboat jetty (and ticket kiosk) is at the south end of the promenade. Loutro's peninsula itself offers a pleasant round walk, taking in various chapels and the two old forts.

Regarding accommodation many rooms here (but not all) may be pre-booked by tour operators at times. However walkers, travelling light, can continue west on the E4 Trail to Phoenix or Likos bays, where there are more rooming houses.

The mule track to Anopolis, which is seen zigzagging up the steep escarpment directly above Loutro, gets the sun all day, making it a hot walk if there is no breeze (see Walks 36 and 37). Note that the Turkish fort mentioned in the route notes is the large ruin just above Loutro Bay, to the west. There is also a small Venetian fort on the south side of the bay.

WALK 45
Hora Sfakion to Loutro (E4 Trail)

Grade	B
Start	Hora Sfakion
Access	KTEL Sfakia bus or coastal boat service
Finish	Loutro
Access to finish	Coastal boat service
Height gain/loss	Undulating coastal walk
Approx distance	6km (4 miles)
Time allowance	2hrs 15mins (each way)

This rugged – but well-tramped – and varied stretch of coastal footpath between two popular centres has good bathing along the way, especially at Sweetwater Beach. Start with a ferryboat transfer from Hora Sfakion to Loutro if you would prefer the 1.5km on the main road at the end of the walk. Boat ticket kiosks can be found beside the bus stop in Hora Sfakion, and by the ferryboat jetty in Loutro.

Leave **Hora Sfakion** up the village street behind and parallel to the promenade. Just beyond the shops, turn up a narrow village lane (turn right, then sharp left) to get to the main road. Turn left (west) for the Ilingas Gorge, where there is a concrete bridge over the watercourse, and then continue on to the uphill right-hand bend where there is a crash barrier and, hopefully, an E4 Trail noticeboard (although recently renewed, it may have been once again shot to bits). This spot is called 'Gleeka-nerah Stro-fee' (Sweetwaters Bend), since the footpath from here heads down to Sweetwater Beach. At first it loses height to negotiate a large rock buttress where a section of the path is hacked out of the cliff. A short section of this feels a little exposed as the sea is directly below.

Follow cairns across a big rockfall to arrive at **Sweetwater Beach**. The west part of the rockfall is fairly recent and it is dangerous to camp on the beach directly under the cliff (anyone who does so hasn't seen what it looks like from the boat). As the name denotes, fresh water,

Loutro Beach and waterfront in May

collected in hollows made by bathers and campers, emerges on this stony beach. Note the waterworks at the west end of the beach – this supplies Loutro by underwater pipe. In the tourist season a small refreshments bar on a rock operates on bottled gas.

The footpath, which is broken up in places due to foot traffic and natural erosion, continues over the next promontory and, after passing small bays, gains height to avoid **Loutro**'s rocky shoreline. Enter the village through a goat gate. The churchyard provides quiet shade away from the otherwise busy waterfront.

The route in reverse The coastal footpath can be seen from Loutro waterfront – the access lane leaves from beside the second restaurant beyond the north end of the beach.

WALK 46
Hora Sfakion to Anopolis

Walk 39 in reverse

Grade	B
Start	Hora Sfakion
Access	KTEL Sfakia bus or coastal boat service
Finish	Anopolis 600m (1968ft)
Access to finish	KTEL Sfakia–Anopolis bus or taxi from Hora Sfakion
Height gain	600m (1968ft)
Approx distance	4km (2.5 miles)
Time allowance	2hrs 40mins (to Kambia)

The Historical Museum in Heraklion has a pre-1950s photograph of the old cobbled road to Anopolis and the hillsides above Hora Sfakion, before the new road was built. Parts of it near Hora Sfakion, east of the Ilingas Gorge, are now difficult to follow; road-widening works have cut out the lower section. West of the gorge the old mule track is more clearly routed up a narrow ravine just behind the hill of the modern road. Walkers can reach the top just to the right of the radio masts on the skyline, although it is easier to finish the last stretch on the main road. Traces of the mule track survived in the ravine quite well until December 2000 when a flash flood washed away most of what was left. Several step-sections in the gorgebed were formed, including one about 2m high, so that minor rock-scrambling ability is needed.

Follow Walk 45 as far as the road bridge across the Ilingas Gorge.

Turn up the stony gorgebed. After a few minutes note the retaining wall of the *kalderimi* descending the eastern side. The lower section has been washed away by the flash flood. The continuation of this track (westwards) is routed up the tributary ravine opposite. Just a few traces of paved track remain in the lower part – look for the retaining wall. Cairns also mark the route.

When the ravine becomes shallow and opens out, follow an undemanding ascending footpath out of it on the right. This leads across to the left again, and later to a waterworks and a track. The track is the route of an underground waterpipe up to the radio masts and Kambi hamlet beyond. Follow this, and then a footpath that passes another waterworks, for the climb up to a left-hand bend on the main road. Here, either take the road (with its dramatic views above Sweetwater Beach) to arrive at **Kambia** hamlet, or keep straight on up to the radio masts where you bear left and walk down to Kambia, or bear right for a track that joins the main road further west – from there it is about 1.5km to **Anopolis** *plateia*.

WALK 47
Hora Sfakion to Mouri

Grade	C
Start/finish	Hora Sfakion (or ongoing walks to Anopolis or Askifou)
Access	KTEL bus service from Chania
Highest point	Mouri church 1010m (3313ft)
Height gain/loss	1010m (3313ft)
Approx distance	5km (8 miles)
Time allowance	Circuit from Hora Sfakion to Kavros: 4hrs up, 3hrs down; total: 7hrs

Mouri was the 'summer' village of the Hora Sfakion community in the days before tourism, when people escaped the worst of the heat by transferring up to the mountains. Mouri ('Moo-ree') was sited in the most suitable place above the coast, and reached after a long but direct ascent of 950m (3117ft) up a spur between the Ilingas (known as Kavis further inland) and Sfakiano gorges. The forested mountains above Hora Sfakion encompass both these gorges and their various tributary ravines. It follows that the old mule track traversing between Niato (Askifou) and Anopolis was made at a height which is clear of the ravines (see Walk 33). From Mouri it is possible to continue up to join this route and then head east for Niato and Askifou, or west for Anopolis. Alternatively there is the option of taking another route to Anopolis from Kavros hamlet.

Looking north above the car park at Hora Sfakion note a small spur above the village, with a ravine either side. The retaining wall of a mule track is clearly seen climbing this spur. This leads up to a ruined hamlet and a small pinewood. Beyond the hamlet the *kalderimi* continues up to the open hillside of the main spur above Hora Sfakion; a shepherds' access road serves this hillside. The footpath route continues from the last shepherds' workstation at the end of this road. Although much of this walk is unfrequented and through forest, the old telephone line (disused) between Hora Sfakion and Mouri can be followed for almost all of the way.

Leave **Hora Sfakion** by walking westwards up the back street parallel to the waterfront, and turn up a steep lane which reaches the main road after passing through an accommodation complex, 'Notos Suites'. The big cave is now above to the left, and there is a small ravine almost in front of you. On the other side of the road, climb up, around the new buildings, and turn right (east) immediately behind them. A flight of concrete steps connects to the start of the old *kalderimi*.

This well-preserved section of *kalderimi* zigzags up the south-facing hillside before taking up a straight traverse above the neighbouring east ravine. With the bustle of Hora Sfakion now out of sight, reach the old hamlet at a spot where there is a ruined chapel, an unsurfaced road, and a white-painted chapel. Follow the *kalderimi* (not a blue-way-marked alternative path) as it passes west of the old houses beyond the chapel. Beyond the houses note another chapel on the right and a house in a large walled enclosure on the hillside in front of you. The path continues up to the left of this walled enclosure. There is no water here: the cistern is disused. At the top, cross a seldom-used car track and climb the opposite bank to find the path again – it now ascends beside a crag. ◄

Note the collapsed telephone line that will later serve to guide you all the way up to Mouri.

The old mule track levels out and crosses shallow upper sections of the 'west' ravine. In direction, it turns north on a sharp step up before turning west again. When this *kalderimi* leaves the more solid foundation of the crags it peters out, leaving you to cross the hillside on a footpath. Head for a lone tree and then join the shepherds' access road at a spot where there is a concrete-topped cistern on the opposite side of the road. Follow the road uphill, keeping right at a junction. About 20mins beyond the junction note a sheep shed on the left, but keep on to the last workstation at the end of the road.

To rejoin the footpath, now climb the ridge, or spur, from behind the hut, on a route less steep than that taken by the telephone line at this point. The old mule track reached the spine of the spur and then crossed over it, to contour along the east-facing side where the underfoot is less rugged. If you miss this section, just make your way up the spine of the spur to a lone tree at 500m (1640ft). There are extensive views from here. The forest treeline is just above, and the mountainside now steepens considerably.

Keeping the telephone line in sight (it has recrossed the ridge and is now over on your left) continue the ascent northwest through the forest to reach a shallow gully orientated north–south. The path climbs alongside this and brings you to a small well-grazed plain 650m (2133ft) in the heart of the forest. There is a large concrete-topped cistern. ▶

The mountainside is now less steep. Leave the plain by bearing left, northwest, at the cistern, to pass near a ruined shepherds' hut. Note a short right-hand turning in the route of the telephone line and follow it; there are also various waymarking cairns. The ascent continues up through the cypress forest, with loose gravel underfoot, and along the eastern side of the Kavis Gorge. At the top of the first ridge the path gradually bears right, and then sharply left, at a point where the old *kalderimi* again reappears. About 100m further on the dense forest ends as you arrive at the first walled enclosures of **Kavros** hamlet. Continue uphill (northwest) until the land opens out. The chapel (locked) at Kavros is over to the southwest.

For Anopolis See Walk 33.

For Mouri A road and the telephone line continue up to Mouri. Mouri is a remote place served only by unmade roads from Anopolis. Although the ascent to it needs yet more effort than from Kavros, it is well worth it. The impressively large church and its site, together with the extensive remains of an obviously once-busy summer village is one of the most evocative sights in all Sfakia.

Either return the same way or, for ongoing routes to **Anopolis or Askifou** see Walks 33 and 44.

Sheep grazing near Mouri, or in the forest, tramp back and forth to this cistern so that the path, or sheep paths, between here and Mouri are more used than the section just walked

WALK 48

*Loutro to Livaniana and
(a) Anopolis or (b) Marmara Beach*

Grade	B (or B/C via the Aradena Gorge)
Start/finish	Loutro
Access	Coastal boat service
Height gain/loss	300m (984ft)
Approx distance	9km (5.5 miles)
Time allowance	Loutro to Livaniana church 300m (984ft) 1hr 45mins; to Aradena Gorge bed 20mins; to Marmara Beach allow 3hrs (several rockfalls to negotiate); to Loutro 45mins; total: 5hrs 50mins

Livaniana's isolated location on the steep, rocky hillside above Phoenix and Likos bays caused it to be the last village of Sfakia to get a road; the junction for this is beyond Anopolis, just before the Aradena Gorge bridge. However, walkers can devise various circular routes by following what is left of the old mule track network that linked Livaniana to Aradena, Anopolis, Ay. Ioannis, and to the coast near Phoenix, Likos, and Marmara bays.

For a walk down the Aradena Gorge, Livaniana ('Lee-van-yan-ah') has old terracing above the gorge and from there a footpath descends to the gorgebed at a point below the big rockfall section (Walk 40a). This makes a varied and interesting circular walk from Loutro, taking in a dramatically scenic section of the gorge, as well as Marmara Beach and the coastal footpath.

Follow Walk 49 as far as the hill beyond Phoenix Bay, which has a chapel and palm trees.

Note the steep gully in the hillside east of Livaniana: a well-built zigzagging *kalderimi* was routed up this. Turn uphill here to reach it via a gate and a short car track.

Livaniana's new road, bulldozed down from the top of the escarpment, has destroyed the last section where it once entered the village. **Livaniana**'s *taverna*, overlooking the view of the coast, now far below, contrasts with an old village cistern alongside it.

Return to Loutro The road (scheduled to be surfaced) cuts through the lower village and continues down to the coast at Likos Bay from where you can walk back to Loutro on the coastal path.

For Aradena Gorge Make your way up the old lanes to the white church at the top of the village and then continue over a large rock (water tap) to the crest of the ridge. The Aradena Gorge and old terracing is now in view and you have a choice of routes.

(a) For Anopolis Walk north along the ridge until you come to a *kalderimi* that, supported by its retaining walls, ascends a steep crag (you cannot see it at first). Once above the crag this old mule track is waymarked with blue dots. The way-marked route does not follow the old trail all the way – it peels off to join the new road when a suitable height is reached. The mule track, cut by the new road, is seen a short way downhill. Purists will choose to walk that last section, but otherwise the new path, and road, provide a faster way of getting to the top. At the top, where the levelled-out hill-side looks like a 'sea of stones', note a white shrine in the distance to the northeast. Perhaps, even in the old days, this was a useful trail-marker. Leave the road at the next bend and head straight for the shrine. The old trail becomes more clearly defined as it leads down to the Anopolis Valley past the ruined *kamara*-style houses of **Giros** hamlet. Follow a car track north to a T-junction. Turn right, east, for **Anopolis** *plateia* (see Walk 36 for the return to Loutro).

(b) For Marmara Beach or Aradena village A footpath descends into the gorge. This leaves from beside the white chapel seen in the far distance across the old terracing. Head for this on a sparsely cairned path at the back of the terracing. From the chapel follow a small footpath downhill, heading northwest over more spurge-covered terraces. Birds may indicate the whereabouts of the spring that emerges beside the path, from under a big rock. A tiny pool collects in a log.

For Aradena At the gorge bed turn up right for the big rockfall section (15mins) and its bypass trail (see Walk 40a).

For Marmara Beach Bear left, over large boulders, for the footpath down the gorge.

Note For alternative routes leading up to Livaniana – from Likos and from a path branching off the trail between Likos and Marmara – see Walk 49.

For Ay. Ioannis The words 'Aghios Ioannis' and an arrow in red paint are seen daubed on a rock face. This old path, which is routed up a steep re-entrant on the west side of the gorge, has lost almost all its original paving. It is waymarked with small cairns and involves a tough climb of more than 300m (984ft) in 1.5km. When you reach a shepherds' road, bear right for Aradena, or left for Sellouda (Walk 42).

Alternatively, continue down the gorge to Marmara Beach
Loose stones in the gorgebed make walking down much easier than up. This is not a made-up trail and vegetation is scratchy in places. Several rockfalls have to be negotiated; cairns indicate the best routes through. Mature pine trees provide shade here and there. Another small spring, with a zinc trough, emerges in the centre of the largest rockfall. Take no risks – if you have to do any real rock scrambling, you have not found the easiest way down – go back and look again.

From springtime, purple oleander in full bloom contrasts with the rich yellow ochre of the massive perpendicular walls. The endemic Cretan ebony, a chasmophyte with clusters of purple flowers, billows out from the walls just before the gorge ends at Marmara Beach, a crag-sided inlet with turquoise water and deep pools. A *taverna* and some overnight cabins (tourist season only) are sited above the west side of the inlet. The *taverna* relies on bottled water since Marmara does not have a drinking-water spring.

WALK 49

Loutro to Ay. Roumeli (E4 Trail)

Grade	C
Start	Loutro
Access	Coastal ferryboat service
Finish	Ay. Roumeli
Access to finish	Coastal ferryboat service
Height loss/gain	Undulating coastal walk
Approx distance	14km (8.7 miles)
Time allowance	Loutro to Marmara Beach 45mins; Marmara to Ay. Pavlos chapel 3hrs; to Ay. Roumeli 1hr 15mins; total: 5hrs

A necessary alternative to the ferryboat service – and now part of the E4 Trail – this attractive and varied coastal path is well tramped and easy to follow. Until you reach the forested section there is little shade, and none at all at midday on Marmara Beach (sunbeds can be hired) except at the *taverna*. Plan your water supply: the south coast can be very hot. There are *tavernas* at Ay. Pavlos and Marmara (tourist season) and Likos (all year) and Phoenix bays. A section of the route between Likos and Marmara needs minor rock-scrambling ability.

Note Winter storms can change any beach along this coastline.

Take the lane behind **Loutro** beach kiosk. Bear left through the goat gate above the church and follow a footpath up to the Turkish fort. Keeping west, bypass **Phoenix Bay** with its chapel and palm trees, and then follow a blue-paint-way-marked path down through the rocks to **Likos Bay** (rooms and *tavernas*) where the footpath passes right across the terrace of Niko's Small Paradise *taverna* and rooming house. This comes from the days years ago when Niko started with a small taverna sited next to a spring in the adjacent crag. Like many establishments along this coastline his premises are now enlarged and completely revamped.

Crags and a large cave border the western end of the beach. Climb up here to rejoin the footpath that traverses above the crags and then descends to **Marmara Beach** (Aradena Gorge).

Before the path starts the descent to the beach, note an old mule track zigzagging uphill – it is blue-dot waymarked. This leads up to Livaniana church and then onwards, right up the escarpment to Anopolis (see Walk 47).

There is no drinking water spring at Marmara, so bottled water and other supplies for the *taverna* and its accommodation cabins are brought by motorboat from Loutro. Depending on sea conditions, there may be occasions when the *taverna* is unable to sell bottled water to passers-by.

From beside a small chapel near the *taverna*, the path climbs steadily to get above the next line of sea cliffs. A 'remote' 4km section follows, with very little shade. ◄

When the bare headland finally ends the path loses height down to a crag, still high above the beach. Pine forest follows: after 10mins pass a concrete-topped cistern (good water), and in another 5mins pass the junction with the Sellouda trail (Walk 53). From this path-junction it is 20mins to **Ay. Pavlos chapel** and *taverna* on a long shady stretch with pine needles underfoot. Depending on winter snowfall conditions in the high mountains, and the action of the sea, the freshwater spring at the shoreline may or may not be seen as you descend towards the beach, chapel and *taverna*, which is opposite a lone rock in the sea. The *taverna* uses water from the spring, and since an old well on the beach has been uncovered it is now easier to see the exact place of the water source.

> The restored chapel of **Ay. Pavlos** marks the spot where St Paul the Evangelist is reputed to have landed on his ill-fated journey from Myra (Demre, Turkey) to Rome in October AD59. October was too late in the year for an easy voyage and his ship was blown off course several times before finally being wrecked at Malta. The proprietor of the *taverna* informs that chapels were sometimes built in isolated spots like this for the deliberate purpose of giving local inhabitants 'something to defend' from pirates and other undesirable visitors.

On a good year Ay. Pavlos spring may run for some months after the thaw. Early in the year, with your back to the chapel, look about 15m to the left. As the waves roll back, a distinct freshwater stream is seen, running out over the stones. Another spring of (unfit) brackish water emerges at the foot of the Eligas Gorge and this is used after dark by goats and other animals of that gorge. Similar springs sustain the *tavernas* at Phoenix and Likos.

Climb the sand dune behind the *taverna* to rejoin the coastal path. In 25mins pass the entrance to the Eligas Gorge (Walk 52) just before you descend over a big sand dune to **Skonyari Beach**, which is long and very stony underfoot.

(To run the sand dune – taking care to avoid compacted areas (which may change every year) – enter the Eligas Gorge, cross over to the west side of it, and find a place that brings you out above the sand dune.)

At the western end of Skonyari Beach, just after you have passed through a collection of huge freestanding rocks below a big cave, the path climbs above the beach again. Finish by crossing the last promontory, the burial site of Tara, the Dorian city which was sited across the river. Ancient glassware has been discovered.

Ay. Roumeli, its heliport protected from wave erosion by a rim of pre-cast concrete staybits, is in view across the Samaria Gorge river now just below. On a good year the river runs well into the summer months. Camping is normally permitted under the trees at its estuary. Green algae grow on seashore stones kept wet by fresh water from the river.

Ay. Roumeli new village does a busy refreshments and midday lunch trade with tour groups walking the Samaria Gorge, finishing up here to be taken off by boat, perhaps after a quick swim.

The ferryboat service includes two large landing craft, the *Samaria* and *Daskaloyannis*, which are able to dock even when the sea is rough. Ferryboats will not run if captains judge the sea to be too rough for safety, or if the gorge is closed. In rough weather they will moor at the more sheltered west end of the beach, or at Loutro.

If a storm lasts for a couple of days, coastal resorts run low on fresh food. For everyone concerned such a change in routine – along with the storm – makes for a memorable visit! It is wise to build in a contingency day if your particular objective is to walk the gorge, or if you need to get back to an airport on a certain day.

After the last boat has left, Ay. Roumeli settles down to the relaxed atmosphere only possible in a place with no road access and thus it is popular with walkers – and, in August, with Greek holidaymakers who may find the other resorts filled with foreign tourists. There is good swimming from the gravelly black-stone beach which, like that at Souyia, shelves away fairly quickly.

This is a fiercely hot place at times. Foliage and flowers are surprisingly well advanced by the early spring. Winter storms prevent tree planting on the beach, but sunbeds can be hired. The water-supply pipe sometimes needs adjusting, but in principle there is no shortage of water thanks to the great spring in the gorge.

Most rooms have individual air-conditioning units, which may suit very well after a hot walk down the gorge. There are two supermarkets selling souvenirs, beach kits and books. Noise in Ay. Roumeli: the sound of the sea (less so at the back of the beach). Although there are several restaurants there are also lots of rooming houses to choose from if you wish to avoid the sound of refridgerator motors, water pumps and so on.

Ay. Roumeli old village, at the head of the wide valley behind the first spur of the gorge, has two outlying chapels that make focal points for short walks. Turkish forts and the nearby Eligas Gorge offer more demanding day walks. The Samaria Gorge itself is a useful passage, north to the Omalos Plain, and westwards there is the challenging two-day coastal footpath to Souyia (Trek 10). The boat service enables transfers (or excursions) to the other coastal villages of Hora Sfakion (for trips to Gavdos), Loutro, Souyia and Paleochora.

Note The mail boat (2005) to Gavdos (tourist office tel: 28230.41507) takes a few passengers and runs from Paleochora (old harbour) and makes a round trip calling at Souyia rather than Ay. Roumeli.

WALK 50
The Gorge of Samaria National Park

Walk 2 in reverse; admission charge € 5 (2007)	
Grade	B
Start	Ay. Roumeli
Access	Coastal boat service
Finish	Xyloscala 1240m (4068ft)
Access to finish	KTEL bus to Chania (last bus departs approx 15.40 depending on its arrival time), or taxi from Chania
Height gain	1240m (4068ft)
Approx distance	18km (11.2 miles)
Time allowance	Ay. Roumeli to Iron Gates 1hr; Iron Gates to Samaria old village 330m (1082ft) 1hr 40mins; Samaria village to Ay.Nikolaos chapel 1hr 30mins; Ay. Nikolaos to Xyloscala 2hrs; total: 6hrs 10mins

Leave **Ay. Roumeli** at 07.00 and you will not meet descending walkers until about 11.00. Alternatively, time it so that you leave **Samaria** old village at 14.00 and the rest of the walk up to **Xyloscala** will be relatively undisturbed (see also Walk 2).

WALK 51

Around Ay. Roumeli

Grade	A/B
Start/finish	Ay. Roumeli
Access	Coastal boat service
Height gain	100m (328ft)
Approx distance	3km (1.8 miles)
Time allowance	Ay. Roumeli to Turkish fort 45mins; to old Ay. Roumeli and return 45mins; total: 1hr 30mins; extra for detours

As seen from Ay. Roumeli old village, the Turkish fort on the spur at the end of the valley features dramatically on the skyline. Mule tracks served the fort on both sides of the spur. A circuit on these offers interesting views of the gorge, the coastline, and both villages. The weather-eroded south-facing slope is best tackled as the ascent.

From **Ay. Roumeli** main street take the gorge-approach modern cobbled road as far as the Byzantine chapel on the outskirts of the village. The 30min-long ascent footpath starts just behind it. This lower section of the mule track has succumbed to winter storm erosion, but retaining wall zigzags nearer the fort can readily be seen. On the northern side a similar path descends to the river at the entrance to old Ay. Roumeli.

Detour Above the fort, the razed remains of what was presumably a signalling post are found some distance further up the spur, and at the very top a trig point marks the summit of **Piskopos** (885m/2904ft), the last peak of the Volakias ridge. The ascent and descent of Piskopos, although within sight of everything going on down below, is unfrequented and also demanding on the knees since it is very steep. Take daysack essentials including 2 litres of water per person, whistle and torch. Return down the same way you went up.

As you descend towards the old village, note a path junction. This traverses the hillside to reach a chapel sited high on a spur above the old village. For the old village, there is a path, or route, down the re-entrant below the chapel. Adjacent to this, since a massive deluge in October 2006 threatened the gorge path and several old houses, flood protection works now channel any future deluge water down to the riverbed.

The footpath up to the little **chapel of Ay. Antoniou** in the east rock face of the valley starts from behind the old schoolhouse, which nowadays is used for storing fire-fighting equipment. Disused, the chapel's panayeri (Saint's Day festival) is in January, when the Ay. Roumeli community is nowadays in Chania. The attractive barrel-vaulted and whitewashed Ay. Roumeli church remains very important to the local community, but as it, and its cemetery, is right beside the gorge main trail it is kept locked for the sake of privacy.

The view from Ay. Roumeli Turkish fort

WALK 52
The Eligas Gorge

Grade:	C/D
Start/finish	Ay. Roumeli
Access	Coastal boat service
Height gain	(a) to Turkish forts 600m (1968ft)
	(b) to Fliskounyas 700m (2296ft)
Approx distance	(a) 9km (5.6 miles); (b) 10km (6.2 miles)
Time allowance	Ay. Roumeli to Eligas Gorge 45mins
	(a) to Turkish forts 2hrs 30mins; to Ay. Roumeli 1hr 50mins; total: 5hrs 5mins
	(b) to Fliskounyas 2hrs 45mins; to Ay. Roumeli 1hr 50mins; total: 5hrs 20mins

On top of the eastern spur of the gorge exit there are two more ruined Turkish forts. One can be seen from the beach, both from the ferryboat. Very few people make the effort to get up to this thought-provoking eagles' eyrie of a site, perched on a thin ridge above two completely contrasting gorges: one a quiet haven for wildlife, the other a top money-earning National Park which attracts thousands of visitors.

The Eligas Gorge itself has an unusual feature: one third of the way up fans of scree descending from both sides block the gorge, forming a fairly deep, humid basin called Fliskounyas. Ancient terracing and varied trees make up its tangled, but passable, floor. Beyond it some maps show a footpath through to the high mountains, but this is misleading.

The top, 7hrs effort from Ay. Roumeli, including 4hrs above the humid basin, ends at 1300m (4226ft) in crags impassable to non-rock-climbers. However, two fixed (apparently nylon – not seen by the author) ropes, installed (July 2004) by the EOS, currently assist the ascent. A cistern on the route up to the forts is the only available water, as fort cisterns are disused. This gorge is seldom visited, in spite of its proximity to Ay. Roumeli.

Take daysack essentials from the entrance to the gorge: a minimum of 2 litres of water per person, whistle and torch.

Follow Walk 53 to the Eligas Gorge.
  A footpath leads up the gorge through sparse pine forest

and over scree. After about 20mins the path bears left in the gorgebed to pass an old stone-built goatfold and a crag with a goatherd's cave (shelter – disused).

Skonyari Beach and the Eligas Gorge from the ferryboat: two ruined forts on top of the west side spur

For the two Turkish forts and the cistern Find the footpath by turning up left behind this crag. Pass the cistern within a few minutes, on top of a first small spur (view). Double back into a re-entrant and then turn uphill, south, again on an old mule track. **Angelokampos**, a large open area of hillside with old spurge-covered terracing, is bordered by a broken-up stone-built wall. Do not cross to the far side of the terracing but turn up, right, beside the wall, for the steep ascent to the forts, part of which is through pine forest. Although Angelokampos seems high above the coast it is only about one third of the way up to the ridgetop, but the pull is well worth it just to visit this remarkable site with its stupendous views. Turkish garrisons of the Sfakia network of forts used trumpeters to pass messages to one another.

For Fliskounyas and beyond Follow the footpath up the gorge and over the dam formed by the scree. Beyond the basin, the gorge narrows considerably and the tree-shaded route is rocky and steep. The gorge opens out at the top, its bed littered with trees swept down by the winter thaw, to end in a 'waterfall' crag worn smooth by the snowmelt of millennia. The tricky pitch that stops non-rock-climbers is found on the left. If you have planned to tackle this climb, treat this as a trekking expedition through to the Potamos Valley from where there are ongoing routes but, of course, take enough water for a downhill return if necessary.

Note
See Treks 5a, 6a and 7 for ongoing routes.

WALK 53

Ay. Roumeli to Anopolis via Sellouda

Walk 42 in reverse	
Grade	B
Start	Ay. Roumeli
Access	Coastal boat service
Finish	Anopolis 600m (1968ft)
Access to finish	KTEL Anopolis bus or taxi from Hora Sfakion
Height gain	600m (1968ft)
Approx distance	14km (8.7 miles)
Time allowance	Ay. Roumeli to Ay. Pavlos chapel 1hr 15mins; to path junction 20mins; to Sellouda clifftop 595m (1952ft) 2hrs 20mins; to Aradena 1hr 5mins; to Anopolis (via bridge) 45mins; total: 5hrs 45mins

From Ay. Roumeli waterfront note the forested escarpment east and the distinct long descending crag between the forest and the bare rocky headland. On the skyline, a short distance in front of this crag, there is a patch of red rock: Sellouda. Easy-to-manage scree slopes are at their highest there. The mule track to Ay. Ioannis, Aradena and Anopolis is routed up through the cliffs at that point. Such is the orientation of the escarpment that if you leave Ay. Roumeli at 07.00 the climb can be done in the shade. Mention Sellouda in Ay. Roumeli. It is a route that has given pleasure to countless walkers over the years.

Water Of the villages above the escarpment, Ay. Ioannis (*kafeneon* closed) is 2km off the direct Aradena–Anopolis footpath and, instead, it is linked to Aradena by 4km of asphalt main road. In the tourist season a refreshments kiosk operates beside the Aradena Gorge bridge. There are no other facilities en route before Anopolis *plateia* is reached. Cisterns beyond the clifftop have poor water (a slightly better one is beside the Aradena bridge car park). Plan your water needs at Ay. Roumeli. Contingency: the *taverna* at Ay. Pavlos can give you water from the spring, but if it is closed, and if the spring at the water's edge is not running, there is an old cistern (you would need your 'water kit') beside the footpath, 5mins east of the Sellouda path junction (Walk 49). Many walkers arrive at the top of the Sellouda trail seriously dehydrated through not having allowed enough water for the ascent on a hot day – and at that point they are still some distance from good water.

Ideally leaving at 07.00, cross the Samaria riverbed, and follow the E4 Trail over the Tara promontory. The coastal footpath is well tramped. The main effort is the long stony beach 25mins from Ay. Roumeli. Take the footpath up the sand dune at the end of the beach; it passes the entrance to the Eligas Gorge. A pleasant forested section follows. Descend over sand dunes to Ay. Pavlos *taverna* and chapel. Pause here no longer than 20mins if you want full morning shade on the Sellouda ascent.

Leave from behind the *taverna* (or turn up sharp left behind the chapel) to regain the footpath through the forest. After 25mins arrive at the path junction (signpost or paint signs).

For Loutro Keep straight on (3hrs 30mins).

For Sellouda (for Ay. Ioannis or Anopolis) Bear left uphill. The path gains height through pine forest and then crosses the scree of a ravine bed. Continue up from the opposite bank on easy zigzags. Fortunately, whatever the time of day, trees provide shade at intervals. Finally, above the scree, a paved *kalderimi* ascends through the crags to the cliff top. **Sellouda**, with its shady pine trees and panoramic view of the coastline, is a favourite picnic spot with walkers. ▸

Head northeast on a walled mule track, past old terracing: in view now are pine-forested and very stony undulating hills under the southernmost peaks of the Lefka Ori. On the left, Zaranokefala 2100m (6889ft) towers behind Ay. Ioannis – a single white chapel showing above the trees marks the location of that village. The mule track leads to a dirt road.

Lammergeiers from the Samaria Gorge glide past this clifftop so often at midday on their foraging trips that it is well worth keeping a look out for them.

Ay. Roumeli from the west

For Aradena Turn right (east) on this road (Walk 41).

For Ay. Ioannis Make your way down to a hollow with a sheepfold and cistern (poor water), which is also served by a shepherds' road – but take the footpath heading northwest up from the sheepfold.

MOUNTAIN TREKS

These treks are backpacking routes that take three days or more (this may include time getting to and from the trailheads). Camping or bivouacking kit, and water and food supplies have to be carried.

The mountains are always snow-covered in winter, providing the all-important water supply for the whole region. In spring snowdrifts may render summit ascents and traverses of high steep slopes dangerous to walkers – how long snowdrifts, shaped by blizzards, remain varies each year. South-facing mountainsides are free of snow earlier than the sheltered high valleys and the northern slopes. Most trekking routes over the range are normally possible by early May, but don't set your heart on any particular summit ascent in the central massif before mid-June. This guide describes various route choices that could be adapted to suit the conditions you may find.

All treks in the mountains – which rise to more than 2400m (7880ft) and attract all weathers, including long hours of relentless sunshine – need careful advance planning. Needless to say, help to conserve the beauty of this rare and beleaguered wilderness by carrying out all your rubbish.

THE MADARES

Above the treeline the mountains are desert-like in character, although in places tiny nutritious plants on the bar-ren terrain sustain flocks of sheep brought up in June from the foothill villages. In the central Lefka Ori these high-level pastures are called the Madares ('Ma-THAR-res'). The grazing rights here belong to the Sfakiot communities of Anopolis and Ay. Ioannis.

Before road access was built, shepherds in the high mountains, using mules, worked in shifts at their family *mitata* (workstation huts or 'bothies') making cheese. Every working *mitato* had living quarters, a water supply, a sheepfold, a cheese-making set-up and a cheese store. Cheeses matured for a month before, wrapped in straw, they were brought down by mule. Workaday mule tracks served the high mountains, and trekkers can still follow sections of those that have escaped the road-making programme.

Although high-mountain shepherding has been in decline for many years, there remains strong community support for those who do work in these remote and lonely places. Anything that happens in the Madares – or anyone who is working up there – is always of great interest to the Anopolis community.

VALLEYS OF THE CENTRAL MASSIF

Three high-level valleys in the heart of the range serve as crossroads for footpaths and mule tracks. The Livada Valley 1800m (5904ft) is the true crossroads of the old north–south, east–west routes still shown on almost all maps of Crete. However, new shepherds' roads, with new cisterns, the E4 Trail, and the location of Kallergi refuge (Omalos) have all combined to shift the emphasis to the Katsiveli Valley (1940m/6364ft). The long and narrow Potamos Valley 1750m (5689ft) is the third crossroads. Orientated north–south it evolves as the Eligas Gorge, the first gorge east of Samaria.

KATSIVELI

The Katsiveli Valley is a natural junction on the mule track routes over the mountains between Anopolis, Omalos, or Theriso. Presumably – since archaeologists have discovered Iron Age remains here – it has been important to shepherds as a grazing area since ancient times. Nowadays the shepherds' road from Anopolis, terminating just below Roussies (2008), enables them (unburdened with backpacks) to reach Katsiveli from that parking place after only 1hr walking. Again –presumably – the road may eventually reach the valley, ensuring its status (in Anopolis) as a viable workstation.

Katsiveli's sheep troughs and large concrete open cistern are fed by snowmelt and a *lastico* (black hosepipe) from a high-level spring (often not running by autumn, or not working if the pipe is damaged). Redundant E4 Trail poles form a trestle on the *mitato* terrace. On top of the adjacent rocky knoll an information panel describes a rare plant and a tough-looking (unlocked) rectangular stone hut, with a zinc-covered pitched roof, is provided as a storm (or overnight) shelter for 'tourists', since the E4 Trail walking route between Kallergi and Anopolis has become quite popular. Like the *mitata* huts, this building is under snow during the winter months so that its contents (eight bunks, with mattresses) could be a mess, especially in the early spring. (Latex gloves are very useful in the clearing-up process.)

In 1992 the EOS opened a stone-built refuge on the northern rim of the valley (locked – information from Chania EOS). No doubt it had to be very solidly built to withstand winter storms. There is no outside terrace or lean-to shelter so it is of no use to passers-by, and this may have prompted the building of the little bunkhouse.

Shepherds will be busy in and around the Katsiveli area from June to October, depending on the water supply.

POTAMOS

Potamos is the northern extension of the Eligas Gorge. Some maps show a footpath down the gorge to the south coast, but this is misleading. At the top, a 'waterfall' cliff face and adjacent crags block the route to walkers or climbers without equipment. In 2004 the EOS installed two fixed nylon ropes to help with this problem. Lone walkers should note that the Eligas Gorge is seldom visited and great care would be needed if you were carrying a heavy pack (see Walk 52).

Potamos, worked by shepherds from Ay. Ioannis and Anopolis, is the valley seen to the southeast from the summit of

Gingilos: the path to the summit. The 'shelf' route of the E4 Trail can be seen on the opposite hillside

Melendaou – it lies between Pachnes and the east rim of the Samaria Gorge. Alternatively, if you arrive from Katsiveli in the east, you will not see much of it in advance.

There are four cisterns and *mitata* in the valley: at the top of the valley's northern extension, just off the E4 Trail, is Pirou. Opposite the mule track from

Katsiveli, on a hilltop to the west, is Petrathe ('Petra-theh'). Down the middle of the valley, on the west side, is Koumi and, lastly, as the Eligas Gorge develops, there is Potamos. All these *mitata* could provide shelter in bad weather, although from June to October they may be in use, or half-use. The barrel-vaulted cistern on the valley floor just beyond

Koumi *mitato* is the most important feature of the valley since it has good water all year. Shepherds use a mule to transport this water between the *mitata* workstations. Water in the open cisterns is only suitable for animals (unless it is boiled).

ROUTE SUGGESTIONS

Various through routes and 'escape' routes can be planned around the options presented by the three crossroads valleys: remotest are the trails to and from Livada which, at present, is far from any roadhead.

Most popular, perhaps because (beyond Melendaou) it is 'basically' downhill, is the trekking route (Treks 6, 5a, 8a) between the Omalos Plain and Anopolis. For a first venture this route is especially recommended because it introduces you to what to expect from this mountain range. It may either leave you saying 'never again' or very keen to explore further! The E4 Trail footpath section is well waymarked, and the path south from Katsiveli is relatively well tramped. There is shelter at Katsiveli, which is about halfway. However, there are times when this little bunkhouse could be full. Your sleeping kit must include a 'bivi' bag or tent. (Commercial groups should plan independent shelter, perhaps at the EOS refuge.)

The other paths and mule tracks have become less easy to follow because lately there are fewer flocks of sheep tramping up and down. For all their spindly appearance, Cretan sheep make short shift of the rocky paths and help to keep them clear. Hopefully for

trekkers the new 1:25,000 GPS compatible Anavasi maps will help to redress the balance. It can be very satisfying to approach the Samaria Gorge on one of the less-frequented routes, such as Treks 1 or 2, and then continue from Katsiveli on the E4 Trail to the Omalos.

A one-week mountain trekking route (after June) that is still almost entirely free of roads is as follows:

- Kambi to Livada (Trek 2); then on to Katsiveli and Potamos (Treks 4, 5).
- Potamos to Ay. Ioannis (Trek 7), followed by the Sellouda trail down to Ay. Roumeli (Walks 41, 42).
- Lastly, the E4 Trail coastal path to Souyia (Trek 10).
  At present, the only facilities certain to be found on this route are at Anopolis and Ay. Roumeli.

For another tough traverse of the range consider:

- Up the Kallikratis Gorge and on to Askifou via Angathes summit (Walks 2, 27 in reverse).
- Niato and the E4 Trail to Livada and Katsiveli, Melendaou and Kallergi (Treks 3, 4, 5, 6).
- Next, over the western massif via Strifomadi, to Souyia (Walk 6). Meals at Kallikratis, Askifou, Kallergi, Omalos (hotel). Supplies at Askifou, and simple supplies at Omalos.

TREK 1
Theriso to Livada via Kolokithas

Grade	D
Start	Theriso 600m (1968ft)
Access	Taxi from Chania
Finish	Livada cistern 1800m (5905ft)
Access to finish	Ongoing from Treks 2a, 3a, 4H
Highest point	Rim of Livada valley 1900m (6233ft)
Height gain	To rim of Kolokithas (Tria Matia) 1160m (3805ft), thereafter undulating with Highest point rim of Livada; total Height gain: 1300m (4265ft)
Approx distance	16km (10 miles)
Time allowance	Theriso to Alyakes spring 850m (2788ft) 1hr 40mins; to Mono Scarfidi spring 1080m (3543ft) 1hr 15mins; to Selya spring 1360m (4461ft) 1hr 30mins; to Kapsekas spring 1600m (1968ft) 2hrs; to Tria Matia 1760m (5774ft) 45mins; to Kolokithas mitato 1800m (5905ft) 1hr; to Livada cistern 2hrs; total: 10hrs

This is the northern section of the old north–south mule track linking Theriso with Anopolis, which wound its way through the Madares by the easiest means possible. Although this northern approach route is well supplied with springs, it is nowadays largely disused. Apart from the first part of the road above Theriso, the area concerned is covered by the 1:25,000 Anavasi map Pachnes, although the old trail is not actually marked (older contour maps mark it). It may be a 'forgotten' trekking route but it does exist, and is much nearer to Chania town than Treks 2 and 3.

For those who have already tackled the more frequented Lefka Ori walking routes, Kolokithas presents another challenge. The fact that there are no waymarks or cairns along the way (2007) will be an additional attraction to those who like being 'right off the tourist trail'. Companions are needed. You need to carry 3 litres of water per person (see route notes).

This trek suits from early May if west-facing mountainsides below 1800m (5905ft) are free of snow. Ongoing routes from Livada in the springtime could be limited to Treks 2a, 4, 8a, and 6a. Take food for three days or more, depending on your ongoing route plan. The trailhead – beyond the scenic Theriso Gorge – is easily reached by taxi (or infrequent KTEL bus) from Chania. Arrive at Theriso (TH'EH-riss-oh) roadend by a monument to Eleutherios Venizelos, the Cretan lawyer and statesman who achieved union for Crete with the Greek nation in 1913. There are various tavernas here: lunch or dinner may suit a late start, if planning to camp at one of the springs.

Theriso lies in a valley between two long low ridges, or spurs, typical of the northern foothills. The shepherds' road is routed along the top of the east ridge, and by following this at first you are able to get on to the mule track at 1190m (3904ft).

Note There is no cell phone contact in the Kolokithas–Livada region or in any of the high mountain valleys.

From the Venizelos monument (water tap in churchyard) walk 1min back downhill to pass a taverna on the right; turn down right immediately after the taverna. Cross a small streambed and bear right uphill on a footpath. Pass through the wire gate of a house with a fenced 'garden' – the path to the shepherds' road continues uphill from there. Turn right at the first road, and then almost immediately left at the next junction. Follow this surfaced road up to a junction (left, east, is for Drakona and Kambi, and south is for the mountains); follow this road up to the ridgetop and continue along the ridge.

Along with ancient terracing, 500-year-old plane trees and a huge oak or two cling to the steep crag at the head of the valley. The first spring and trough, **Alyakes** ('Al-ya-kez'), is found in this shady woodland. A parking place and a disused stone hut (shelter of sorts) marks the path to the spring.

For Zourva (45mins) A footpath continues east from the spring, across a meadow and down to the next low ridge.

For Kolokithas The road continues to climb. After about 40mins arrive at a *phrygana*-filled open valley 990m (3248ft); continue uphill on the road and then double back at a junction for a stand of plane trees and other woodland further uphill, but over on the left. This marks the location of the second spring and trough, **Mono Scarfidi**. A short uphill path cuts off a road loop. To continue from the spring take a short cut that climbs over the crag above the spring, or follow the road west as it passes around the wooded crag. Clear of this, the road contours, in a wide loop, around a re-entrant descending to the northwest.

The old mule track is routed up the steep and rounded hillside now towering above the road (south) but you cannot see it from here. To reach it, first get onto the ridge (east) above the road: at the end of the road-loop a footpath 1190m (3904ft) leaves the road. This spot is marked (2007) with a metre-high wooden post. Walk straight up (110°NE) to the top of the low ridge (20mins) and then turn uphill (south) on an obvious path through the *phrygana*. After another 20mins arrive at a flat area where there is an old *mitato* (shelter) named **Kastelos** on the Anavasi map. The next spring is its water supply. Look west to find the ascending footpath.

After 15mins the path levels out, rounding the hillside to reach a large well-preserved stone-corbelled hut (shelter) and sheepfold. Just beyond, on the path, a trough marks **Selya**, the third spring.

A trekker pauses for a last look down to the north coast: the Rothopo peninsula is seen in the distance

Few springs of the White Mountains emerge over such a tremendous view of the foothills and the north coast and, as hut locations go, this must be one of the best. It is a great place to camp if the timing of about 3hrs 45mins from Theriso, and settled weather, allows; the priority is route-finding in good visibility.

A junction of footpaths develops just beyond the spring. Straight on is new – a traverse and descent to the shepherds' road, now far below – whilst left, heading steadily uphill, and much less distinct, is the correct route. After about 20mins of ascent, turn into a re-entrant (a valley descending to the northwest). Make your way up this (the terrain becomes more rugged), then bear right to climb up to a saddle on the skyline 1600m (5249ft).

Keeping left across the hillside, follow the faint footpath as it continues the ascent, traversing to the next shoulder, or spur, on the mountainside – and from there it continues to another one. At that point 1660m (5446ft) you overlook a large and very wide re-entrant rimmed with crags.

On the far side, lower down (120°SE), note two narrow watercourse gullies. The faint footpath, tramped by sheep at least, loses height to pass across these gullies before climbing again – up the spine of the spur that encloses the far side of the re-entrant. **Kapsekas**, the fourth and last spring, is found just after the path crosses the second gully. It emerges in an area of solid rocks, clear of *phrygana*. In the autumn, if the spring is not running, there should be usable water in the small rock cistern (not fully covered) to the left of the trough. **Note** Fully replenish your water supply here as the north–south watershed is now imminent.

The faint path, or route, now leads steeply up the bordering spur. It levels out near the top and contours southeast to a low pass on the rim of the Kolithas Valley – a spot called **Tria Matia** 1760m (5774ft). **Kolokithas** appears as 'remote' and forbidding as it actually is. There are chains of sinkholes, (and isolated sinkholes here and there) various crags, and big rocks. However, directly below, note the flat floor of the valley and, due east, a low hill and ridge on the far side of this. Kolokithas *mitato*, which is en route for Livada, is on the top of that ridge.

Make your way down to the valley floor and then climb uphill, east, to reach the *mitato* (disused). There is a large corbelled hut (shelter) and a sheepfold. Corbelling construction cannot sustain large openings and the entrance to the main hut is typical – be careful not to hit your head. The rectangular stone hut alongside was not completed before shepherds abandoned this workstation in the mid-1980s (it was a 10hr mule ride from Anopolis). A water cistern exists but it is not found (shepherds' minimal directions include 'to the right of the *mitato*'). Since no use of concrete is apparent, it might be a small traditional type, somewhere in amongst the thorny burnet. Do not rely on finding it – bring your required water supply from Kapsekas spring. The next reliable water source is in the Livada Valley, still a couple of hours away over rocky paths.

Looking southeast across the valley from the *mitato*, the perfectly shaped cone of Grias Soros is seen in the distance at 130°SE whilst a nearby conical hill, with a 'pimple' on top (probably a wind shelter), is at 140°SE. The path to Livada contours southeast around the lower slopes of this hill to reach a pass that forms the entrance to the next valley.

To get there, walk southwest along the ridge from the *mitato*. The path soon bears left, losing height to cross a 'bridge' of relatively easy terrain between rugged rocks on one side and chains of sinkholes on the other. Join the contouring path (a rocky route) of the conical hill; bear right and make your way around and up to the pass. At the entrance to the valley leading through to Livada there is a sheepfold with some orange paint marks (2007). Continue southeast along this valley – there are various sheep trails but, if anything, as you approach the end of the valley, bear to the right. An unusually large freestanding rock is just about the only landmark until you get within sight of **Pirgos**, a stone-built rectangular *mitato* (still used) perched high above Livada.

The ongoing mule track to Katsiveli is routed down a gully on the right-hand side (west) of the *mitato* hill. However, from below the *mitato*, yet above the gully, another path leads directly down to Livada cistern, which is in a small doline of the valley floor. (There may be a black *lastico* pipe that you can follow downhill.) As you descend, note **Livada** *mitato* (disused, provides shelter), directly above the cistern on the opposite side of the valley.

Note The next water supply is found at Katsiveli (Trek 4). If the spring at Katsiveli is not running, good water can be found either at the covered cistern halfway down the Potamos Valley (Trek 5) or at Roussies (Trek 8a).

TREK 1A
Livada to Theriso

Trek 1 in reverse

Grade	D
Start	Livada cistern 1800m (5905ft)
Access	Treks 2, 3, 4a
Finish	Theriso 600m (1968ft)
Access to finish	Taxi from Chania
Highest point	Rim of Livada valley 1900m (6233ft)
Height loss	Undulating route between Livada and Kolokithas (see Trek 1): 1300m (4265ft)
Approx distance	16km (10 miles)
Time allowance	Livada to Kolokithas mitato 2hrs; to Kapsekas spring 1hr 30mins; to Selya spring 1hr 30mins; to Theriso shepherds' road 1190m (3904ft) 40mins; to Theriso 2hrs; total: 7hrs 40mins

Note Read the route notes of Trek 1 to familiarise yourself with what to expect from this unfrequented route.

Starting from Katsiveli, follow Trek 4a.

Starting from **Livada** cistern, leave the northwest side of the hollow on a footpath that bears left, climbing steeply uphill, towards **Pirgos** *mitato*, directly above. When the path levels out, join the path that ascends the adjacent gully. This mule track now heads northwest along a wide valley. As you near the end of the valley, bear left to find a sheepfold that marks the end of this section.

Kolokithas *mitato* is on top of a low ridge, part of which is just in sight from the sheepfold, at 320°NW. To get there, bear to the right to pick up a rocky route that contours around the next hillside. It then loses a little height to pick up the path that leads to the bridging piece of land that gives easy access to the *mitato* ridge. Walk northeast along the ridge to the *mitato* complex (disused). Tria Matia, the pass on the west rim of the valley, is seen due west of the *mitato*. Head straight for **Tria Matia** by first descending westwards to the flat floor of the valley.

From there, reverse Trek 1.

TREK 2
Kambi to Livada via EOS Volikas Refuge

Grade	D
Start	Kambi 600m (1968ft)
Access	KTEL Kambi bus or taxi from Chania
Finish	Livada cistern 1800m (5905ft)
Access to finish	Ongoing Treks 1a, 3a, 4
Highest point	Stavrou Seli pass 1920m (6299ft) ; variation to summit of Spathi 2048m (6719ft)
Height gain	1320m (4330ft)
Approx distance	12km (7.5 miles)
Time allowance	Kambi to Volikas refuge 1300m (4265ft) 3hrs 15mins; to Spathi pass 1900m (6496ft) 3hrs; pass to Stavrou Seli 1920m (6299ft) 2hrs; to Livada cistern 1800m (6854ft) 1hr; total: 9hrs 15mins

EOS Volikas refuge 1300m (4265ft) is sited under a long crag with a spring on the north–south footpath between Kambi and Livada (not a mule track). Spathi 2048m (6719ft) is the peak commonly climbed from this path. However, beyond Spathi the route continues south less easily, crossing an area of confusing ridges and hollows (chains of sinkholes) to reach the northeastern rim of Livada.

Although the ascent of Spathi is due south from Volikas over relatively easy terrain, a crossing of the sinkholes area (named 'Gourgoutha tou Spathiou') would be very difficult in poor visibility even for those who are familiar with it. Even if the weather seems settled you must be equipped to camp anywhere if mist develops, and be prepared to retrace your steps if it persists. Mist with drizzle and rain sometimes lasts for three days. Alternatively, ordinary afternoon mist may clear by the evening in a pattern that lasts for a few days at a time.

In settled conditions this is a scenically superb route in a very rugged part of the mountains still almost free of access roads. EOS Volikas refuge is locked (details from the EOS) but its terrace makes a pleasant camping spot on the total ascent to the rim of the Livada Valley. A side shed provides shelter in bad weather.

This trek suits from early May if snow on the northern slopes lies in streaks, but ongoing routes from Livada may be limited to Treks 1a, 4, 8a and 6a. Take food for three days, or more, depending on your ongoing route plans.

Crossing the Gougoutha tou Spathiou (May): Ay. Pnevma in the background

Follow Walk 13 to **Volikas** refuge. Take on water here for the ascent to Livada for – unless there is snow to melt – the next water source is the cistern halfway along the Livada Valley.

Climb up through the crags (a lone E4 Trail pole marks the spot) above and a little to the left of the refuge, and ascend due south to the top of the spur. Beyond, the path continues up beside a minor watercourse draining from a small amphitheatre-shaped valley. Turn right in this valley and ascend through rocks to the west rim. An old stone-corbelled hut at the end of this ridge is the last man-made shelter on the route. Looking west, the mountainside now comprises a mass of black ridges, hollows, sinkholes and crags.

Continue south up the ridge on easy gravel to a level area divided by a shallow furrow running northwest. A rocky conical peak rises beyond. Bear left across the meadow to find the easiest route to the summit. The view from the top suits those who do not want to do the full climb to Spathi – the higher peak now just along the ridge. Spathi's north face is a sheer cliff above a deep circular valley, Gournes, which is accessed (Walk 15) from Kares (Apokorona district). Gournes' chapel can be seen far below. Some footpath maps show the path crossing the cliff, but it heads, of course, to the pass on the right, southwest of the peak.

Now descend to the small saddle below and head straight for this **pass**, gradually gaining height (40mins).

Alternatively, for **Spathi** summit, turn up left and then descend to the pass from the summit.

The pass overlooks the sinkholes depression, with the mass of Ay. Pnevma on the far side. The rim of Livada is not in sight from this position as it is around the corner to the right, below Ay. Pnevma (about 1.7km direct).

Select a route across these various hollows and rocky ridges in the general direction of 160°SE, starting off by bearing right over a large rock below the pass. If snow is still thawing in the hollows take extra care at the weak edges of these drifts. Cross this area with patience. As you cannot always see your way, it is quite normal to arrive at a dead-end crag: in this situation, just try another option.

Near the rim of Livada the terrain gets back to normal: easy gravel underfoot. This is the **Stavrou Seli** 'cross pass' between Ay. Pnevma and Ornio. The steep and unattractive 100m descent to the valley floor is not clearly defined –

On the path above Volikas refuge

Livada from Stavrou Seli pass in May

choose your route. The cistern is about 1.5km down the valley to the southwest in a hollow just below Pirgos *mitato* (still used), which appears as an apparent pile of rocks on the southwest rim. Similarly, **Livada** *mitato* (disused, provides shelter) blends into the hillside opposite Pirgos: this, too, is just above the water source.

Keep straight down the centre of the valley heading southwest on a footpath that crosses various rocky hollows. In springtime the cistern may be buried under a big snowdrift, in which case you could melt snow for water or continue on to Katsiveli (Trek 4a) where the cistern will have snowmelt at least (essential to boil it), even if the spring is not running.

TREK 2A
Livada to Kambi

Trek 2 in reverse; see also Trek 4a

Grade	D
Start	Livada cistern 1800m (5905ft)
Access	Treks 1, 3 and 4a
Finish	Kambi 600m (1968ft)
Access to finish	KTEL Kambi bus or taxi from Chania
Highest point	1920m (6299ft)
Height gain	To Livada rim: 120m (393ft)
Height loss	1320m (4339ft)
Approx distance	12km (7.5 miles)
Time allowance	Livada cistern to Stavrou Seli pass 1hr 20mins; to Spathi pass 2hrs; to Volikas refuge 2hrs; to Kambi 2hrs; total: 7hrs 20mins

Reverse the route notes for Trek 2. Note that northern mountainsides are steep and extremely rugged in places so that good visibility is needed for this descent. Apart from the correct footpath, the only 'escape' route is the Madaro shepherds' road (a long tramp eastwards), which crosses the footpath below Volikas refuge – a 6km tramp downhill eastwards. Madaro (Walk 14) has no *kafeneon*.

TREK 3
Askifou to Livada via Niato
and Grias Soros (E4 Trail)

Grade	E
Start	Ammoudari–Askifou 790m (2591ft)
Access	KTEL Sfakia bus or taxi from Vrisses or Hora Sfakion
Finish	Livada cistern 1800m (5905ft)
Access to finish	Ongoing Treks 1a, 2a, 4
Highest point	Grias Soros saddle 2060m (6758ft)
Height gain	1270m (4166ft)
Height loss	260m (853ft)
Approx distance	16km (10 miles)
Time allowance	Ammoudari to E4 Trail trailhead beyond Niato 1280m (4199ft) 2hrs 30mins; to last cistern 10mins; to Koutala Seli pass 1800m (5905ft) 3hrs 45mins; to Askifiotikos Soros saddle 2040m (6692ft) 2hrs; to Grias Soros saddle 50mins; to Livada cistern 1800m (5905ft) 1hr 30mins; total: 10hrs 45mins
	Optional round detour to Grias Soros summit 2331m (7647ft) 1hr 45mins

Note Timings for the E4 Trail route over Kastro – option (b) below – are similar

This challenging, unfrequented branch of the E4 Trail gives access to the summit of the distinctively cone-shaped Grias Soros, a remote high peak of the Lefka Ori. This is not an old mule track, just an east–west route across the range between Livada and Niato. British Army cadets have used it for (voluntary) training purposes. Build up skills and experience on other Lefka Ori routes before you tackle it so that you are familiar with what to expect, what you need to carry, and your likely rate of walking. In common with some other trekking routes, it is not an expedition for those who have to get back to the airport as bad weather might delay progress.

The main problem is the traverse of the north flank of Kastro, a 2hr 30min struggle across a steep scree-lined slope, eroded and loose, to reach Koutala Seli pass. The EOS has waymarked the E4 Trail on an alternative route, which bypasses part of the old loose-surfaced traverse. This climbs the south side of Kastro's north ridge, to cross over the spine at an altitude above the level of the pass. Waymarking (1998)

E4 Trail: Kastro – the view east from Koutala Seli pass

ends here: installation of the poles is very difficult for amateurs on foot in such a remote place.

The approach from Livada in the west is not much easier (although food supplies will now weigh less) as there is no escaping the Kastro traverse, by which time there may be no alternative but to hurry on because water supply is low. If the Kastro scree slope is very bad it is possible to descend to the valley below and work your way through the rocky terrain. An initial escape option is more available to those who start from Niato and it could be useful to tackle the main effort first, even though you have more to carry. Either way, from Livada or Niato, stages, food and water supply need careful planning.

Note Whilst some maps mark the E4 Trail where it actually is on the ground, others mark it as being on the traditional route: read the map contours in conjunction with these notes. Do not set off in unsettled weather as you need good visibility the whole way and, once you are on the trail, keep a constant note of your position. If a mist develops, stay in place, on low rations (food digestion needs water) so that you can then move safely on, or back, when conditions allow. Take a water bottle on any detours. Remember that nights are colder at higher altitude and for a good night's sleep you need to be warm; a three-season sleeping bag is more practical than lots of clothes. Take food supplies for three days and a minimum of 6l of water per person: 2 litres on the trail, 3 litres for the overnight camp and 1 litre spare for the morning. Although melted snow provides drinking water, steep drifts – which can linger through June – could block your passage (unless you are suitably equipped for such conditions). As a rule the best time of year for this venture is mid-September to mid-October – after the heat of summer and in between the unsettled periods that are normal over the summer–autumn seasonal change.

In the afternoon, follow Walk 30 to Niato (E4 Trail signpost notes 'Livada 6.5 hours'), then continue on to the E4 Trail trailhead beyond the northwest pass. Note the water supply options mentioned in Walk 30 and camp nearby for an early morning start. In the evening check out the route options:

(a) Follow Walk 30 down the valley from the Niato northwest pass to the second old barrel-vaulted cistern under the lone tall kermis oak tree. The huge grey slab of Kastro's north flank now looms above (although you cannot see around the corner to the 'essential' pass from here). The traditional route starts from a short distance up the gully behind this cistern. A faint path bears right, up through rocks, to get onto the hillside where there are sparse trees. Beyond, and out of sight of the cistern, it crosses beneath a big open dip in the mountainside before gaining more height for the traverse proper. From there the pass is in sight, and it is then a matter of working towards it. The valley below this traverse comprises passable, but tortuous, rock formations, which is why this old route crosses the scree slope above it.

(b) Alternatively, consider the E4 Trail waymarked up to the south side of the north-flank ridge (EOS members describe the going as 'very bad'). Very rocky terrain is a feature of the initial strenuous ascent and loose rocks make descents (with a backpack) very trying. ◄

Koutala Seli (pass), once it is reached, is the entrance to a high valley of much more hospitable appearance, rather like Roussies on the way to Katsiveli. There may be faint footpath options made by goats, or the occasional shepherd, or hunters, walkers and quartz collectors.

Your next objective is the saddle on the north side of **Askifiotikos Soros** 2210m (7250ft) a conical peak (unnamed on maps) just east of Grias Soros: from the west end of the 'hospitable' valley, make your way up to approx 2000m (6561ft), under the ridge, which is the northern rim of the sinkholes depression now in full view to the southwest. This is the **Pavlia Harlara**, a 6km^2 'moonscape' of black, white, grey and red rock formations, slabs and hollows. Its appearance fascinates some and appals others. Minor rock-scrambling ability, and care, is needed for crossings of this remote area. ◄

Whichever route you choose set your mind to tackling it with patience and care for, as you can see, there is no room for errors on these remote mountainsides.

The nearest access road serves the Ammoutsara Valley under Kakovoli (see Trek 8).

From the saddle north of (below) Askifiotikos Soros your next objective is the **pass** 2100m (6889ft), north side of the next conical peak, which is **Grias Soros**. Ay. Pnevma (Mount of the Holy Spirit) with its ruined summit chapel and south-east facing crag is 310°NW. Weather permitting this pass is a good place to camp for an evening summit ascent – take daysack essentials on this detour.

Detour: ascent of Grias Soros In places, veins of solid rock punctuate a thin layer of eroded scree as the gradient gets steeper, providing welcome hand and footholds for the climb. The summit area of this huge cone is small, so that you feel even more like an ant in a vast landscape. Grias Soros 2331m (7650ft) is the seventh-highest summit of the Lefka Ori, although it does not feel so. It is beaten (by a small margin) by the peaks grouped south of Pachnes. The busy north coast road is in sight far below, but southwards the panorama from Kastro to Pachnes is undoubtedly the most extraordinary view in all Crete. The 'sinister' Pavlia Harlara is such a deterrent to development that not a single man-made object is in sight. It looks its weird best just before sunset. The lengthening shadows define west-facing hillsides and yellow and orange hues replace the stark midday glare on the scree. After dark, the lights of the north coast twinkle below, but no unnatural light or sound disturbs the Pavlia Harlara.

For Livada From the Grias Soros pass take a compass bearing 300°NW (down the valley under Ay. Pnevma) to part of the Livada Valley, which is now in sight beyond it. In advance, assess the best route down to and along the valley, where low rocky ridges separate sandy, flat plains. At the northwest end a footpath beside a huge rock funnel (sink-hole), of the type that holds thawing snow for many months, gains height to the rim where a small stone wind shelter and an E4 pole heralds your arrival at **Livada**.

The shepherds' footpath heads downhill straight for the cistern in a flat-floored hollow on the valley floor, but halfway down E4 Trail poles direct you left, past Livada *mitato* (disused) which looks like a pile of rocks. This route bypasses the cistern and is a quicker way west to Katsiveli (Trek 4).

TREK 3A

Livada to Niato and Askifou (E4 Trail)

Trek 3 in reverse

Grade	E
Start	Livada cistern 1800m (5905ft)
Access	Treks 4a and 1, 2
Finish	Ammoudari–Askifou 790m (2591ft
Access to finish	KTEL Sfakia bus, or taxi from Vrisses or Hora Sfakion
Highest point	2060m (6758ft)
Height gain	260m (853ft)
Height loss	1270m (42166ft)
Approx distance	16km (10 miles)
Time allowance	Livada cistern to Grias Soros saddle 2060m (6758ft) 2hrs 10mins; to Askifiotikos Soros saddle 2040m (6692ft) 40mins; to Koutala Seli pass 1700m (5577ft) 1hr 45mins; to E4 trailhead 3hrs 40mins; to Ammoudari–Askifou 1hr 30mins; total: 9hrs 50mins

See Trek 3. From Livada, take food supplies for two-and-a-half days and minimum of 6l of water per person: 2 litres on the trail, 3 litres for the overnight camp and 1 litre for the morning.

Starting from Livada cistern, leave the hollow, east, on a footpath up to the pass on the southeast rim where there is a small stone wind shelter and the last E4 Trail pole (1998). The pass overlooks a remote valley under Ay. Pnevma with the conical Grias Soros in the distance. On a bearing 120°SE, note a dip, or pass, on the skyline north of Grias Soros – this is your first objective. The footpath along the valley directs you to the best route through the rocks and up to this spot.

From there reverse the route notes of Trek 3.

Grade	C/D
Start	Livada cistern 1800m (5905ft)
Access	Treks 1, 2, 3
Finish	Katsiveli cistern 1940m (6365ft)
Access to finish	Ongoing Treks 5, 8a, 9b
Highest point	Katsiveli EOS refuge 1980m (6496ft)
Height gain	180m (590ft)
Height loss	40m (131ft)
Approx distance	3km (1.8 miles)
Time allowance	1hr 25mins

Leave **Livada** on the central footpath leading up to the southwest rim (E4 Trail pole). Continue a short distance to the next E4 pole and then turn sharp left (south), traversing above a valley. As the path ascends the next ridge, note an E4 Trail signpost on the left, above the path: 'Livada 1 hour, Niato 7.5 hours, Askifou 9.5 hours'. The stone-built EOS refuge (locked) appears on the skyline. The refuge overlooks **Katsiveli** and the path down (5mins) continues just to the right of it.

This is a mule track between two valleys used for grazing but, even so, this trail is now less distinct than it was in the 1990s.

Katsiveli 'tourist' bunkhouse

TREK 4A
Katsiveli to Livada (E4 Trail)

Trek 4 in reverse

Grade	C/D
Start	Katsiveli 1940m (6365ft)
Access	Ongoing Treks 5, 8a, 9b
Finish	Livada cistern 1800m (5905ft)
Access to finish	Treks 1, 2, 3
Highest point	Katsiveli EOS refuge 1980m (6496ft)
Height gain	40m (131ft)
Height loss	180m (590ft)
Approx distance	3km (1.8 miles)
Time allowance	1hr 10mins

Katsiveli from the north, September

For the EOS refuge, on the north rim of **Katsiveli**, take the footpath through the cutting between the bunkhouse knoll and the *mitato*. On the way up there is a rock with two

names and the year '1992, Geneva, Syria' tooled in Arabic. The mule track continues north steeply downhill from the refuge (note an E4 Trail signpost above the path on the way down). Two more E4 Trail poles mark the southwest rim of Livada. From here Livada's two *mitata* are in sight, one third of the way down the valley: both are old style, looking like piles of rocks. Pirgos (still used) is on the skyline to the left, on a spur (northwest), and Livada (disused) is opposite it on the other side. The cistern is in a rocky hollow on the valley floor, directly below the *mitata*. A central footpath leads 3km straight down **Livada** to the northeast rim (for Volikas refuge and Kambi, Trek 2a).

Note The trail to Kolokithas (Trek 1a) leaves from near Pirgos *mitato,* and the E4 Trail via Grias Soros to Askifou, leaves from behind Livada *mitato* (Trek 3a).

TREK 5
Katsiveli to Potamos (E4 Trail)

Grade	C/D
Start	Katsiveli 1940m (6365ft)
Access	Trek 8
Finish	Potamos Valley north 1750m (5741ft)
Access to finish	Ongoing Treks 6a, 7
Highest point	1980m (6496ft)
Height gain	40m (131ft)
Height loss	180m (591ft)
Approx distance	2km (1.2 miles)
Time allowance	1hr

Now part of the E4 Trail to Omalos and Kallergi, this is also a well-used shepherds' mule track that is waymarked and easy to follow. Unfortunately for walkers it may eventually be replaced by a road from Katsiveli as there is good grazing at Potamos.

From **Katsiveli** cistern, turn west alongside the outer wall of an enclosure; the path leads up to the low west rim of the valley. After 45mins arrive to overlook the Potamos Valley. Klissida, a ruined *mitato*, is below the path to the left. Petrathe *mitato* is on top of a hill across the valley to the west and an open cistern is seen on the valley floor.

Note Good water is found, even late in the year, at the covered cistern halfway down the Potamos Valley.

For Trek 7 Make your way down to the valley floor and turn south.

For a rare view of the Samaria Gorge (no through route) Detour west to the end of the smaller valley below Petrathe *mitato*.

For the E4 Trail to Kallergi See Trek 6a.

TREK 5A

Potamos to Katsiveli

Trek 5 in reverse

Grade	C/D
Start	Potamos Valley north 1790m (5872ft)
Access	Ongoing Treks 6a, 7
Finish	Katsiveli cistern 1940m (6365ft)
Access to finish	Trek 8
Highest point	1960m (6430ft)
Height gain	180m (591ft)
Height loss	20m (65ft)
Approx distance	2km (1.2 miles)
Time allowance:	1hr 20mins

Follow route notes for Trek 5 in reverse.

The Potamos Valley in May

TREK 6

*Omalos (or Kallergi Refuge) to Potamos
(for Katsiveli) via Melendaou (E4 Trail)*

Grade	D
Start	Kallergi refuge 1680m (5511ft)
Access	Walk 4 from Xyloscala
Finish	Potamos Valley north 1790m (5872ft)
Access to finish	Ongoing Treks 7
Highest point	E4 Trail 2090m (6856ft); detour to summit of Melendaou 2133m (6998ft)
Height gain	410m (1345ft)
Height loss	310m (1017ft)
Approx distance	10km (6.2 miles)
Time allowance	Kallergi to E4 turn-off 1600m (5249ft) for Melendaou 1hr 15mins; to summit area 2hrs 45mins; to Potamos Valley north 1hr 30mins; total: 5hrs 30mins

This waymarked branch of the E4 Trail to Katsiveli via the summit of Melendaou 2133m (8122ft) is the first stage of a two-day route from Omalos to Anopolis. From Katsiveli a mule track continues south (Trek 8a) meeting the Anopolis shepherds' road just below Roussies (2008).

Although unavoidably downgraded by the new road, this very scenic trekking route takes in almost all the elements that characterise the Madares and the heart of the White Mountains. Start with 2 litres of water and take food for two days.

Water supply Water from open cisterns needs boiling. Katsiveli should have good water at least until the end of September. Although good water is always available from the barrel-vaulted cistern halfway down the Potamos Valley (Trek 7), this opportunity comes before you get to Katsiveli and requires a detour from the E4 Trail. Going south from Katsiveli, the next good water is at Roussies cistern (Trek 8a) whilst, going east, the next good cistern is at Livada. Shepherds will make sure the Katsiveli *lastico* is running during the grazing season, but if it is damaged, it will not be repaired until after the winter. If west-facing mountainsides are free of snow, this route suits from May to November.

Note Potamos and Katsiveli offer other route choices, but these extend the trek to two-and-a-half days at least: consider this before setting off.

From **Xyloscala** follow Walks 4 and 5 to Poria, beyond Kallergi refuge. For the E4 Trail continue along the shepherds' road as far as a picnic shelter, where E4 Trail waymarks mark the start of the ascent up to the ridgetop. The first section is steep (see Walk 5) and brings you to a high-level valley. From there it is still some distance up to the ridgetop.

At the ridgetop the E4 turns due east and, after gaining some height, follows a shepherds' workaday route (that bypasses the summit) on a traverse across the mountainside high above Melendaou's great stratified cliff. Along this section there are tremendous views across the Samaria Gorge now far below. The trail then loses height and turns away from the gorge, crossing rocky outcrops on a steady descent to **Plakoseli**, a flat-floored valley with an open cistern. Continue southeast to a pass with a small stone wind shelter. Turn sharp left for Pirou *mitato* (shelter), or keep straight on down a gully and across the next valley (open cistern), where you bear right to reach another gully which is the entrance to the Potamos Valley. Downhill is for **Potamos**, but the E4 Trail footpath avoids this descent by bearing left and contouring around the hillside above the gully. The next landmark is Klissida, an abandoned *mitato* (serving as a mule shed) seen below the path just as it turns east for Katsiveli.

From there follow Trek 5a to **Katsiveli**.

TREK 6A
Potamos to Kallergi Refuge (E4 Trail)

Trek 6 in reverse	
Grade	D
Start	Potamos Valley north 1790m (5839ft)
Access	Treks 5, 7a
Finish	Kallergi refuge 1680m (5511ft)
Access to finish	Walk 4 to Xyloscala, or shepherds' road to Omalos plateau
Highest point	E4 Trail 2090m (6856ft)
Height gain	310m (1017ft)

Height loss	410m (1345ft)
Approx distance	10km (6.2 miles)
Time allowance	Potamos to Melendaou summit area 3hrs 30mins; to Kallergi refuge 2hrs 30mins; total: 6hrs

Follow Trek 5 to **Klissida** *mitato*.

The waymarked trail now continues around the hillside to reach the next valley (open cistern), which is at a higher level. Pirou *mitato* is on the north side of the valley. The E4 Trail leaves this valley via a pass over on the left (northwest side). A corbelled stone wind shelter marks the entrance to the next level, the Plakoseli Valley. Follow E4 painted stones along the valley (open cistern) to where the ascent of **Melendaou** begins. Since this high mountain often attracts mist, this well-marked trail is useful and reassuring. The ascent is gradual and almost due west in direction for the whole way across the south-facing flank of the mountain. There are stupendous views across the Samaria Gorge.

Once clear of Melendaou's great cliff, the path begins the long descent. When the path reaches the 'Poria' ridge (see Walk 3) there is a choice: either turn northwest on the waymarked E4 Trail, or keep west for the ridge walk. The E4 Trail tackles the descent in various stages including one section across a level valley, which is followed by a steep descent to the shepherds' road. The red-roofed **Kallergi** refuge is in sight – as is the 4km road-tramp to reach it. Unfortunately this otherwise excellent trekking route finishes on this road (note an uphill short cut across one road loop).

The refuge is normally open from May to end October, although it may close for a time in midsummer if there are no walkers about. A stop-off here for food or refreshments will set you up, perhaps, for the final descent to the Omalos (see Walk 4).

TREK 7
Potamos to Ay. Ioannis via Zaranokefala

Grade	D
Start	Potamos Valley north 1780m (5839ft)
Access	Treks 6, 5
Finish	Ay. Ioannis 800m (2624ft)
Access to finish	Taxi from Hora Sfakion, or ongoing Walks 40, 41
Highest point	1900m (6233ft)
Height gain	From Potamos mitato 1540m (5052ft): 360m (1181ft)
Height loss	1100m (3608ft)
Approx distance	11km (7 miles)
Time allowance	Potamos Valley north to Potamos mitato 40mins; ascent to Zaranokefala spring 1900m (6233ft) 3hrs 15mins; descent to Kroussia 1240m (4068ft) 2hrs 20mins; to Ay. Ioannis 1hr 15mins; total: 7hrs 30mins

Contouring along a shelf on the southwest-facing summit crag of Zaranokefala, high above the Eligas Gorge, this ancient droving trail between Anopolis (or Ay. Ioannis) and the Omalos grazing pastures is the most dramatic of all mule tracks, affording stupendous views down to the south coast. A small but permanent spring is the all-important treasure of the crag. Once you know where to look, the line of the shelf can be seen from the boats that ply the south coast, or from the summit of Gingilos (Walk 3).

However, there is a problem: after climbing out of the Potamos Valley, the path contours into a deep re-entrant above a long steep drop and, sheltered from the sun, a last snowdrift can block the trail here well into June. Reserve this trek for the period between July and November and avoid it in strong wind as some sections are rather exposed. Remember, also, that shepherds from Ay. Ioannis probably no longer drive flocks of sheep up and down this trail, since it is now much easier to reach the Potamos Valley from the roadhead below Roussies (Trek 8). The old trail will be far less distinct as a result.

Halfway down the **Potamos Valley**, 300m south of **Koumi** *mitato*, take on water at a barrel-vaulted cistern: allow 2 litres for the long ascent. The ascent starts from Potamos

An overhang in the crag on the Zaranokefala path

mitato, another 20mins down the valley. Pass the remains (on the east side) of an aeroplane that crashed in 1957. Throughout the mountains, almost every *mitato* has some useful piece of its aluminium fuselage. Avoid the path from the aeroplane as it is loose and rather exposed at high level, even though it does join the main trail. Instead, continue down to **Potamos** *mitato* on the west side of the dry riverbed. ▶

The ascent to the crag takes more than 3hrs, which is why, on a hot day, you will need lots of water. Potamos cistern is another 100m down the riverbed, on the right-hand side.

Take the path up the opposite bank to reach the main trail which now zigzags up the scree slope of a steep, shallow re-entrant. After this initial ascent, and now high above the Eligas Gorge, contour around a rocky spur into the deep re-entrant that retains the snowdrift in the spring. Beyond it, the path climbs to a long shelf. This is a barren and grim-looking place high above an awesome drop into the gorge. In summer a dancing heat haze enhances its inhospitable appearance.

Note the rare ambelitsia tree, endemic to the Omalos region, in front of the mitato, from which the traditional katsouna – shepherds' crook of Sfakia – is made.

241

Heading up to the Zaranokefala crag, with the saddle in the foreground

The next objective is a distinct saddle on a spur at higher level, in the middle distance. Continue along the shelf almost to the point where it ends in an outcrop of ugly black rock. Unless high winds have dispersed them, cairns mark the best route across this. With the saddle as your known goal, make your way up, gaining height steadily on this traverse. The Zaranokefala crag looms above and beyond the saddle.

On the saddle, face east into the mountain To the left (northeast) it is possible (not walked by author) to make your way up to the ridgetop and across another outcrop of slabs and sinkholes to reach the saddle near Pachnes summit. This is said to be a difficult route to find unless you are already familiar with it. Another consideration is that the 2220m (7284ft) level is very confusing in conditions of poor visibility because everything looks much the same.

However – far easier – once you reach the **Zaranokefala** crag you are less than 1km from the top of a mountain spur, from where you start your descent to Ay. Ioannis. Therefore look to the right, up to the big crag, and note the brown (or green) horizontal line of spiny burnet that marks the contouring shelf. Directly in front of you, a vein of vertical rock guides you up the continuation of the route. After about 200m turn off to the right and cross to the next descending spur. Beyond it the mule track is easier to see as it zigzags up the steep hillside to reach the crag. About 5mins along the shelf, pass a walled-in overhang inevitably much used by sheep and goats. There are more overhangs beside the spring further on, but this particular one is the only real shelter in the crag. However, these overhangs appear – unless the crag is high enough – to fit the profile that should be avoided in an electric storm.

Be very careful not to contaminate the spring as you get drinking water by removing protective stones – use your cooking pan as a baler. If you camp here, and defecate, do this onto a stone and throw this (not the toilet paper – burn that or carry it out) carefully down the steep cliff, because (despite its feeling like an 'eagle's eyrie') this mule track is still in occasional use. Also, in this apparently remote spot, during the hunting season (mid-September onwards) do not be alarmed if parties of hunters pass in the night. Cretans like walking after dark, because it is cooler. Shepherds accustomed to the terrain can even run at night on some of these rocky trails.

Take on 2 litres of water for the long descent to Ay. Ioannis. Continue along the shelf to the southwest-facing corner of the crag, where layered flat rocks make good seats as you pause to look at the view of the coast far below. The western end of Ay. Roumeli beach is in sight, as are the two Turkish forts high above the west side of the Eligas Gorge (Walk 52).

Now enhanced by the welcome reappearance of mountain cypresses, the path turns east under the south face of the crag, and heads for the level top of a spur. From there, Anopolis is in view far to the southeast. Walk south for 200m along the spur, and then turn east steeply down a main footpath in amongst splintered goat paths. Still very far down, the rooftops of Ay. Ioannis are seen below pine-forested slopes.

On the Zaranokefala path: the view down to the coast

Cross a shallow gully and enter sparse pine forest, keeping straight on southeastwards down the mule track to **Kroussia**, a large clearing with three open cisterns (poor water). A shepherds' road from Ay. Ioannis comes in from the south. Follow this for 200m to **Vitside** ('Vit-see-theh') *mitato* (shelter). From there it is a long road-tramp to **Ay. Ioannis**. Alternatively, the old mule track to Ay. Ioannis, down a forested ravine, is quicker, although in the usual way, it is broken up and stony underfoot. After that (unless you are heading for Sellouda and Ay. Roumeli) there follows 5km of asphalt road from Ay. Ioannis to Aradena (for Anopolis). Forest trails are lately almost disused so that the old short-cut route to Anopolis through the forest is not an easy option. Get lost and it could be more demanding than the other choices – but see Walk 43 for details.

For Ay. Ioannis via old mule track Leave Kroussia on the road, peeling off it after a couple of minutes, to the left (south) on a stony footpath. The path gains a little height before starting the descent of the ravine. Pass a walled, disused orchard on the right. The path winds its way seemingly endlessly down the ravine. However, just when you think you must have missed the village altogether, a *kalderimi* leaves the east side and heads for a big concrete water tank. Walk down the road and bear left. What was a 1920s-style schoolhouse used to operate as a *kafeneon* but it is now closed. There may be an 'honesty box' drinks dispenser – otherwise the nearest 'refreshments' are found either at the kiosk, Aradena Gorge bridge, or at Ay. Pavlos *taverna* on the coast below Sellouda, or at Anopolis. The old schoolhouse is the last building of the village (or the first if you had arrived from Aradena). Pass through the village entrance gate and either turn down right near a chapel on a footpath to Sellouda for Ay. Roumeli (Walks 40, 41) or tramp the road to Anopolis (1hr 40mins), via the bridge over the Aradena Gorge and short-cut footpath route to Ay. Dimitrios hamlet (see Walk 40).

TREK 7A
Ay. Ioannis to Potamos via Zaranokefala

Trek 7 in reverse	
Grade	D
Start	Ay. Ioannis 800m (2624ft)
Access	Taxi from Hora Sfakion
Finish	Potamos Valley north 1780m (5839ft)
Access to finish	Ongoing Treks 5a, 6a
Highest point	1900m (6233ft)
Height gain	1100m (3608ft)
Height loss	360m (1181ft)
Approx distance	11km (7 miles)
Time allowance	Ay. Ioannis to Kroussia 1240m (4068ft) 2hrs 20mins; to Zaranokefala spring 1900m (6233ft) 3hrs 20mins; spring to Potamos mitato 1600m (5249ft) 2hrs 30mins; to Potamos Valley north, E4 Trail 1740m (5708ft) 1hr; total: 9hrs 10mins

The long steep ascent above Ay. Ioannis makes this a more strenuous way of doing it, but an approach from the south may suit your itinerary. Take food for two-and-a-half to three days and at least 2 litres of water for the ascent effort, to be supplemented by a brew up at Kroussia if necessary. Take on supplies at Hora Sfakion (or at The Platanos, Anopolis *plateia)* and arrange a lift or a taxi to Ay. Ioannis.

Trekkers above Kroussia meet a shepherd on his way down from Potamos and Zaranokefala

Walk up to the concrete village water tank and, just beyond it, bear right (west) onto a stony footpath that heads for the steep, forested ravine above the village. From **Kroussia** cisterns, the mule track continues the ascent northwestwards (reverse Trek 7).

Grade	D
Start	Anopolis 600m (1968ft)
Access	KTEL Sfakia–Anopolis bus or taxi from Chania
Finish	Katsiveli cistern 1940m (6365ft)
Access to finish	Ongoing Treks 4a, 5
Highest point	2140m (7020ft)
Height gain	1540m (5052ft)
Height loss	200m (656ft)
Approx distance:	17km (10.6 miles)
Time allowance	Anopolis plateia to Vigla cistern 1400m (4593ft) 3hrs 30mins; to Roussies pass 2140m (7020ft) 3hrs 30mins; to Katsiveli 1hr 30mins; total: 8hrs 30mins

This route, a mule track, is shown on all maps. Part of it may be shown as a foot-path, and part of it as a road, since the latter has been under construction in stages. It is the easiest approach to Pachnes and other parts of the Madares, especially now that the road terminates just short of Roussies (2008), the customary 'base camp' for the ascent of Pachnes. From Anopolis or Hora Sfakion it may be possible to get a lift to this roadhead (enquire). At present, the road surface is very rough. Purists will want to use what is left of the old mule track where possible and, initially, this is routed up the steep forested ravine almost due north of Anopolis *plateia*.

Take food supplies for two or three days according to your ongoing route plan, and at least 2 litres of water for the initial ascent, to be supplemented by a brew-up at Vigla if necessary, after which the next good water is at Roussies. This trek is usually suitable from May until the first snow of winter – but can hold one particular snowdrift (passable) until mid-June.

Leave **Anopolis** *plateia* on the west side. Turn north at the next junction, at Kostas' *taverna*, on a road that heads straight for the mountains. After 12mins the road forks: bear left (on the shepherds' road to the Madares) for 1min, as far as a large animal shed on the right, inside a fenced

On the path up to Roussies

Note This road to the Madares is also for Scarfidia (Walk 44).

enclosure. For a useful short cut, walk around the enclosure to pick up a track as though from the shed, and then continue north through the forest. This path heads straight for the forested ravine – keep straight on across the shepherds' road when you re-join it. ◄

The road turns east at the foot of the ravine, on the start of its long, winding but very scenic climb. As ever, the mule track takes the direct route, zigzagging up the ravine. After the ravine opens out (for at least the second time) **Vigla** cistern (named Sopata on the Anavasi map) appears at last – a huge barrel-vaulted creation entirely in keeping with this very old trail. The shepherds' road is seen traversing the steep hill above, and a slip road from it connects down to the cistern.

The old mule track continues uphill, west from the cistern, gaining height before zigzagging up the final section of the ravine. The hillside finally levels out beyond the last cypress trees at 1600m (5249ft) at a place called **Angathopeoi** ('Ang-garth-oh-pee-ee'). Here, you re-join the shepherds' road as it enters a long valley – the true entrance to the high mountains. The road gains height in loops, but walkers can take the mule track short cut up the centre of the valley. Just before the pass at the top, turn up right to rejoin the road. Beyond the pass the Amoutsara Valley, a moonscape of black rocks and sandy basins, is bordered on the northeastern side by the Kakovoli ridge.

Below the pass a small hut (disused, poor shelter –leaks) and a concrete cistern, once important to the old trail, are now redundant. Continue on the road. The rock is black so that the road does not show as an unsightly scar. In the distance, Grias Soros and other peaks border the far side of the Pavlia Harlara depression, its weird rock formations partly in view as you gain height.

Tramp the road to its terminus (2008), just below a steep slope of black rock 18km from Anopolis. The great bulk of Trocharis 2410m (7906ft), the second-highest peak of the Lefka Ori, with its fascinatingly long scree slopes, is now just across a deep valley to the southwest. The ascent to Roussies ('Roo-see-ess') from here takes about 20mins. Roussies is a small 'hanging'-shaped valley with a small stone hut (overnight space for three people) and a covered cistern with good water. This base-camp spot for the ascent of Pachnes (Trek 9) is often very draughty: campers have built windbreaks. For shepherds it is a useful water point for their animals on the trail.

At 2140m (7020ft), **Roussies** is the highest pass on the whole south–north mule track over the mountains (hence the windy conditions). An E4 Trail signpost marks the turn-off uphill for Pachnes summit while the mule track continues north along the valley, with easy gravel underfoot. This 1km stretch ends at another high pass where a snowdrift may block the trail until mid-June. Sheep and mules are not brought up from Anopolis until this snowdrift has thawed. (Before that, perhaps eager for springtime, some older sheep make their own way up.) If the trail is blocked, climb up around the snowdrift on the east side, which is less steep. Descend from the pass to a small rocky ridge between two valleys: the east valley is quite deep. Gingilos crag is in view to the northwest, across the Samaria Gorge. Continue above the deep valley to the next pass. The **Katsiveli Valley** is now just below, with the EOS refuge on its northern rim.

TREK 8A
Katsiveli to Anopolis

Trek 8 in reverse

Grade	D
Start	Katsiveli cistern 1940m (6365ft)
Access	Treks 4 and 5a
Finish	Anopolis 600m (1968ft)
Access to finish	KTEL Sfakia–Anopolis bus, or taxi from Hora Sfakion
Highest point	2140m (7020ft)
Height gain	360m (1181ft)
Height loss	1100m (4608ft)
Approx distance	17km (10.6 miles)
Time allowance	Katsiveli to Roussies pass 2140m (7020ft) 1hr 40mins; to Vigla cistern 2hrs 30mins; to Anopolis 2hrs; total: 6hrs 10mins

Katsiveli is about 150m lower than two high passes that are crossed on the mule track route south to the roadhead. Scenery along the way is spectacular and varied, although the shepherds' new road, when it is reached, may render this walk somewhat disappointing to trekkers. This route is not part of the E4, so there are no E4 poles, but it is well tramped and, in reasonable visibility, not difficult to follow.

Note In 2008 the road ended below Roussies but if – or when – it is extended it is likely to replace the rest of the mule track, in which case you would just follow this road southeast from Katsiveli.

From Katsiveli cistern turn 130°SE for the mule track that first passes between big rocks and then zigzags up to the south-eastern rim of the valley. A long traverse south, above a deep valley, now follows, ending at a small rocky ridge that forms a division between this and another, smaller valley. Above and beyond the ridge, bear right to reach a wide saddle on the skyline. From there, Roussies pass is in sight, 1km down the valley to the southeast. If a snowdrift still blocks the trail here, pass around it on the east side.

Katsiveli mitato with the EOS refuge on the skyline

At **Roussies**, where there is a small stone hut and cistern, an E4 Trail signpost marks the turn-off for the ascent of Pachnes to the southwest (Trek 9). Trocharis 2410m (7907ft) with its long scree slopes, dominates the view south across the deep, almost semi-circular, valley beyond.

The trail now descends steeply, over black rock lower down, (keep right) to reach the shepherds' road (15mins). Just beyond, a fairly long section of the old mule track can be seen. It provides an optional short cut down to the **Amoutsara Valley**, which is now in sight below the Kakovoli ridge.

At the south end of Amoutsara, where there is a small stone hut and cistern (disused), continue over the pass to overlook the next valley. About 100m further on, red paint marks the place where you can clamber down over rocks to rejoin the mule track: a useful short cut down the centre of the valley. Rejoin the road as it heads south out of the valley. In a few minutes, as the first cypress trees appear, leave it again, to the right, on a footpath heading straight down a steep ravine. This eventually bears left (east), down to a small valley: **Vigla** cistern is here. From Vigla continue south down the ravine to the Anopolis Valley. This rocky ravine is well known for being 'endless' – tackle the descent with patience.

Reverse Trek 8 for the last stage to **Anopolis**, which is almost straight on across the valley once you emerge from the ravine.

251

THE ASCENT OF PACHNES

TREK 9
Roussies to Pachnes Summit

Grade	C/D
Start/finish	Roussies pass 2140m (7020ft)
Access	Treks 8, 8a
Highest point	Summit of Pachnes 2453m (8047ft)
Height gain/loss	313m (1026ft)
Approx distance	5km (3 miles)
Time allowance	2hr 20mins

This is the easiest ascent of Pachnes, a round trip from Roussies base camp (Trek 8). Note the daylight hours, and if possible (in settled conditions) plan a late afternoon ascent, because the high mountain views look their best just before sunset. Deep shadows define the hillsides and, under a dark blue sky, the light-coloured scree slopes take on a golden glow that develops into a rich orange at sunset. By twilight the magic hour has gone and the slopes, robbed of shadows, all look alike. Therefore as you leave Roussies, note the valley of the north–south mule track to Katsiveli. If you lost the footpath on the descent, this valley would be your 'aiming-off' destination for the return to Roussies.

If there is no one to look after your gear at Roussies, conceal it behind rocks as this is not a remote place in terms of the mountains. Take daysack essentials including 1 litre of water, and allow 3hrs minimum before sunset for the round walk. This ascent suits between July and October and months either side if the route is suitably free of snow.

Start up on the footpath to the west from **Roussies** pass (E4 Trail signpost). After gaining some height, the path traverses northwestwards to the top of the first shoulder above the mule track valley. Pachnes summit is now in view on the skyline – not the false summit that looks likely, but the group of rocks right along the ridge (240°SW). It is not as far as it looks.

With easy gravel underfoot, gain height up this main spur by traversing across, or zigzagging up, rocky slopes, scree and gravel slopes, bands of rock, all the time heading for the ridgetop by the easiest means. Cairns and waymarks guide you. At the top of the ridge, continue along it for the final pull up to the summit where there is a trig point.

On a late afternoon ascent avoid the twilight – leave the summit 1hr 15mins before dark at the latest, and return the same way.

The Madares: a group returning from the summit of Pachnes

253

TREK 9A
Pachnes Summit to Katsiveli

Grade	D
Start	Pachnes summit 2453m (8047ft)
Access	Trek 9
Finish	Katsiveli cistern 1940m (6375ft)
Access to finish	Treks 8, 8a, 4a, 5
Height loss	513m (1683ft)
Approx distance	3.5km (2 miles)
Time allowance	1hr 10mins

This is a shepherds' route between Katsiveli and high pastures of the Pachnes area.

Katsiveli is due north of **Pachnes** summit, just behind the distinctive conical peak of Modaki 2224m (7296ft). The route passes the west side of Modaki. Clear visibility is needed as the path, which descends steeply northeast of the summit to a saddle, is not well tramped, nor very well placed for an easy 'escape' overland to the main mule track.

TREK 9B
Katsiveli to Pachnes Summit

Trek 9a in reverse	
Grade	D
Start	Katsiveli cistern 1940m (6365ft)
Access	Treks 8, 4a, 5
Finish	Pachnes summit 2453m (8047ft)
Access to finish	Trek 9
Height gain	513m (1683ft)
Approx distance	3.5km (2 miles)
Time allowance	2hrs 20mins

Leave **Katsiveli** on a footpath ascending the southwestern rim of the valley. Turn south under the west flank of Modaki. **Pachnes** summit is in view (170°SE), and the faint path takes the easiest route to it, following the lie of the land.

THE SOUTH COAST

TREK 10
Ay. Roumeli to Souyia (E4 Trail)

Grade	D
Starting point	Ay. Roumeli
Access	Coastal boat service
Finish	Souyia
Access to finish	Coastal ferryboat or KTEL bus service
Height loss/gain	Undulating coastal footpath: two high points of 300m (984ft) and 400m (1312ft)
Approx distance	18km (11.2 miles)
Time allowance	Ay. Roumeli to 400m (1312ft) first headland 2hrs 30mins; to Domata Beach (Klados Gorge) 1hr 30mins; to bay with shepherds' huts 2hrs; to Tripiti Gorge 30mins; to Turkish fort 300m (984ft) 1hr 15mins; to Souyia 2hrs 30mins; total: 10hrs 15mins

This challenging and scenically varied footpath along the rugged coastline between Ay. Roumeli and Souyia is undoubtedly one of the best wilderness walks in Crete. In springtime particularly trekkers may choose this route if lots of snow still lies in the high mountains. However, vertigo sufferers would not enjoy this path because sections of it, over steeply shelving hillsides, are in poor condition.

When bad weather affects the mountains the south coast may be clear, and much warmer. On the other hand, even early in the year, it may be very hot. You need less clothing, but you have to carry enough water to suit one long stretch where there is none to be found. Part of the E4 Trail, this walk can be done in one very long day especially if you are familiar with it (it has its springtime 'regulars'), but that would be a waste. There are not many places like this left – make the most of it by planning a two- or three-day trek. As water is scarce, avoid this route in the midsummer months when the south coast is extremely hot, and also (see route notes) when a storm at sea looks likely.

Route planning Starting from Ay. Roumeli and walking west is recommended, as in this way you head towards the water supply at the Tripiti Gorge ('Trip-pit-tee') and tackle the more strenuous sections first. Starting from Souyia you are faced with a steep knee-taxing descent at the end, followed by a fairly exposed traverse, downhill, above Ay. Roumeli Beach, when your water supply might be very low. Another option is to start with a boat transfer from Souyia to Ay. Roumeli, which allows you a preview of the coastline (although – unless there are walkers on it – it is hardly possible to see the footpath from the boat). Although mobile phones do work along this route, avoid walking it alone because of the remoteness of the main section, and the bad state of the path in some places.

The route The headland cliffs at the far end of Ay. Roumeli Beach extend west to the next gorge: the Klados Gorge and Domata Beach. To get over this headland, the footpath crosses the slope above Ay. Roumeli Beach and then climbs the steep forested gully just beyond it. From Domata Beach, in the next bay, it continues west as an undulating coastal footpath, mostly high above the shore, to the Tripiti Gorge. After climbing steeply to a Turkish fort, on the west side of the gorge, the path descends to take up an undulating route, again inland, for the last 6km to Souyia.

From Ay. Roumeli as far as one third of the way (but not throughout) the route is well marked with E4 Trail poles correctly positioned to suit sightlines. The rest of the route is not too difficult to find, but over 1km or so, east of the Tripiti Gorge, where the coastal cliffs are unstable, there are several bad sections of path to be negotiated.

Water supply (from west to east) A few minutes west of the Turkish fort a tiny spring emerges on the footpath. The little white chapel of Profitas Ilias Tripitis along the ridge from the

fort has a small water cistern needed for its Panayeri festival in August, which is very popular (participants arrive by boat). Huge crags border the Tripiti Gorge as it meets the sea in a rocky cove. A private source (from high in the crag) supplies two shepherds' houses in the gorge. There is a cistern beside the disused chapel under the east crag. Shepherds' huts (fenced off) in the bay, east of the Tripiti Gorge, have private cisterns. There is another at the east end of that bay under a crag. The next and last water point eastwards is the open cistern beside the path in the pine forest above Domata Beach east side. It was lined with polythene sheet in 2001, probably by the local goatherd before he retired; while this sustains it will be full, at least early in the year. The Tripiti Gorge is the most reliable water point on this route. From whichever end you start plan your supplies accordingly and, as with the high mountain treks, if your supply gets too low do not eat because this draws on body-moisture reserves.

Directions Leave **Ay. Roumeli** by walking up the second street west of, and parallel to, the village main street. Pass

Ay. Roumeli: The E4 Trail passes above the crags (and below the caves) at the back of the beach.

through a gate in the fence at the top. Follow a steep path up through the pinewood to the E4 pole marking the start of the traverse above the beach. To some people this short section with the beach cliff yawning below may be the 'worst' on the whole route. However, there are several stretches of one sort or another on this walk to Souyia that need extra care – opinions vary on which is the worst and whether these sections are enjoyable or awful (a light backpack helps).

Beyond the traverse the path soon feels much more secure. A small rocky spur provides a last view of Ay. Roumeli. From here, lose height to negotiate a rockfall. Enter the forest of the steep gully and ascend almost right to the top on eroded zigzags marked with cairns and E4 paint.

Now high above the headland and other crags – and with just one more gully to negotiate – the footpath leaves the trees on an undulating and contouring route around open shrub-covered hillsides. Ay. Roumeli is now out of sight, and the south coast appears completely undeveloped in both directions as far as the eye can see. Inland, the inaccessible crags and gorges under Volakias, Strifomadi and Psilafi are coming into view, forming the spectacular backdrop which accompanies much of this walk.

Returning from the chapel to the Turkish fort

But first, the headland path turns inland before zigzagging downhill to a pine forested, high-level valley. Here it turns south again, climbing to reach the south end of the next spur (this section can be seen from across the valley before you start the descent).

At the top mature pines and traces of old terracing mark the start of the waymarked descent to **Domata Beach**. As you leave the trees to overlook the coast, note an isolated pinnacle of rock on the hillside above the beach: the forest cistern is under that crag. Isolated from the usual pollutants, its green-coloured water is most probably drinkable or certainly good for a brew-up if you wish to conserve your water supply. A large tree has fallen across it so that some walkers do not see it as they pass by.

The **Klados Gorge**, with its intriguing tree-capped pinnacles and various tributary ravines, is now in full view, reminding you that every Sfakiot gorge really is different.

The Klados Gorge ends with a wide shelf of conglomerate rock, high above the stony beach (a postcard of it, wrongly titled 'Crete Aradenas' Gorge', is often found in souvenir shops). This is (or used to be) Ay. Roumeli goat-grazing territory, accessed by motorboat. In remote locations like this, goats are (or were) raised for meat rather than milk.

Leaving the cistern, descend steeply through crags to the pine-forested shelf and then bear left for the route down to the beach. At the west end of the beach, turn a short way up the gorgebed to pick up the footpath (E4 poles), just across on the left. This is the start of a fairly long climb up to the next open hillside, where one or two large pine trees provide some shade. This section ends as you arrive to overlook a rocky inlet. A bee-keeper's cottage is seen on its western shoreline. Beyond this viewpoint various sections of the footpath, over the next 1km, are in poor condition. The route is also less well waymarked from here onwards. ▸

To continue descend the crag and, after traversing above the inlet, arrive at a rocky ravine, where there is shade. After climbing out of the ravine and crossing open hillside, the path descends to the crags just above the shore-

Note If you are on an out-and-return walk from Ay. Roumeli this is the best place to turn back.

259

line. At this point a cliff face, from which there are landslips, blocks the whole hillside so that the trail has to cross unstable ground with no easy alternatives. About 4m of path have fallen away between two crags, obliging walkers to dash across shifting gravel to a precarious perch over a long, steeply shelving slope. It is the sort of place that needs a steel wire handrail to make it safe. Various bad stretches of path follow but the route is easy to find except at one point: as you approach a large bay with a pebble beach, pass a goats' pen and a water hollow (probably dry). From here the path heads downhill to crags above the shoreline. Look carefully for cairns that mark the point where you climb down to reach the footpath, or route, that then continues along below the crag. There is a cistern under the crag at the east end of the beach. Two goatherds' huts have private cisterns that may be locked.

The Tripiti Gorge is next, beyond the bay: the footpath continues around the rocky headland on the seashore. A section of this passes very near the main cliff. ◄

Note

This seashore section would be impassable in a storm – take no risks. If you have to wait for conditions to improve, and use the goatherds' water, take care not to contaminate or waste any of it.

Either follow an E4 waymark that guides you through to the landing stage, or pass through a deep cave – a huge low arch in the cliff used as a goats' pen – that brings you out at the chapel (disused) and cistern (good water) of the **Tripiti Gorge**. High cliffs border the riverbed here. An astonishingly long ladder, made in sections out of steel bars, is draped down the 40m-high cliff face near the landing stage. A fenced-off hut and a house both use spring water piped down from the western crag.

A big freestanding rock beside the bulldozed track that goes up the gorge is level with the E4 footpath turn-off for the steep climb to the Turkish fort. Not much further up the gorge, also on the west side of the valley, the ruins of the Dorian city of Pikilassos can be found. Goat paths from this site to the fort are strenuous – it is easier to return to the E4 Trail.

For Souyia direct The footpath crosses the saddle north of the fort.

For Profitis Ilias Tripitis chapel From the fort detour for 15mins south along the forested spur. If possible, do not miss this detour as the chapel is one of the best sited in all Crete. On the ascent of Gingilos (Walk 3) you may have seen this tiny white chapel on the coast, far below. Here now is that view in reverse – the mountains bordering the Omalos Plain from quite another angle. Linked directly to the south coast escarpment without a break, this south-facing flank of the western massif tumbles to the sea as a tangled mass of precipitous cliffs, inaccessible high pastures, forests and caves. Opposite Pikilassos, faint zigzags of an ancient mule track can still be seen, climbing the spur. By looking east, you can review all your efforts from the Klados Gorge. To the west, Souyia and Paleochora may, or may not beckon, depending on your inclination. Lastly, dominating the whole panorama, is the vast, glittering expanse of the Libyan Sea. Those who enjoy watching events in the night sky rate this an excellent spot (if they like camping) since there is no adjacent light pollution.

On the way down from the fort, just beyond the spring – which has a small zinc trough across the footpath – note an old-style phallic-shaped shrine that marks where the crag contours around the head of a crag. Thereafter the 6km path to **Souyia** is easy to follow, even though there are few E4 trail markers.

TREK 10A
Souyia to Ay. Roumeli (E4 Trail)

Trek 10 in reverse	
Grade	D
Starting point	Souyia
Access	Coastal ferryboat or KTEL bus service
Finish	Ay. Roumeli
Access to finish	Coastal boat service or ongoing Walks 50, 53
Height loss/gain	Undulating coastal footpath: two high points of 300m (984ft) and 400m (1312ft)
Approx distance	18km (11.2 miles)
Time allowance	Souyia to Turkish fort 300m (984ft) 3hrs; fort to Tripiti cove 45mins; Tripiti to Domata Beach (Klados Gorge) 2hrs 30mins; Domata to 400m headland 1hr 30mins; headland to Ay. Roumeli 2hrs 30mins; total: 10hrs 15mins

The E4 coastal footpath from Souyia to Profitis Ilias chapel and back makes a good day's walk if you are based in Souyia. However, if you intend to continue on to Ay. Roumeli, reverse the route notes for Trek 10 and allow the same time schedule. Perched on top of a great rock buttress, Profitas Ilias Tripitis chapel can just be seen from Souyia – the limit of the view east along the coastline. To get to it, the coastal footpath (E4 Trail) which once served old terracing, undulates fairly high above and a little distance inland from the seashore.

From halfway up **Souyia**'s main street, walk down to the promenade beside the stony riverbed where an E4 pole marks the start of the route. Cross the riverbed to pick up the short-cut footpath that takes you up to a dirt road. Turn right, up the road, to reach the hilltop where waymarks direct you on to the coastal footpath. Rehydrate at the **Tripiti Gorge** and resupply with a minimum of 3 litres of water per person from that point. Do not rely on getting water from the uncovered cistern above Domata Beach. It will be subject to evaporation and at some point its polythene sheet lining will fail.

PART 2
PSILORITIS – MOUNT IDA

Near the top of the Rouvas Gorge (Walk P2)

Nearing the Timios Stavros summit chapel in May: looking west (Walk P12)

The Oros Idhi – or Psiloritis – mountain range of central Crete, 'Mount Ida' in English, is not quite as large and impressive as the Lefka Ori in the west, but the limestone terrain is just as challenging. As you might expect there are several good walking and trekking routes.

Towering above the Amari Valley, Mount Ida's huge 8km-long 'whaleback' summit ridge includes the highest point in Crete at 2456m (8056ft). The ridge is snow-capped for several months of the year, and on a clear day can be seen from the length of the island. Consequently the view from the summit makes the climb to it especially rewarding. The most popular route, a round walk that takes a full day, starts from the Nida Plain in the heart of the range. At 1400m (4270ft) Nida is the highest of the four large mountain plains of Crete.

In or near the mountainous rim of Nida there are several high peaks, all of which are seldom visited, except perhaps Kousakas 2211m (7253ft) and Skinakas 1750m (5741ft), which has an observatory on its summit.

Northwards, the massif comprises an extensive area of undulating foothills, largely within the treeline (approx 1200m/3930ft). This region is punctuated by snowmelt watercourses which drain to the Milopotamos Valley where there are several shepherding villages, the largest of which is Anoyeia.

To the south, the outer edges of the mountain are quite different. Here gigantic cliffs, ravines and steep spurs rise abruptly to over 1500m (4600ft), above the Amari Valley and the plain of Messara. This is the huge mass that, together with the summit ridge, forms such an impressive backdrop to the much-visited archaeological sites of Gortys, Phaistos and Ayia Triada, near the large village of Mires.

THE SUMMIT

The great ridge is narrow at the summit point, giving wide, unobstructed views in almost every direction. Inevitably it attracts 'all weathers' at any time of year but late summer to early autumn is likely to be the most settled period. In spring large snowdrifts lie across the paths in places and can be a hazard.

On most summits you may find a cairn and a concrete trig point, but the summit of Mount Ida, probably the most exposed place in Crete, is also the site of a centuries-old three-roomed chapel built entirely of drystone corbelling. This is Timios Stavros, chapel of the Holy Cross. It can be seen as a tiny pimple on the skyline from the Arcadi monastery (near Rethymnon) and from many places throughout the mountain. Its Panayeri (saint's day festival) is 13–14 September by which time the interior, inevitably full of wind-driven snow after the winter, will have long since dried out. As with many other summit chapels in Greece, the Panayeri is nowadays also celebrated at lower level since many participants are likely to need car transport.

A small cistern, its access framed with flat stones lying flush with the ground, lies about 5m from the northeast corner of the chapel. There is no other water to be found on the ridge after the thaw.

THE NIDA PLAIN

Nida ('Nee-tha') is a spring-to-autumn grazing pasture for the large flocks of sheep kept by shepherds particularly from Anoyeia. Roughly oval in shape, some 2.5km long and 1km wide, the plain (also called 'plateau') is dead flat in some places and soft underfoot. Unlike the other large mountain plains of Crete it is too high for the cultivation of crops.

For at least 30 years there has been a vehicular road from Anoyeia to Nida, and the full 22km is surfaced throughout. The making of the road presumably prompted an attempt to form a recreational ski centre near the northwest corner of the Nida Plain, but the scheme was abandoned before full completion. The ski-lift restaurant building and the half-finished three-storey hotel stand as two separate ruins on the mountain. However, the restaurant wing of the hotel was completed, and this *taverna* at the road-end car park overlooking the Nida Plain is open daily about 10.00–19.00 from April to end October. It is mainly a lunchtime facility to suit day-trippers who leave their cars here for the short walk up to the Ideon Andron cave. First explored in 1885, the cave yielded artefacts associated with Late Minoan cult ceremonies dedicated to Zeus. These, and other precious finds from the region, are held in the Archaeological Museum of Heraklion.

On the hillside just above the car park the Analipsi spring (open the hatch for drinking water) sustains several sheep troughs, a small plane tree and a patch of green grass. This is just beside a

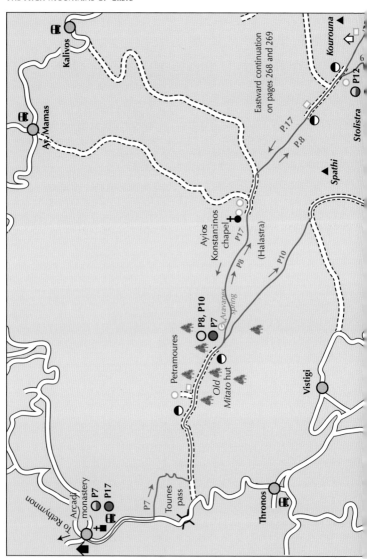

Eastward continuation on pages 268 and 269

Kalivos

Ay. Mamas

To Rethymnon

Arcadi monastery

P7
P17

P7 →

Tounes pass

Petramoures

P8, P10
P7

Old Mitato hut

Ayios Konstanjinos chapel

P17

P8 →

P8 →

(Halastra)

Aravanes spring

P10

Thronos

Vistigi

Spathi

Stolistra

P8

P17

Kourouna

P12

6

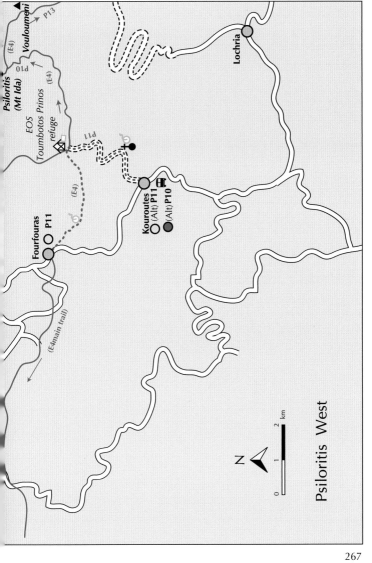

Psiloritis West

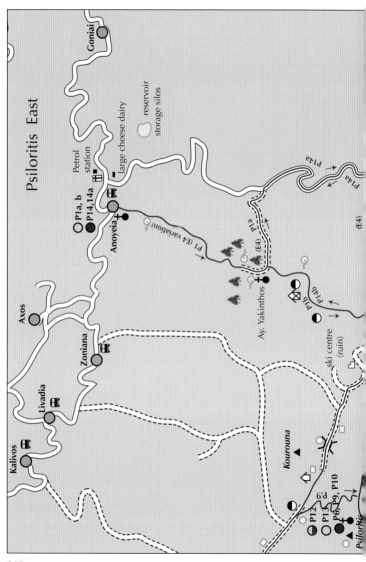

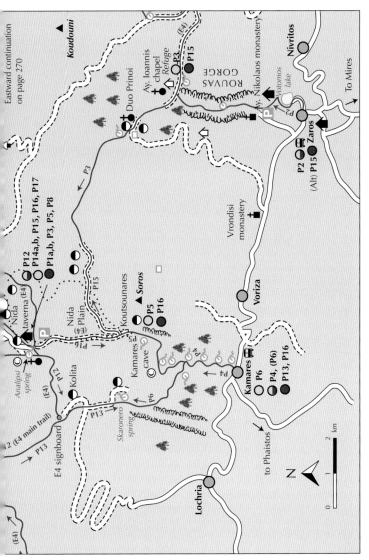

Eastward continuation
on page 270

269

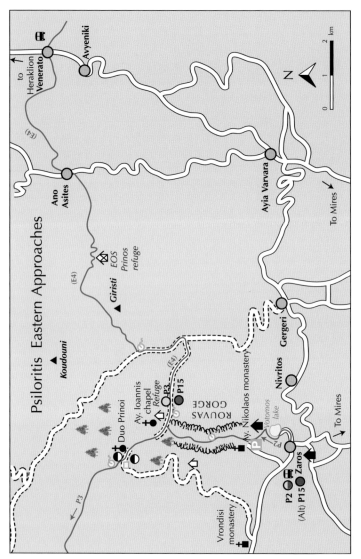

stone-built former cheese dairy on the unmade road that leads up to the cave. The footpath to the summit is way-marked off this road (Walk P8).

The Ideon Andron *Taverna* (The Nida *taverna*), a building much battered by winter storms, offers two modest double rooms for rent as well as midday and early evening meals. The proprietor, Stelios Stavrakakis (tel: [Anoyeia] 28340.31141) commutes daily from Anoyeia, since customers are normally only present from mid-morning to early evening. Note that all supplies are brought up from Anoyeia. Bread, cheese or tomatoes for a packed lunch can sometimes be spared to customers, but not at busy weekends; bring your own supplies. This high mountain location is no place for formalities, and Mr Stavrakakis may allow larger groups to sleep on the floor if they wish. To be certain of overnight accommodation telephone his home in advance (Greek only). Alternatively, for enquiries, his family house is just near the triangular-shaped *plateia* of Anoyeia's lower village, and anyone will direct you to it. It is usually possible to find someone in the *plateia* who will help you with the language if necessary.

It follows that those who want an evening meal and a bed for the night must arrive at the Nida *taverna* by early evening before the proprietor has left for Anoyeia. (Guests who want an early start let themselves out in the morning.) As mentioned, the *taverna* is attached to the abandoned and unfinished ski centre hotel. If you arrived to find the *taverna* closed, the car park entirely empty, and the weather turning bad, you could at least find shelter in this ruined building, bleak though that prospect might be. Inevitably, Mr. Stavrakakis will decide to retire at some point since he has run the business for many years. Hopefully, since visitors will keep coming, someone else will take on the lease of this *taverna* which is so useful to walkers.

On the plain, at the foot of a low hill (110°SE from the *taverna)*, there is a stone-built installation in the form of a figure set into the ground. Entitled 'The Partisan of Peace', this is the work of a German sculptress who lived for some time in Anoyeia. It is intended to represent a huge winged angel or, alternatively, a World War II partisan wearing a goats'-hair cloak – the weatherproof garment that all mountain peoples of the Balkans wore before the advent of synthetic materials. The work should be viewed from the low hill just above it. Unfortunately there has been no annual maintenance and it has attracted a growth of spiny burnet and thistles. The *taverna* sells postcards, including photographs taken when it was new, together with a few other souvenirs relevant to the area.

Other man-made features in and around Nida include various shepherds' huts, old and new. Many of the traditional *koumi* complexes constitute fine examples of vernacular architecture in the form of corbelling work (drystone igloo-shaped construction). Mount Ida is particularly rich in flat stones suitable for this. Nowadays, where there is road access, some *koumi* complexes have been abandoned in favour of modern huts, or used for storing materials.

A very dominant feature, the asphalted road from Anoyeia, enters from the northeast corner at a height above the plain of about 100m (328ft). For walkers this road forms a barrier to comfortable walking. This is one reason so many walkers skip the E4 Trail northern approach route and arrive by car – or by truck, as Anoyeia shepherds, and others, may give individual walkers lifts up the road.

APPROACH ROUTES TO THE MOUNTAIN

Mount Ida (*Psiloritis* –'P'sill-or-ree-tis' in Greek) provides important sheep- and goat-grazing territory for the many villages around its perimeter. Consequently there are many new access roads that target grazing areas and springs. Here, as in other places on Crete, road-making may be ongoing so that some footpath routes described here could be affected. Note also that new roads, or even roads in existence for some years, may not be marked on maps – or if they are, may not be accurately marked. There is (2007) only one road that passes north–south over the massif: the road from the Skinakas Observatory area, just north of Nida, that runs for 30km to Gergeri ('Yer-yer-ree') near Zaros. In all the mountain ranges of Crete shepherding communities may prefer roads that fall short of joining up, as this helps to deter animal rustlers and unwanted parties of hunters from the towns.

Naturally, there are lots of shepherds' paths on Mount Ida, but for recreational walking the EOS has chosen those for the E4 Trail (and variations) which target the Nida Plain, or the summit, and which take in freshwater springs and points of interest. By combining two or three of these routes you can choose how you would like to cross the mountain.

Coming from Heraklion is clearly the shortest and easiest way of getting to the trailheads at Anoyeia, Zaros and Kamares. If you are travelling from Chania, bus connections from Rethymnon access trailheads also at Anoyeia, the Arcadi monastery and Amari Valley.

To aid with planning your route, details of trailhead points are as follows:

From the north
Anoyeia
This large village – with upper, middle and lower parts – clusters along the spine of a steep spur more than 1km in length. The *plateia*, and therefore the main bus stop, is in the middle village which has a paved square, open on one side to the main road, and bordered on the others by the town hall, a large church, and war memorials. The World War II memorial includes a transcript of the order given by General Muller listing his reasons for inflicting a devastating massacre on male inhabitants in August 1944. The same fate was suffered by many other villages around Mount Ida, because the mountain was a refuge for partisan fighters of the Resistance and Allied Forces intelligence agents during the years of the Occupation. After the war, bereaved women, no doubt already skilled at the craft, took up weaving to make a living, and Anoyeia's souvenir shops still reflect this

Mitato complex southwest of the crag; Vitsinela pass (Walk P17) is seen in the background (Walk P1)

tradition. The lower and middle districts offer accommodation, shops and *tavernas*; the upper village has shops and a *taverna*. Anoyeia is served by KTEL bus from Heraklion (every day) and Rethymnon (weekdays only).

Arriving from Rethymnon the bus terminates at the very top of the hill, 700m (2300ft) above the upper village, where there is a petrol station and a crossroads.

The petrol station (bottled water on sale) is on the main road that heads downhill (east) for Heraklion. The road to the village cemetery is 40°NE; north is a road leading up beside a cypress wood to a (restored) former weather research station (viewpoint); and 160°SE is the approach road to the Nida Plain. The large Anoyeia cheese dairy is on this

road, near the junction, and further uphill there are sheep fodder storage silos and a reservoir. Hikers who hope for a lift up to Nida in a shepherds' wagon should start up this road, or the main road of the middle-to-upper village (where Nida shepherds live), at least by 06.00 (especially during April to June, during the milking season).

Although the upper village has a *taverna*, the nearest rooming house (2007) to this crossroads is in the middle village. For an early morning lift up to Nida, it can be useful to camp (for those with bivouac kit) near the Nida road as this spot is not far from open mountainside. Since village accommodation options attract summit walkers, especially in the autumn, it is sometimes possible to meet others and share car or taxi

273

transport to Nida. Do not plan a later start, however, because the round walk to the summit from the Nida Plain takes a very full day. The whole venture is certainly not a 'doddle' (see Walk P12).

Arriving from Heraklion, the bus stops first at the top of the hill (at the Nida road junction). Look out for the petrol station, and cemetery, if you wish to alight here. Otherwise ask for the *plateia* and you will alight in the middle village.

The E4 Trail Anoyeia shepherds speak of not just one, but three ancient droving trails to the Nida Plain. The E4 Trail (variation) from Anoyeia follows one of these routes (Walk P1) and is fairly well waymarked. The trailhead starts from the lower village (see Walk P1).

From the south
Zaros
Zaros village, 320m (1049ft), is sited 3km downhill from a small artificial lake formed beside the entrance to the Rouvas Gorge, where the great Votomos spring emerges from the mountain. A built recreational footpath up the gorge starts at the lakeside restaurant and bar and passes the Rouvas monastery (car park and WC) at the entrance to the gorge. Its destination is the chapel of Ay. Ioannis 950m (3116ft), where there is a permanent spring and where the municipality has provided picnic tables and an unlocked refuge. Since there is also road access to this place, via Gergeri village, it is a popular picnic spot on Sundays with excursionists from Heraklion. A section of the E4 main trail passes the chapel and can be followed either west,

up to the Nida Plain, or east, over a pass beside Giristi 1774m (5722ft) to the EOS Prinos mountain refuge.

The three-storey Hotel Idi, on the road up to the lake, accommodates tour bus groups, and others, visiting the nearby archaeological sites of Phaistos, Ay.Triada and Gortys, and perhaps Matala, a beach resort. Thanks to the Votomos spring, this mid-priced hotel (tel: 28940.31301) has a green and leafy garden and, in the warmer months, an outdoor swimming pool that could be just the thing after a long trek over the mountain. Beside the hotel and on the way up to the lake, two or three *tavernas* specialise in grilled trout. Taxis come from Mires (€12–15 2005), a small workaday town on the plain of Messara. Zaros also has a 'bed and breakfast' hotel and two supermarkets. A corner *kafeneon* beside a supermarket serves as the bus stop (enquire), and a nearby restaurant offers good home cooking. There are weekday buses between Kamares and Heraklion (Chania Gate bus station) and to Mires, from where there are frequent connections to Heraklion, Matala and Ay. Galini (for Rethymnon).

Kamares
Kamares ('Kam-mar-rezz') is served by twice-daily weekday bus, via Zaros, from Heraklion. (Otherwise take a bus to Mires, then a taxi to Kamares.) For the trailhead, alight at Zakarias Saridakis' *taverna* Kamares Cave (tel: 28920. 43040), the first building of the village. The footpath (E4 Trail variation) to the Kamares cave, and/or to the summit of Mount Ida – an old mule track which

Crossing the small hollow:
Kampos Tigani in the background, October (Walk P8)

zigzags up a steep spur above the village – starts just opposite. The *taverna*, with its shady terrace, provides refreshments and hearty meals to those who have tackled the fairly popular but demanding day-walk to the cave and back. Kamares also has a lodging house with '24 beds'– enquire in the *plateia*.

In terms of archaeological finds, the Kamares cave is the second most important cave on Mount Ida. It was here that a distinctive Early Bronze Age pottery style, later named Kamares ware, was first discovered in 1904. Alternatively, for walkers coming from the north (from the summit or the Nida Plain) the Kamares path forms a steep, but stupendously scenic, route down from the mountain.

From the west
The Arcadi Monastery

It is possible to trek right across the mountain, and/or climb to the summit, from this prime tourist destination which has a seven-days-a-week bus service from Rethymnon. The monastery, famous for a heroic 'last stand' battle in the 1866 revolution against the Turkish Occupation, is sited on a fertile shelf high above the northern end of the Amari Valley. In historical times when the monastery thrived, the route of Walk P7 would have been the monks' path to the summit chapel. An early traveller, Richard Pococke, described climbing the mountain by this means in 1739. Nowadays it is a route seldom used by recreational walkers who naturally tend to follow the paths chosen for the E4

Trail. As an approach to the mountain it cuts down bus transport time from western Crete but, since the seldom-used footpath sections are rough underfoot, it is not a fast option to the summit, or to Nida. Nevertheless, it may suit you to climb over the summit from this direction and then continue east on the E4 Trail down to Nida, or to Kamares; or you might care, since water can be found, to spend two or three days camping 'away from it all' in the pleasantly wooded lower foothills.

Initially, there is a 10km tramp from the monastery on unmade shepherds' roads through wooded foothills. This road ends at the foot of the great summit ridge where you have a choice of ongoing paths: either to the Nida Plain on the north side of it, or to the EOS refuge above Kouroutes on the south side. Steep ascents are not involved unless you tackle the branch paths to the summit either side of the ridge.

The Amari Valley

Villages of the Amari Valley, including Gerakari ('Yerra-ka-ree') (for Mount Kedros), Fourfouras and Kouroutes, are served by the Amari KTEL bus from Rethymnon bus station. Its terminus (1hr 30mins) is the village of Apodoulou. Villages further east as far as Lochria ('Loch-ree-ah') appear to be responsibility of the Rethymnon bus service (enquire), but note the gap in transport arrangements, since Heraklion buses serve only as far as Kamares. It is useful to know also that taxi drivers choose to travel between Rethymnon and Ay. Galini on the modern Spili main road, since the Amari Valley road is long and winding. Tourists tend to bypass Amari altogether. Well watered and particularly lush in the spring, with fields of mown hay, orchards and woodland, the Amari Valley is a hidden oasis of greenery. The southern end is enhanced by the bright light that is reflected off the bay of Messara.

ROUTE SUGGESTIONS

Mount Ida has a lot more to offer than just the round walk to the summit from the Nida Plain, although circular walks and Grade B walks are in short supply. This is partly because the massif has no coastline.

However, for those who enjoy two-day treks, there are fine choices that do not involve the summit ridge, partly thanks to the facility of the Nida *taverna*. On the other hand, for strong walkers who arrive at the Nida Plain in the early morning (the shepherds are generous in giving lifts up the road) any of the adventurous 'Nida trailhead' routes down off the mountain can be done in one day (in conditions of good visibility).

On most routes it is helpful to be able to refer to both the Anavasi and Harms Verlag maps, and an altimeter (and/or GPS) will also be useful. Directions are written with backpacking trekkers in mind – those who carry more weight than just a daysack and therefore may need to take extra care in some places. However, using the *taverna*, long-distance walkers travelling light could cross the mountain on any two-day route of their choice. There is also the option of a tough circular day-walk (during long daylight hours), or a two-

Snowdrift on the summit ridge in May: looking west (Route P12)

day trek, which arguably takes in 'the best of Mount Ida'.

- Starting from the Nida car park, combine Walks P12, 13, 4 and 5 to visit the summit, descend to the Kamares cave, and return to Nida from there.

For those who are left to wait while their companions are off on the long day-walk to the summit, first sections of other walks could be a good way to pass the day.

- For vernacular architecture (and views to the south) there is a fine complex of corbelled huts near the Koutsounares spring (Walk P15).
- The 'hidden valley' of Amoudara is worth a visit (Walk 14).
- For those interested in geology there is a fascinating, recently formed sinkhole to be seen on the second section of Walk P17.

WALKS AND TREKS FROM TRAILHEADS OF THE FOOTHILLS

For further information also see the Approach Routes in the Introduction, and the walking routes in reverse where applicable.

WALK P1
Anoyeia to the Nida Taverna

Grade	C/D
Start	Anoyeia (lower village) 700m (2296ft)
Access	KTEL bus from either Rethymnon or Heraklion
Finish	Nida *taverna* 1420m (4658ft)
Access to finish	Road to Anoyeia, or ongoing trekking routes P12, P15, P16, P17

This walk leads from Anoyeia to Ay. Yakinthos chapel, from where there are two options:
(a) Via the E4 Trail and Nida main road (Grade C)
(b) Via the E4 Trail and the old droving route (Grade D).

Section 1
Anoyeia to Ay. Yakinthos Chapel 1200m (3936ft)

Height gain	500m (1640ft)
Approx distance	6km (4 miles)
Time allowance	2hrs 45mins

Section 2
Walk P1a Ay. Yakinthos to Nida *taverna* on the E4 Trail

Road walking route
Height gain	200m (656ft)
Height loss	100m (328ft)
Approx distance	13km (8.1 miles)
Time allowance	3hrs 25mins

Walk P1b Ay. Yakinthos to Nida *taverna* via Old Droving Trail

Mountain paths
Height gain	300m (984ft)
Height loss	240m (787ft)
Approx distance	9km (5.6 miles)
Time allowance	3hrs 45mins

This undulating route gains height very gradually, following much of the still definable remains of a very old road, or *kalderimi*, once used as a droving trail. It leads almost due south from Anoyeia to the Nida Plain through a series of low hills within the treeline. The second part of the route described here (b) is more remote and steeper than the designated E4 Trail (a) that, halfway along, turns off to join the modern main road.

Note the church of **Ay. Nektarios** ('Eye-ee-oss Nek-TAR-ree-oss') on the hillside above **Anoyeia** lower village. It has a bell tower and is roofed with two red-tiled barrel vaults. The E4 Trail is found on the left-hand side of this church. (If you are in the middle village, take a short-cut lane downhill from the rear of the *plateia*.)

Once past the church, note traces of paved zigzags and an E4 waymark of yellow and black paint on a rock and a tin triangle sign on a tree (2003). The route has been waymarked by someone who understands sightlines, but unfortunately flocks of sheep scramble over the waymarks and wear down the paint. Take it slowly so as not to miss the paint marks.

On the E4 Trail (variation) from Anoyeia: nearing Ay. Yakinthos

Above the church the path continues up the right-hand side of a shallow gully, then passes a cypress wood before gaining the top of the hill 800m (2625ft) above Anoyeia. Note a green-painted shrine on a large flat rock, over on the left.

Mount Ida's summit chapel is now visible on the skyline as a tiny pimple at the western edge of this great ridge. From several places along this route you will be able to establish your approximate position on the contour map by taking bearings off this chapel.

The path now bears slightly left and heads downhill alongside a low wall to a valley with a sheep shed, concrete cistern and troughs. From between the troughs and a large oak tree, look uphill (south) to spot a yellow waymark. Further yellow waymarks direct you uphill to reach a shepherds' road, 890m (2920ft). Cross the road for the continuation of the uphill trail, just beside another large oak tree. Descend from the crest of the ridge, cross the shepherds' road again, and continue straight down a track to a fenced sheep shed.

For the continuation of the old trail, look to your left to spot a faded yellow arrow on a rock face. Follow this uphill to cross a dirt road. Continue on a path over the ridge and down to re-join the road. Follow this around to a second re-entrant to find yellow waymarks directing you up a gully. Bear left around a fenced enclosure near the top, cross the road and walk over the next ridge 920m (3019ft). There is a new concrete cistern in the distance, over on the left.

Re-join the road, which now heads southeast, running parallel with the old road (now seen just above it in sparse woodland). Leave the road at the next right-hand bend (E4 waymark) to re-join the old trail. After a section through woodland arrive at a meadow 990m (3248ft). From this spot, identify the next pass on the route at 225°SW. Keep to the right as you cross the meadow. Another meadow, with sheep troughs, is just beyond it. However, do not enter that meadow (waymarking is poor just here) but turn sharply left on a wide, sparsely wooded spur strewn with rocks. Keep to the centre, and then bear left as you near the top 1030m (3379ft). The old trail now continues through woodland but since this section is overgrown it is easier to follow the shallow watercourse alongside it. ▸

A shepherds' road leads uphill from the spring. Follow this and, around the corner, arrive at a road junction, 1090m (3575ft). Right is for Rousa Limni, and straight on is for the E4 and Ay. Yakinthos. Follow the road uphill (part of it is surfaced with concrete) and continue across an open flat area of green (springtime) meadows. At the crest of the next hill 1140m (3740ft) there is a pipe-fed animal trough and, just below, the beautiful, recently built chapel of **Ay. Yakinthos** (no shelter, but a spring adjacent) with its associated terracing, benches, and theatre seating, all constructed of corbelling and other drystone building methods by local craftsmen.

(a) To the Nida taverna on the E4 trail Continue on the unmade road (shelter: there is an old corbelled hut on the left) heading eastwards to join the Nida main road (fairly busy in fine weather during the tourist season). This is a pleasant part of the mountain, with open views, but it is not always possible to avoid walking on the hard-surfaced main road as there is no side footpath. (Some maps mark two short-cut paths between loops.)

After passing across the bleak-looking area west of Skinakas peak, the road finally rounds a corner and the Nida

This leads uphill to a ravine where an old stone-built cistern collects spring water from a crag. Amongst the animals that use this water point in the woods may be one or two pigs. If the pool in the crag is dry there should still be water in the cistern.

Plain comes into view. A roadside panel informs on the geology of the plain and surrounding mountains. The *taverna* is seen 260°SW across the plain under the great east-facing flank of the summit ridge. Just before this point, the E4 Trail leaves the surfaced main road on a stony slip road heading down to the northeast corner of the plain. Rather than follow this all the way down to the bottom, take a short cut off it, down the spine of a spur marked by a ruined stone hut and sheepfold. From there walk straight across the plain to the *taverna*.

(b) To the Nida taverna on the old droving trail This route is one of two 'footpaths' shown dotted on the Harms Verlag map but not on the Anavasi map (showing the wisdom of reading one in conjunction with another). Keeping south from the **Ay. Yakinthos chapel**, leave the road at the first bend (2005 – wooden signboard 'Ay. Yakinthos').

Follow a shallow watercourse down through woodland to a partly cultivated flat-floored valley. The path continues alongside a fenced enclosure. Climb a short distance up the hill beyond the enclosure fence (south) to join another dirt road. Turn uphill to reach a pass (viewpoint). Note a two-storey 'house' in the distance (west). Keep on the road, which now descends to the next valley. Note an E4 pole and other E4 waymarks (these guide you to the next spring, where they end). The road brings you to the crest of the next ridge where a lone kermis oak marks a T-junction. The ridge forms one side of a large snowmelt watercourse. ◀

Bear right for the house, a (locked) well-built refuge (perhaps of the forestry service) alongside a shepherds' workstation and sheepfold.

However, from the oak tree, look about 5m to the left to find a yellow arrow painted on a rock at the roadside. It is pointing southwest but should probably be pointing left (eastwards), down towards the ravine now seen in the distance, emerging from the mountain. (The rock may have been moved during road-making.) At the entrance to the ravine, if the light is right – or through binoculars – you can just see the next spring, *Tria Yortho*, with its stone-built cistern under a crag beside the riverbed.

For an advance understanding of the next stage, now look straight across the watercourse to the crag on the skyline opposite. The hillside across the watercourse at this point is a fat spur with a flat top. Above the flat top, the hillside continues up to the crag.

To continue from this oak tree road junction, take the path which now takes an easy downhill gradient through the woodland directly towards the ravine (on what soon appears as a very obvious section of old mule track), and then continues up the riverbed to reach the spring. From the spring, the climb to the fat spur flat top is fairly easy – and then you continue on a footpath straight up to the crag. Beyond the crag there is still some way to go, because the mountainous rim of the Nida Plain is fairly wide at that point. ▶

On the steep hillside above the spring you may see, as you climb, just one short section of retaining wall still remaining (without that you would have supposed the old mule track had ended at the riverbed). Therefore, now leaving from the right-hand side of the cistern, make your way up this steep slope on sheep trails and then across to the fat spur, using as a guide at first a lone round-headed oak tree on the skyline above the spring. On reaching the 'flat' area, take the small central footpath leading straight up to the crag. Above the crag, bear right, on a faint rocky path that leads, gaining a little height, around to a saddle where there is an old roofless *koumi* hut and sheepfold. Dates carved on its stone bench suggest this place was used up to the 1950s. You cannot see the Nida Plain from here, but you can identify Kourouna 1850m (6070ft) and the flank of Mount Ida's great summit ridge. Your next destination is a pass at 1465m (4806ft) directly north of the plain (not visible from this point).

A small valley just below the *koumi* complex is separated from a larger valley by a low ridge. Over on the right (west) a shepherds' road is seen leaving the larger valley. Make your way over the low ridge to join this road and follow it out of the valley. It gains a little height before arriving at a smaller flat-floored valley with a modern shepherds' hut in the northwest corner.

Continue on the road as it goes steeply downhill and keep straight on when you arrive at a T-junction. It does not seem logical to lose height at this stage, but this move positions you looking south once again – up a narrow valley that leads to the correct pass. A minute or so beyond the T-junction, you have a view through the trees (160°SE) of the ascending valley, and the pass. Leave the road on a footpath that traverses above the valley, left-hand side. It is easy to follow at first but at mid-height in the valley, various choices

Note The E4 Trail has followed an easier option by heading for the main road. It would be a useful escape route in bad weather, since route-finding on this last section needs good visibility.

evolve. Make your way up to the pass, which is just west of Timbanatoras 1577m (5174ft). Thickets of spiny burnet, which thrives at this altitude, variously dictate which section of path is best. **Note** Maps other than the Anavasi mark the 'ski-centre' road on this pass, when in fact it is some distance further west along the mountainous rim. Do not think of it as an escape route in bad weather.

The area of the pass includes a meadow with clumps of spiny burnet and an old stone hut up on the left. Keeping south, cross the meadow and make your way downhill on the left side of a re-entrant. The Nida Plain, usually looking dauntingly bleak thanks to its altitude, soon comes into view. Join the main road at a deep bend in the road marked with a large concrete culvert. The road is at least 100m (320ft) above the plain.

Either Turn right (west) and tramp about 3km to the road end and the *taverna*.

Or To continue on footpaths: various spurs descend to the plain, and it is not possible to leave the road where it contours around steep re-entrants. However, it also slices through two nearby spurs and you can use either of these for the descent. Either follow the road west for 3mins to find one spur after a couple of bends, or – perhaps easier – turn left (east) around a major bend, to find a slip road down to a spur where there is an old stone hut and sheepfold. The footpath continues, not down the spine of the spur, but down a gully directly behind the hut – make your way around a fenced enclosure to reach it. The ***taverna*** (and unfinished hotel building) is in sight across the plain, at 210°SW.

WALK P2

Zaros to Ay. Ioannis Chapel via the Rouvas Gorge

Grade	C
Start/finish	Zaros 350m (1148ft)
Access	KTEL bus from Heraklion or taxi from Mires
Highest point	Ay. Ioannis chapel 950m (3116ft)
Height gain/loss	590m (1935ft)
Approx distance	15km (9.3 miles)

Time allowance	Zaros to trailhead at Votomos lake 420m (1378ft) 50mins; to monastery 440m (1444ft) 20mins; to path junction beyond crag 640m (2100ft) 50mins; to Ay. Ioannis chapel 1hr 30mins; ascent total: 3hrs 30mins; descent total: 2hrs 30mins; total: 6hrs

The footpath in the Rouvas Gorge above Zaros, with its focal point the spring and chapel of Ay. Ioannis 950m (3116ft), forms a steep but easily followed round day-walk from the Votomos lake, or the Rouvas monastery car park. This is a pleasant gorge since there is shady woodland along much of the way. Unfortunately (2005) maintenance of the once well-executed trail has halted for some years. Wayside water taps no longer operate, but there are two natural springs – one in the lower gorge, and the other at Ay. Ioannis chapel.

For trekkers, the main E4 Trail passes Ay. Ioannis chapel. Westwards takes a well-marked but challenging shepherds' route up to the Nida Plain (Walk P3), and eastwards follows roads and footpaths to Prinos EOS mountain refuge via a pass northwest of Giristi 1779m (5837ft).

Walk north up the **Zaros** main street as far as a Y-junction signed (bear right) for the Hotel Idi and Votomos lake, an uphill road walk of 3km.

The gorge footpath leaves from behind the lakeside bar and restaurant. The monastery functions as a quiet retreat, so the footpath bypasses the whole complex. It climbs through woodland to join a car track where you turn right. The hillside above the monastery is cut with unsightly bulldozed tracks and an unfinished project (2005) in the hillside behind the buildings interrupts this first track that you have encountered. It links with the car park – 'car tour walkers' clamber over the debris as best they can.

The track soon ends at a well-made wire gate and a footpath takes over, loosing height to follow the bed of the gorge. This climbs, and after passing an L-shaped trough and spring, the path crosses over to the west side of the gorge to reach a big crag (shelter) where there is a goats' pen and an access track.

This goatherds' track was once used as a return route to the monastery but is now fenced off, and the original short-cut footpath is also now disused. A devastating bush fire in

Ay. Ioannis chapel and Rouvas refuge

the 1990s destroyed these routes and most of the trees in this part of the gorge.

Leaving the crag, look carefully on the roadside for the continuation of the footpath, which now heads uphill to reach a T-junction of footpaths in the mountainside 640m (2100ft). Uphill is for the gorge and left (south) is for the road system above the monastery. Since that now involves a long road-tramp on zigzags, you may prefer to return down on the footpath in the gorge.

The path, balustraded in places, now starts to climb in earnest as the formerly wide-open gorge becomes a narrow ravine. There are timber stepladders, ramps, walkways and high-level trails, all of which are needed to get around obstacles typical of steep ravines: large boulders, 'waterfalls' and smooth rounded rocks. The path starts to level out at about 800m (2625ft). This is a pleasant stretch through evergreen oak forest and alongside the shallow stream fed by the spring from Ay. Ioannis meadow. The stream comes in from the right (east): this turn-off is marked with a roofed timber noticeboard. Walk up beside the stream to reach the meadow, with its picnic tables, the chapel and the refuge hut where there is an information panel on the protected forest of this attractive high-level valley.

Apart from a table, two benches and a sink, a fireplace (seemingly never cleared of ashes) and a disused WC, there is nothing inside the refuge. It is not locked, presumably in case excursionists need shelter in this remote place. As with most such refuges it has no protection from misuse.

Note There is vehicular access to Ay. Ioannis via an unsurfaced slip road that descends from the Skinakas–Gergeri mountain road. The E4 Trail heading east over Giristi (not walked by author) takes this road at first. The route is well waymarked since it forms a link between the Rouvas refuge at Samari (via Duo Prinoi) and the EOS Prinos refuge above Ano Asites.

WALK P3
Ay. Ioannis Chapel to the Nida Plain (E4 Trail)

Grade	D
Start	Ay. Ioannis chapel 950m (3116ft)
Access	Walk P2 or by car from Gergeri
Finish	Nida Plain 1400m (4493ft)
Access to finish	Road from Anoyeia or ongoing trekking routes P12, P14, P5
Highest point	1400m (4493ft)
Height gain	450m (1476ft)
Approx distance	12km (7.5 miles)
Time allowance	8hrs; less if the Amoudara Valley road is complete

The popular day-walk up the Rouvas Gorge from Zaros (Walk P2) links to this section of the E4 main Trail. Following a steep and unfrequented shepherds' route up to the Nida Plain this path immediately feels much more remote. There is also an option for a circular walk from Ay. Ioannis chapel.

For an overview of the first stage, walk downhill a few metres from the tomb beside **Ay. Ioannis chapel** for a clear view of the hillsides of the Rouvas forest. At 315°NW note a white chapel, at a place called Duo Prinoi ('The-oh Prinee'). Note the two forested spurs descending from the chapel to the riverbed. The E4 Trail is routed up the right-hand spur. From the chapel it continues the ascent by traversing the forested hillside towards a pass on the skyline, 319°N. In addition, a pan-Cretan mountain-biking course used (2005) an alternative and perhaps easier route up to Duo Prinoi, marking it with red-paint waymarks.

The two forested spurs from the chapel converge at the riverbed. The E4 waymarks direct you onto the right-hand spur by the shortest route possible. This involves a minor rock scramble up a crag that is found about 3mins walk up the riverbed from the Ay. Ioannis stream turn-off.

For the rock scramble, start off by following the track from the tomb straight down to the riverbed. Turn up the

E4 Trail: the pass above Duo Prinoi seen from Ay. Ioannis chapel

riverbed to find an E4 waymark and arrow on a rock in the riverbed. This waymark may be designed to be seen by walkers who are coming down from Nida, not going up, which is why this particular point on the trail is so hard to find. Continue up the riverbed for a minute or so, looking out for signs and arrows on the left, which indicate the (short) rock-scramble route. Once you are above it, head uphill towards the spine of the spur. There are several E4 enamelled tin 'flags' nailed to the trees (2003), although you may have to keep looking back to spot them.

Alternatively, if you wish to avoid the rock scramble short cut take a small unfrequented footpath that leaves the riverbed a little further downstream from the Ay. Ioannis stream outlet. Keeping to the right, steadily climb the hill until you reach a small saddle, bare of trees. Walk over this and down to join an earthen track – follow the red-dotted mountain-biking route along the track. Red paint waymarks guide you sharp left up the next spur on a path that leads to Duo Prinoi chapel.

Option: round walk from Ay. Ioannis If you made your way up the spine of the spur with the small saddle you would also get to **Duo Prinoi**. If there is good visibility, it follows that if you want to extend the day-walk beyond Ay. Ioannis, you could go to Duo Prinoi – up one spur and down the other. It is unfortunate that most walkers return down the gorge without having climbed just a little bit higher to get above the trees and be rewarded with much wider views of this remote forested valley.

The chapel at Duo Prinoi, 1155m (3790ft) and shepherds' workstation nearby, is at the end of a road (said to be 9km) that first climbs to a pass before descending to the main Zaros–Kamares road via the Vrondisi monastery. If the water tap by the chapel's stone benches is not working, water is obtainable at a cistern a little further uphill on the E4 route.

For the Nida Plain From the **Duo Prinoi chapel** the pass to Nida is seen at 325°NE. Just beyond the shepherds' huts bear right on a track that ends at a concrete water tank (water tap). The trail now traverses the hillside as a footpath (pass another spring in about 4mins) heading for the start of a steep traverse that leads up, through the forest, to the relevant pass.

About 13mins from the water tank the path starts this main ascent at a crag 1245m (4085ft). This is clearly a shepherds' route that would be difficult to find were it not so well waymarked. By starting, in effect, from the top of the Duo Prinoi spur, the route has avoided a very steep climb from the valley floor. Even so, this forested section is still not easy because the steep mountainside is carpeted with slippery oak leaves. In places there are gaps between the rocky outcrops that provide reassuring handholds.

This first part of the traverse ends at a T-junction of footpaths in the forest: straight down is a sheep trail, presumably to the valley floor. Turn uphill, carefully following the E4 paint waymarks on rocks, which now guide you up a very steep spur. At the top there is a short traverse where you have to 'put hand to rock'. This passes above a huge crag that, as you see later, forms one side of a 'vertical' watercourse

Note

In 2005 a road from Nida was under construction. If it now serves the whole length of this valley, you could simply tramp this road to Nida, perhaps finding sections of the footpath along the way.

which develops from a shallow gully. Beyond the traverse the path takes you down into this gully, then turns up it to continue the ascent. Waymarks guide you around thickets of spiny burnet and over big rocks until, the ascent largely completed. you arrive at the tunnel-like entrance to the long and sparsely wooded **Amoudara Valley**.

Waymarks are also sparse here. To pick up the trail again, walk straight across the wide open space (260°W) now in front of you. Waymarks reappear and guide you through the undulating rocky terrain of this 'hidden' high-level valley in the region just east of the Nida Plain. If anything, the main landmark is a huge vertical cave in the cliff face that borders one of the flat areas. This spot is marked with an E4 pole on a small round rock. ◄

A final low pass (E4 pole) at the end of the valley brings you down to a fairly large flat grazing area called **Arulokampos**, where you bear left for the final climb up to the **Nida Plain**. As the land levels out, follow the unmade road for at least 2km, around thorn thickets, before reaching the entrance to the plain itself. At a T-junction, turn right, north, for the *taverna* – or turn left for Kamares cave via Koutsounares spring (Walk P15).

WALK P4

Kamares to the Kamares Cave

Grade	C
Start/finish	Kamares 600m (1968ft)
Access	KTEL bus from Zaros or Heraklion or taxi from Mires
Access to finish	Round walk, or descent route from Nida (Walk P15)
Highest point	Kamares cave 1524m (5000ft)
Height gain/loss	924m (3031ft)
Approx distance	5km (8 miles) to the cave
Time allowance	Kamares to E4 Mandra Kalamafka (spring) path junction 1300m (4265ft) 3hrs; to Kamares cave 1hr; descent to Kamares 2hrs; total: 6hrs

This popular but challenging E4 Trail variation follows an old mule track which climbs a steep spur above Kamares. When you reach 900m (2950ft) a deep belt of oak forest provides welcome shade. There are five springs on the trail up to the cave and for the whole way, especially above the treeline, there are panoramic views across the plain of Messara. A modern water supply pipe links all the springs. The pipe is set into a concrete channel that can be seen, or followed, as you ascend or descend. This makes the walk to the cave seem less 'remote' than it otherwise might – weather conditions on the mountain are very changeable and often include thick mist.

This may be a 'straight-up-and-down' route on a well-trodden trail, but it is also a high mountain walk. Be sure to take your '12 essentials', including adequate spare clothing. Such relentless ascent/descent routes are very taxing on the knees. Allow sufficient time for taking it slowly if necessary, especially on the descent.

Take the steep concreted village lane opposite the Kamares Cave *taverna*. There are several wooden signs stating 'Hohle' (German for 'cave') on this route, perhaps because Zakarias (of the taverna) spent time in Germany in his youth. From the lane, up on the right, a gate in a fence gives access to the footpath (it does not resemble a main footpath at first).

Just after passing a few isolated trees, encounter the first cistern 640m (2100) in a fenced enclosure. Pass through this enclosure to continue up the bare hillside on a much more distinct trail infrequently marked with E4 Trail poles. The second spring, and deep trough, is at 910m (2986ft). After reaching the forest and crossing westwards, the path follows the water pipe 1110m (3642ft) above a steep ravine. The Kamares cave can now be seen as a big black hole high on the mountainside above the forest at 13°N.

The path climbs to a flat area, where there is another spring and several sheep troughs. If you wish to camp on this trail note that this is just about the only flat spot near to any of the springs. (Sheep come to drink here, so take care to camp away from the spring.) Continue up alongside the water pipe to the fourth spring 1300m (4265ft) and junction of paths, marked with an E4 pole and a 'Hohle' pointer signboard. ▶

Notes The Anavasi map marks this spot on the 1300m contour.

E4 Trail (variation): looking down on Kamares from the climb to the cave

In the direction 45°NE above the spring note some shepherds' fencing and an overhang in the crag. This place, called **Mandra Kalamáfka**, is the only shelter on the mountain at this point. The Kamares cave is still another hour's climb and, even so, is not the type of cave that provides much shelter because, pothole-style, it 'yawns' back into the hillside.

For the summit of Mount Ida (Walk P6) Bear left here.

For Kamares cave Bear right; the path is well tramped and easy to follow (80°E) through the forest. As the treeline ends, the fifth spring is encountered at approx 1420m (4659ft). Next, pass the last spring, in a concrete water tank with a steel door (not locked). An easy rock scramble at the head of this steep valley brings you to the top of the wide spur descending from the cave. In early May or so beautiful

Note There is an unfrequented path, or route (not walked by author), starting to the east of the cave, that climbs over Digenis to reach a grazing meadow not far from Skaronero spring (see Walk P6). However, whilst this is a route from the cave to that level, note that from there, there are no similar paths down the steep-sided western rim of the Nida Plain other than that taken by the E4 Trail down to the Analipsi spring (Walk P12).

yellow lilies are found here, and at the cave. Kamares rooftops are seen far below; since the cave can be readily spotted from Phaistos archaeological site (if you know where to look) you should, in reverse, be able to identify the hill of Phaistos, seen almost due south.

Return to Kamares by the same route.

WALK P5

Kamares Cave to the Nida Plain

Walk P16 in reverse	
Grade	C/D
Start	Kamares cave 1524m (5000ft)
Access	On foot via Walk P4
Finish	Nida taverna 1420m (4658ft)
Access	By road from Anoyeia, or ongoing trekking routes P12, P14, P15
Height loss/gain	Undulating route: approx 100m (328ft)
Approx distance	6.5km (4 miles)
Time allowance	2hrs

Due to its position in relation to access roads, this footpath is not often used as part of a day-walk, although (2005) it is well waymarked. It suits those who intend, perhaps, to overnight on the Nida Plain. At first losing height rapidly from the cave, the path heads eastwards through forest to a spot where it contours around the next spur. It then gradually gains height, traversing high above the steep ravine at the south exit of the plain. The terrain becomes very rugged at the point where, with Nida in sight, the path passes Koutsounares spring and a complex of expertly built old *koumi* huts (shelter).

The path starts in the direction about 170°SE from the cave mouth. To get on to it, follow the main path just a short distance down from the cave to where the hillside levels out a little (not right down to the lower part of the spur), and then bear left to find a red-dotted path that heads for the trees. It looses height rapidly through the woodland. Take this section slowly, in order not to miss seeing the waymarks. This is a very steep slope – if you have not seen a waymark for a minute or so, and are feeling puzzled, retrace your steps and check again.

The path levels out to cross a first rocky part of the spur at approx 1470m (4823ft), then descends another 20m to where it again levels out. Through the trees the

Koutsounares mitata

Note In addition to the spring at Koutsounares, the Anavasi map marks a spring just above the path after it has rounded the spine of the spur. This may explain the presence of a very old ruined stone hut which otherwise would have been unusually far from a water source.

shepherds' road from Voriza can be seen on the opposite side of the next ravine. ◄

If you are on the correct level, when you leave the forest and start the traverse along the east-facing side of this ravine, heading towards Koutsounares ('Kootsoo-nar-rezz') complex (which is in sight), you should be on an obvious, rocky, but waymarked path. **Koutsounares**, with its spring 1460m (4790ft), is still used by shepherds from Voriza, but not for the milking operation because the road (2005) does not reach it. Albanian shepherds will gladly agree to work in remote places like this, especially now that cell phones enable instructions to be passed from village to mountain.

The path takes you past the spring, which is in a re-entrant just beyond the complex, and then crosses steep and very rocky terrain to join the car track from Nida, seen ending on the opposite side of the ravine (not on the west side as marked on some maps). There is a gap (2005) between this road end and the shepherds' road from Voriza, which approaches it from far down on the spur.

Walk north about 3km along the plain to the **Nida taverna**, passing a T-junction with an E4-waymarked rock indicating the route of the E4 main Trail down to Ay. Ioannis chapel (Walk P15).

WALK P6
Kamares to the Summit of Mount Ida

Walk P13 in reverse	
Grade	D
Start/finish	Kamares 600m (1968ft)
Access	KTEL bus from Zaros or Heraklion or taxi from Mires
Access to finish	Round walk, or Walk 12
Highest point	Mount Ida summit 2454m (8051ft)
Height gain/loss	1854m (6082ft)
Approx distance	28km (17 miles)
Time allowance	Kamares to E4 Mandra Kalamfka spring 1300m (4265ft) 3hrs; to Skaronero spring 1760m (5774ft) 2hrs 30mins; to Kolita E4 signboard 1840m (6036ft) 1hr; signboard to summit 2hrs 30mins; ascent total: 9hrs; descent total: 5hrs 30mins; total: 14hrs 30mins

This steep route to the summit and back, if done in one day (during the months of long daylight hours), is the most strenuous of the regular routes to the summit. It attracts those with extreme physical fitness. Warnings for Walk P4 also apply here: shorts and T-shirt, and a hand-held water bottle, will not do. You must carry the '12 essentials' for high-mountain walking and have confidence in your hillwalking ability and fitness to cope with both ascent and descent.

Follow Walk P4 to the spring and trough where the path divides (uphill, right, is for the Kamares cave).

However, left, the route no longer follows the water pipe. To find it, take a couple of steps down from the 'Hohle' spring and trough at the E4 Trail junction, to spot the continuation of the mule track, heading 305°NW through the forest. This leads to the next rocky spur by first contouring around a re-entrant and crossing a watercourse in the forest. Thereafter it gains height to reach the top of the spur at a place where there is an open area of flat rock. (Note a roofless stone hut beside the path, just before you reach this spot.)

Skaronero spring

Although the Kamares cave is fascinating in its way, the panoramic view from this flat rock is even better because it allows a wider field of view. Kastro, the mountain above Askifou in the Lefka Ori, can be identified (276°W) far across the Rethymnon hills. The immediate view westwards, however, is across a massive steeply descending ravine. You may be able to see a small grazing area mid-height on the opposite side, which is used by shepherds from Lochria.

The path now continues from the west side of this thin spur, and takes up a pleasantly level traverse above the large ravine. After the second re-entrant note a walled-in overhang in the crag (shelter). Cross a small snowmelt watercourse and arrive at the foot of a fat spur. Cairns and waymarks mark the zigzags of the path, which goes up the middle of the spur. On reaching the crag at the top it levels out before continuing the climb northwards, following a rocky 'shelf' high above the ravine. Waymarks here are very faded (2005), but there are cairns. This steep, but dramatically scenic, section of the ascent ends at **Skaronero spring** which has a couple of concrete benches, two troughs, and road access for shepherds.

This single water source is all-important to those who work the high-level grazing area named Kolita, now about 2.5km up the valley. The bare rock location of the spring is not pretty, but since local shepherds have a deep affection for their mountain, it is no surprise to see it celebrated with a little poem set into the rock (translated): 'Cold water – gift of God – to old Psiloriti – highest altitude [mountain] in all Kriti'.

Naturally, a mule track once took a direct route from Kolita to the spring, and what is left of this – a useful short cut but still high above the ravine – is found just up the road on the left-hand side, marked with a cairn or two. If you miss this unassuming path, just continue up the road. It climbs over the spur, and descends, past two workstations, to a T-junction where you turn left for Kolita.

Now walking north on this road, pass a junction with the shepherds' road from Lochria (a possible very long tramp 'escape' route, along which you would find shelter) and keep straight on up the valley to reach **Kolita** meadow and old stone huts (not disused). Continue north to where the road ends at the foot of a crag in the middle of the valley. In the spring the crag shelters a long-lasting snowdrift that provides drinking water for goats.

Continue by bearing right on a footpath around the crag. This brings you to an important junction of footpaths, marked with a yellow E4 double-pole wind-battered aluminium signboard.

For the Nida Plain Turn east, and climb the spur to the top of the ridge now above you – it borders the west side of the plain.

For the summit Continue northwestwards on the well-tramped E4 main Trail (see Walks P12, P13).

WALK P7

The Arcadi Monastery to Aravanes Kampos

See also Walk P17

Grade	B/C
Start	Arcadi monastery 480m (1574ft)
Access	KTEL bus from Rethymnon
Finish	Aravanes Kampos 940m (3084ft)
Access	Return to Arcadi or ongoing Walks P8, P9, P10
Height gain	460m (1509ft)
Approx distance	(to Aravanes) 10km (6.2 miles)
Time allowance	4hrs to Aravanes; 3hrs return to Arcadi

The monastery forecourt is served by a thrice-daily KTEL bus from Rethymnon. Forecourt facilities include a well-appointed toilet block and a pleasant 'Touristico Periptero' – a souvenir shop with a terrace and a bar serving refreshments and grills (tel: 83127.23227) – which closes at about 19.00. There are no other shops nearby: bring trekking food supplies from Rethymnon. The monastery, an important pilgrimage destination for many Cretans and their descendants from overseas, is open 08.00–20.00 daily.

Facing the monastery, and moving a little to the right, note the great 'whale-back' summit ridge of Mount Ida and the tiny pimple of the summit chapel, behind the first peaks of the ridge, Spathi and Stolistra. The foothills between Arcadi ('Ar-car-thee') and the summit ridge are sheep-grazing territory served by an unmade road. This branches off from the main Arcadi–Thonos road (now in front of you) at a junction just beyond Tsounes pass, about 3km from the monastery. However, walkers can reach it by taking an erosion-damaged older road no longer passable to vehicles. This is the dirt road that can be seen climbing the *phrygana*-covered hillside at 150°SSE.

Note The 1:100,000 Harms Verlag map includes the first part of this route, which is outside the coverage of the larger-scale maps.

Note Unless you get a shepherds' vehicle lift from Arcadi to Aravanes, the length of the ongoing walks P8 and P9 would mean that you should expect to camp.

Follow the main road to Thronos past woodland (including some magnificent umbrella pines) and after 10mins arrive at a T-junction, signed for Thonos: turn up this road. Just across the junction's concrete culvert, pass through a gate on the left, which gives access to a dirt road. This is the disused road – follow it as it crosses over to the next valley, then turn south-southeast again. The usable part of this road ends at a concrete dam, built to control flash flooding.

Pass though 'gates' in the fences here, and continue for about 1km up the valley on a badly damaged section of the road. At the head of this valley, where there is a shepherd's house (with a slip road leading up to the main Thronos road on the right) the disused road crosses the riverbed and starts to climb the hillside you saw from the monastery. At the top of the hill what is left of the road continues across a flat area to join the shepherds' newer road at 640m (2100ft). Turn right for the main road to Thonos (a long downhill tramp) or left (east) for the foothills and Aravanes. An old hut is seen under a nearby crag.

Beyond a long, level section above a ravine, the road starts to gain height. There are good views westwards across the Amari Valley to the Rethymnon hills and, now far from the tourist trail, it is unlikely that you will meet any other walkers. If a shepherd offers you a lift your destination is Aravanes ('Arra-varn-ezz'). However the first shepherds' workstation is at **Petramoures** ('Petra-moor-rezz') 870m (2855ft). A Y-junction of tracks in the oak forest, about 3hrs walk from the monastery, marks this turn-off – but keep right for Aravanes.

Petromoures has two concrete water storage tanks, including a huge one with a concrete apron. A track opposite this leads to an old stone hut (shelter, but not disused), and there are one or two vehicular tracks that give access to grazing areas nearby.

The Aravanes road, continuing now through oak forest, gains height to a pass at 905m (2969ft), followed by a pleasantly level contouring route above a valley. Leave the valley, and at a minor T-junction (zinc water pipe) keep right. The Akrotiri peninsula and Kefalas, perched on the clifftop above

Georgioupoli, is seen 288°WNW. **Aravanes Kampos** 940m (3166ft), a flat-floored grazing area, is now just around the corner, about 3km from Petromoures. There is a stone-built shepherds' hut over on the right (shelter, but not disused). Although disfigured with a breeze-block addition, its interior is formed, unusually, with a single large barrel vault.

Called 'Old Mitato' – its water supply is the Aravanes spring – the hut may indeed be very old because the 18th-century traveller, Richard Pococke, describing his ascent of Mount Ida, mentions an overnight camp at this *kampos*, which belonged to the monastery.

Ongoing routes At Aravanes meadow – at the foot of the western end of the summit ridge – your approach route divides and you have a choice. Right is for the 'shelf' high above the Amari Valley (Walk P10), and left is for an ascending valley that leads up to the Nida Plain (Walk P8) or to the summit of Mount Ida (Walk P9). For Aravanes spring, follow Walk P8.

WALK P8
Aravanes Kampos to the Nida Taverna

Grade	D
Start	Aravanes Kampos 940m (3084ft)
Access	Walk P7
Finish	Nida taverna 1420m (4658ft)
Access to finish	Road from Anoyeia, or ongoing trekking routes P14, P15, P16
Highest point	Vitsinela pass 1720m (5643ft)
Height gain	760m (2493ft)
Height loss	300m (984ft)
Approx distance	17km (10.6 miles)
Time allowance	Aravanes Kampos to Ay. Konstantinos (Halastra) 1300m (4265ft) 2hrs; Halastra to summit path junction (old cistern) 1580m (5184ft) 3hrs; to Vitsinela pass 1720m (5643ft) 1hr 40mins; Vitsinela pass to ski-centre building 35mins; to Nida taverna 45 mins; total: 8hrs

This continuation of Walk P7 passes Aravanes spring before starting up the long valley directly below the northeast-facing flank of the summit ridge – a route marked as a footpath on older contour maps. Long, winding roads from several Milopotamos villages access the valley in three places, and unfrequented rocky footpaths link each of these road heads.

Continuing from Walk P7, keep on the Aravanes unsurfaced road as it climbs northeast to the crest of the wooded hill at 1075m (3527ft) that divides the *kampos* from the next valley. At the hilltop, turn left down a track and then sharp right at the first junction on this track. The spring, with its trough, is in sight from this junction. ▸

Note If you prefer, follow an old footpath across Aravanes Kampos and up through the woodland (65°ENE) since it leads more directly to the spring.

Aravanes is marked as a chapel on contour maps, but the chapel is long ruined (no shelter). The ruined chapel is near the end of the long valley below the summit ridge and, leaving from the spring, you are now on the footpath that goes up this valley. The route up the valley is not a straightforward ascent. There are several passes to cross, making it an undulating route, even though you are steadily gaining height to a final pass, Vitsinela 1720m (5643ft), from where the descent to Nida begins.

For the Nida Plain and/or Mount Ida summit From the spring follow the footpath up through the woodland 70°ENE. You may see what is left of the chapel, looking like a pile of rocks, over on your left. The watercourse narrows, obliging the path to continue over a big rock before taking up a more normal route again, occasionally leaving the valley floor if that makes the passage easier. After you leave the woodland and reach a wide, fairly level pass, the valley opens out and the footpath descends to a flat grazing area and a dirt track. Bear left, uphill, on this to find **Ay. Konstantinos chapel** (formerly ruined, rebuilt 1998) at a place called **Halastra** 1300m (4265ft) where meadows and three seepage wells are surrounded by low crags. Overhangs in the crags provide shelter. There is a table and seating benches, possibly left by those who rebuilt the chapel. This pleasant camp spot is about 6hrs walking from Arcadi.

Re-join the dirt track as it continues over the next pass and descends to another flat plain, **Kampos Tigani**, which has oak trees and, before midsummer, carpets of white

Ay. Konstantinos (May)

asphodel. The dirt road now climbs the hillside to the north, on its long return route to Ay. Mamas. However, another road leads southeast up the valley to a shepherds' hut (and beyond). Follow this uphill for a few minutes and identify the next pass, which is in sight – a small cutting at 130°SE.

For the next 5km the valley has widened out and is not a clear 'V' shape. It looks as though the main path might go to left or right. However, keep to the right for a marginally easier passage. Also, since there is a gap here between shepherding districts, together with the decline in sheep-raising, paths between the road-ends are no longer well tramped. High mountain trails, under snow all winter, soon show signs of being reclaimed by Nature if they are not used.

Now leave the road, cross over to the opposite hillside and make your way up to the pass (which turns out to be a small rocky hollow). Climb across this, then around a thicket of thorny burnet, to continue the climb on a section of foot-path that traverses the hillside to reach an area of rocky basins. Once you have crossed this it is not far to the top of the next pass, marked with a tin plaque, an old stone sheep-fold at 1560m (5118ft) and a road. Pass a new concrete cistern (**note** if you plan to climb to the summit, or to camp, get water here rather than from the path-junction cistern further on since that needs boiling). Keep straight on up the valley, ignoring a junction with the road down to Livadhia. The road ends beside an old stone *koumi* hut and sheepfold on your left, and an old-style open cistern on your right 1580m (5184ft).

For the E4 Trail and Mount Ida summit (3hrs 30mins) Start the climb here (Walk P9). The path goes up beside a distinct re-entrant (160°SE) in the summit ridge (the ridge has loomed above you for most of the way).

For the Nida Plain Leave the road-end and continue up the valley on another rocky footpath section of about 2km, bearing to the right about 110°SE. This eventually brings you to a small flat-floored plain, or doline, which has a breeze-block hut (shelter) on the left, and, directly in front of it, a large recently formed sinkhole more than 5m (16ft) deep (a serious hazard in thick mist, or after dark).

Beyond the sinkhole join a road-end. The road passes a large modern cistern before continuing to the final pass 1720m (5643ft) just below **Vitsinela** peak. There is another newly built cistern and shepherds' hut here, and an old stone shelter in an adjacent hollow. This is the shepherds' road to Zoniana, and it now begins its long, winding descent.

Note the communications antennae on top of a hill called Harkias (110°SE), seen across the valley as you walk down the road. The ruined ski-centre building (your next destination) is sited in a southeast-facing hollow under this hill. To get to it, leave the road at a T-junction beside a big grey rock, and pass through a 'gate' in the fence. This track brings you to the 'Harkias' road; turn right for the ski centre. You cannot see it until you have turned a corner and started downhill towards it. It is a large two-storey stone-clad 1970s-style building at the foot of the broken ski-lift. Since it is roofed but open to the elements, flocks of sheep now use it as a storm shelter. Humans, too, might be glad to pause here during one of Mount Ida's fierce storms (note there is no water supply). Part of the Nida Plain is now in sight.

To get there, **either** tramp the ski-centre road (long and winding)

Or take a short cut down the valley: leave the road (just beyond the building) on a footpath than heads downhill, bearing right to reach a narrow overgrown track. There is a concrete cistern tank halfway along this track, which soon joins the road-end of a wide newer track. In turn this leads down to the main road; turn right for the *taverna* and car park. Alternatively, leave the road-end on a footpath that traverses southwards across the hillside above the main road. (There are several sheep paths here.) This leads to the stone-built chapel on the road between the *taverna* and the Ideon Andron cave. Turn downhill at the chapel.

WALK P9

Mount Ida Summit: Northern Approach Path

Grade	D
Start	Cistern at 1580m (5184ft) on Walk P8
Access	Via Walk P8
Finish	Summit of Mount Ida 2454m (8051ft)
Access to finish	E4 Trail (Walk 12) to Nida or to Toumbotos Prinos EOS refuge
Height gain	864m (2834ft)
Approx distance	4km (2.5 miles)
Time allowance	Old cistern 1580m (5184ft) to E4 path junction 2200m (7218ft) 2hrs 30mins; path junction to summit 1hr; total: 3hrs 30mins

This unfrequented, very steep, but non-hazardous path is marked on older contour maps. Years ago it will doubtless have been marked by the construction of the water cistern. Shepherds occasionally use it to pass over the summit ridge, but for walkers its usefulness is that it joins the E4 Trail to the summit.

If there is no snow – and although water at the summit chapel may sometimes sustain all year – start with an adequate supply from the valley, even if you have to boil the cistern water. Weather conditions on the summit ridge, which is very exposed, can change so rapidly that by the time you reach the main trail you might have to alter your plans. You would then be a long way from the two nearest water sources, the Analipsi spring above Nida *taverna*, and Skaronero spring, 2.5km down the Kolita Valley.

Look southwards (160°SE) beyond the cistern of Walk P8 to identify a distinct re-entrant between Vouloumenou and Angathias peaks. The steep path that joins the E4 Trail leaves from the cistern and heads towards this. It eventually bears to the left in order to avoid scree slopes at high level. When you reach the E4 Trail path junction, follow Walk P12.

The steep path to the E4 Trail

WALK P10

Aravanes Kampos to
Toumbotos Prinos EOS Refuge

Grade	D
Start	Aravanes Kampos 940m (3084ft)
Access	Via Walk P7
Finish	Toumbotos Prinos EOS refuge 1450m (4757ft)
Access to finish	On foot or by car from Kouroutes (see Walk P11), or KTEL weekday service from Rethymnon
Height gain	Undulating route: 500m (1640ft)
Approx distance	10km (6.2 miles)
Time allowance	4hrs 30mins

At the foot of the southwest-facing flank of the summit ridge, approx 1400m (4593ft), there is a long 'shelf' in the mountainside which tops the huge cliffs that border the Amari Valley. Available contour maps seldom mark cliffs or crags. To get to the refuge you can make your way along this shelf from Aravanes Kampos, gaining height gradually on various footpaths and a shepherds' road. There are minor ascents and descents, flat areas and patches of forest. Water is not too diffi-cult to find because there are shepherds' workstations served by the road from Vistigi ('Viss-tee-yee').

The stone-clad refuge, which belongs to Rethymnon EOS, has a distinctive round tower and a large covered terrace. Its water supply comes from a fenced cistern just behind, on the right-hand side. The E4 Trail to the summit leaves from the cistern. An unsurfaced road links the refuge with Kouroutes ('Kor-route-tezz'). It follows that, for a round walk to the summit, you could drive up by car to reach the trailhead at the refuge.

Note The Anavasi map does not cover Aravanes Kampos, but it is useful for the latter part of this route.

There is no well-defined obvious footpath linking **Aravanes Kampos** to the Vistigi road presumably because these are two different shepherding districts. However, start off by tak-ing the footpath straight across the Kampos, heading south-east towards the first bordering hill, then keep going to encounter the Vistigi road at about 1100m (3608ft). Gain height from there, bearing in mind that the 1500m contour is about right for the **refuge** and the Vistigi road is your 'escape route' should you need it.

WALK P11
The Amari Valley: Fourfouras and Kouroutes

Grade	C/D
Start	Fourfouras 500m (1640ft)
Access	KTEL weekday Amari bus from Rethymnon
Finish	Toumbotos Prinos EOS refuge 1450m (4757ft)
Access to finish	Road from Kouroutes, or Walk P10
Highest point	1450m (4757ft)
Height gain	950m (3116ft)
Approx distance	Fourfouras to EOS refuge 7km; refuge to Kouroutes (road walk) 14km
Time allowance	Fourfouras to EOS refuge 4hrs 30mins (not walked by author); to Kouroutes 3hrs 30mins; total: 8hrs

From contour maps it appears that the Fourfouras section of the E4 Trail could be an attractive footpath between Fourfouras and the EOS refuge, and therefore a welcome escape from the long road-tramp to, or from, Kouroutes. However it is not a mule track or proper footpath, but just a route up through the massive cliffs and steep ravines above the Amari Valley at Fourfouras. The underfoot is rocky and loose, and neglected waymarks are both indistinct and scarce. Presumably, as with other trails of this sort, it is easier to find, and safer to climb, as an ascent rather than as a descent.

The Kouroutes road from the refuge may be a very long tramp but at least it is not hazardous. The first stage includes one or two short cuts across road loops. The main landmark is **Ay. Titos chapel** and spring, 1000m (3280ft), after which the road crosses to the north side of the steep valley and winds down at great length to **Kouroutes**. Up to 1995 at least there was an old mule track/footpath route down to the village from the meadow that is seen on a spur below the chapel area. Beyond the meadow it passed by some big rocks before zigzagging down more open hillside. It made a good short cut but lately it may be overgrown. If so, there is no practical sideways escape. You would have to return to the chapel and take the road.

The Toumbotos Prinos EOS refuge

From Kouroutes to the EOS refuge The road up to the refuge can be seen and it is clearly marked near the bus stop. You could enquire at the *taverna* for transport possibilities, but do not rely on this.

The E4 Trail from Fourfouras to Toumbotos Prinos EOS Refuge For those who want the challenge of what the locals call 'a really bad path', getting to the trailhead is as follows.

Follow the Fourfouras main road south. One minute from the last supermarket of the village, note an E4 aluminium yellow signboard on the left. Turn up here and almost immediately find a yellow paint arrow pointing sharp right alongside a wall. At this point you have a more open view of the cliffs above the village. Various steep ravines punctuate the cliffs. The E4 is routed up the ravine and steep buttress at 100°E. The arrow directs you to an ancient chapel (restored) in an olive grove. From the chapel follow a service track uphill to a T-junction of tracks 600m (1969ft). Turn uphill (northeast), and then southeast at the next junction. Arrive at a spring and troughs at 700m (2297ft). It is here that you climb up above the road to get onto the path which, marked with cairns, now heads up the bed of the ravine. A wire gate in the fence above the spring gives access to the ravine (next section not walked by author but the route is said to be passable).

WALKS AND TREKS FROM TRAILHEADS ON THE NIDA PLAIN

Apart from Walk 12 (the round walk to the summit), these trailheads are for Walks P1, 2, 3, 4 (in reverse). Before starting out on any of these routes, stock up with drinking water at the *taverna*, or at the Analipsi spring.

WALK P12
Nida to the Summit of Mount Ida (E4 Trail)

Grade	C/D
Start/finish	Nida taverna car park 1420m (4658ft)
Access	By car, taxi, shepherds' wagon, or via approach walking routes P1, P3, P5, P8
Highest point	Summit of Mount Ida 2454m (8051ft)
Height gain/loss	1056m (3465ft)
Approx distance	17km (10.6 miles) round trip
Time allowance	Nida taverna car park to top of first ridge 1910m (6267ft) 2hrs 45mins; ridgetop down to Kolita signboard 1840m (6037ft) 15mins; signboard to summit 2hrs 30mins; summit down to signboard 1hr 15mins; signboard up to ridge (rim of Nida Plain) 25mins; ridgetop down to car park 1hr 30 mins; ascent total: 5hrs 30mins; descent total: 3hrs 15mins; total: 9hrs

This rugged but well-tramped path, starting from the *taverna* car park, is popular with experienced mountain walkers, most of whom plan it as a round day-walk, using rented cars to get to the trailhead. It is a long day: start as early as you can. The *taverna* stays open until 19.00 or 20.00, hopefully long enough for walkers to return in time for refreshments.

At the car park there is very steep mountainside above you (west); looking south, note the first steep gully that punctuates it. The path climbs that gully to the top of the ridge and then makes a short descent on the other side to reach the

Kolita Valley, where a battered yellow E4 signboard marks an important path junction – either to the summit, or downhill to Kamares. For those without a car, there is the option (during long daylight hours) of returning down from the summit to that spot and then finishing the walk by making the long descent to Kamares (Walk P4).

Note Since there is a shepherds' road from Lochria up to the Kolita Valley, perhaps the easiest way to get to the summit is to hire an ATV and drive up to that spot. If you do this, remember that – as a precaution against rustlers – shepherds sometimes lock the gates across village-specific mountain roads. Obviously you are welcome as someone not about to rustle any sheep, but for your own convenience it may be useful to enquire about gates in advance at a Lochria *kafeneon*.

To get to the ascending gully, leave the *taverna* car park on the short-cut path up to the Analipsi spring (drinking water), where you join the road up to the cave. Turn uphill at the next bend, and look out for E4 paint waymarks marking the start of the footpath on your left. This small, rocky path heads straight for the gully, gaining height fairly rapidly. Alternatively, when the road to the cave bears to the right at higher level, find another access path which heads for the gully. This is the worst section of the route – once you reach the gully the underfoot gets easier. Waymarks guide you up the gully.

At the top of the ridge (the west rim of the plain) there is a choice of routes, and both paths may be marked as the E4. North is for the summit via Kousakas and Vouloumenou, and southeast is down a spur to the Kolita Valley where there is a path junction signboard. You lose height on this second path, but nevertheless this is the easiest and most popular route.

From the signboard the path continues northwest, up a well-defined valley – later a rocky gully – to a pass between the summit ridge and the Vouloumenou ridge. ◄

A seldom-used shepherds' path (Walk P9) from the valley below (north) joins the main trail at this point.

Beyond the pass the path continues to climb, taking a direct route across the steep east-facing flank of the summit ridge. In the spring a long-lasting snowdrift may cover the footpath here and, depending on conditions, you may have to climb above it. As you approach the summit, the large 'pile of stones' – the three-roomed **Timios Stavros summit chapel** – is easily recognised as it is the only feature of note on the bare ridge.

The summit-ascent gully as seen from the car park

Called a 'hovel' by Royal Navy surveyor Captain Spratt when he climbed Mount Ida in the 1860s (ill-equipped but keen to see the dawn – he spent a very cold night inside) the summit chapel nevertheless provides shade, or shelter, and a welcome seating bench for modern-day hikers.

Note that in springtime the three rooms may still be full of snow, leaving little space for shelter (this is a building entirely in tune with its environment!). In summer, if you need to use the water in the cistern (boil it) be careful not to waste any since there is no other supply on the ridge.

Of the three nearest alternative water sources the one beside the EOS refuge may be the nearest, a one-way trip since it is such a long way down. The other alternatives are Skaronero, 2.5km down the Kolita Valley (Walk 13) or Analipsi above the Nida car park.

On the descent to Kotila E4 Trail signboard, May

For the Toumbotos Prinos EOS refuge 1450m (4757ft) From the chapel, turn southeast to find E4 Trail waymarks and cairns that lead you across to a point where it is easiest to make the 1000m descent. In the spring this south-facing mountainside may retain patches of snow so that, in some places, it is possible to slide safely down the drifts – but be sure to remain in control because there are rocks under the snow, or on the edge of it. There is shelter at the refuge since it has a large covered terrace, but it is a very long road-tramp down to Kouroutes (see Walk P11).

WALK P13

Summit of Mount Ida: Descent to Kamares

Walk P6 in reverse	
Grade	D
Start	Summit of Mount Ida 2454m (8051ft)
Access	E4 Trail (Walk 12) to Nida or to Toumbotos Prinos EOS refuge
Finish	Kamares 600m (1968ft)
Access to finish	KTEL bus from Zaros or Heraklion or taxi from Mires
Height loss	1854m (6082ft)
Approx distance	14km (8.7 miles)
Time allowance	Summit to Kolita E4 trail signboard 1840m (6036ft) 1hr 15mins; to Skaronero spring 45mins; to E4 Trail Mandra Kalamafka path junction 1300m (4265ft) 1hr 30mins; to Kamares 2hrs; total: 5hrs 30mins

From the summit chapel take the E4 Trail eastwards down to the path junction in the Kolita Valley (see Walks P6 or P11). The battered yellow E4 signboard is just above a big rock and crag that blocks the centre of the valley in the downhill direction. The diagram on the board refers to Skaronero spring, at least a couple of kilometres down the valley. Take the footpath on the left-hand side of the rock. This joins a car track that continues down, passing **Kolita** grazing area where a rocky outcrop protects a complex of old stone *koumi* huts. (The footpath, if you prefer it, passes to the right of this complex.) Continuing down the valley, keep left when you arrive at a road junction. ▸

The road now gains height as it approaches a large, wide ravine and, upon reaching it, makes a turning to the left. At this point note the original footpath, poorly marked with cairns (2005), remaining sections of which have taken a direct, but undulating, route down the valley. It now crosses the road and continues straight on for Skaronero spring. This section of path forms a short cut from the road to the spring, and joins the road again just above the spring. If you miss the path, keep on the road to the next junction, where you turn uphill (south). The road climbs, passing a

The right-hand option leads (at great length) down to Lochria; a possible escape route in bad weather.

Walkers enjoying the view at Timios Stavros chapel in October: summit of Mount Ida

couple of shepherds' workstations, to get over a spur, before making a steep descent to the spring.

The footpath now follows a shelf in the crag on this east side of the ravine. This place is somewhat forbidding in appearance as there is little vegetation. Waymarking (2005) is poor, but there are cairns to mark the trail. Pass through the wire gate beyond the spring to get onto the 'shelf'. After a short ascent, the path loses height as it heads for the top of a (much less exposed) wide spur. The path zigzags down the spur to reach another shelf, but this lower one is pleasantly wooded. Turn left, and walk along the shelf to a steeply descending rocky spur, where there is a large open area of flat rock and stupendous views across the Messara. Note the next spur east and a ruined stone hut on your left as you continue eastwards, first losing height to enter kermis oak forest. After losing a bit more height in the forest - look carefully for the waymarking cairns – the path contours across the mountainside to the next spur which has the spring and the Kamares 'Hohle' path junction.

Either turn uphill for the cave, or down to **Kamares** on a well-marked trail beside the water pipeline.

WALK P14
Nida to Anoyeia on the E4 Trail

Walk P1a in reverse

Grade	C/D
Start	Nida taverna 1420m (4658ft)
Access	By road from Anoyeia, or from Walks P3, P5, P8
Finish	Anoyeia lower village 700m (2296ft)
Access to finish	KTEL bus service from Rethymnon or Heraklion
Highest point	Rim of plain at Damaki: 1500m (4921ft)
Height gain	160m (524ft)
Height loss	800m (2624ft)
Approx distance	19km (11.8 miles)
Time allowance	Nida to Ay. Yakinthos 3hrs 55mins; to Anoyeia 2hrs 15mins; total: 6hrs 10mins

Starting from the north-facing flank wall of the *taverna*, make your way down to the plain and cut straight across 80°NE to the E4 slip road (see Walk P1a) and follow this up to join the main road. The road junction to **Ay. Yakinthos** is about 10km further on. It is well signposted. If you have been given a lift you could ask the driver to drop you off at this spot. It is then about 2km to the chapel complex on an unmade road.

Thereafter, reverse the route notes for Walk P1. In general, if you hope for a lift to Anoyeia note that shepherds working on the Nida Plain leave in the late afternoon/early evening. The *taverna* proprietor may be able to advise.

WALK P14A
Nida to Anoyeia on Old Droving Trail

Walk P1b in reverse

Grade	D
Start	Nida taverna 1420m (4658ft)
Access	By road from Anoyeia or via Walks P3, P5, P8
Finish	Anoyeia lower village 700m (2296ft)
Access to finish	KTEL bus service from Rethymnon or Heraklion
Highest point	Rim of plain at Timbanatoras: 1500m (4921ft)
Height gain	160m (524ft)
Height loss	800m (2624ft)
Approx distance	15km (9.3 miles)
Time allowance	Nida taverna to rim of plain 1hr 15mins; to spring 2hrs; to Ay. Yaklnthos chapel 45mins; to Anoyeia 2hrs 15mins; total: 6hrs 15mins

For those who want to walk down to Anoyeia, rather than ride the road, this is an adventurous route with several footpath sections, panoramic views, and lots of variety along the way as you make your way down through the wooded northern foothills. You need good visibility for the first section since the path crosses the high northern rim of the plain. It leaves from the main road at a place that cannot be seen from the *taverna* because it is in a deep re-entrant. Therefore the first stage is to get to this point on the road.

Note the descending spur 30°NE from the *taverna*, a spur with vegetation at road level. From the east-facing wall of the **taverna**, make your way down to the plain and walk straight across it to the foot of the spur. Climb the gully on its right (east-facing) side (see Walk P1b). On reaching the main road, turn west around a large outer (left-hand) bend to get to the correct re-entrant which is marked by a large concrete tunnel culvert and an old stone hut on the hillside beyond it. Follow sheep paths up the right-hand side of the re-entrant to reach a pass.

The correct ongoing direction is now some distance over to the right (eastwards), but the trail avoids difficult mountain terrain here by first descending the valley below this pass. Make your way downhill. The path is on the left-hand side at first but eventually crosses over and leads up to a shepherds' road hidden in a stand of mature oak trees that can be seen from the pass. When you reach the road, turn right and walk uphill, ignoring a downhill junction on the left. Your next destination is a point on the clifftop high above a large watercourse valley now to the northeast (you cannot see it from here).

At the top of the hill the road crosses a level meadow with a shepherds' hut in the near left-hand corner. Continue through to the next open valley, which is much larger. Walk halfway along this, and then bear left to climb the north side of it. This is a hill in the centre of the valley; there are one or two old stone huts on it. Make your way over it and cross the next small valley on the other side. Climb its northern rim on a path that leads up to a roofless *koumi* hut and sheepfold. A clear footpath with flat stones here and there leads northeast from the *koumi* to the crags above the large watercourse valley. The main landmark to be seen, in the extensive view across the foothills, is a 'house' (refuge) which is in sight far below on the other side, along with a road to it. ▸

The short route down through the crag is easy, even for sheep, although you have to 'put hand to rock'. You are aiming for a small path that goes down the centre of a wide spur which is now directly below you. When the spur levels out, bear right on sheep paths that lead down to **Tria Yortho** spring, in the ravine of the riverbed. This is the easiest way, but if you prefer just keep straight down the spur to the riverbed. It is steep, but there are no crags.

From the spring, reverse Walk P1.

Notes The house and road are not marked on maps even though they are not new; and some maps show a road to Zoniana in the bed of the watercourse. Its correct position (not reached from here) is presumably as marked on the Anavasi map.

WALK P15
Nida to Ay. Ioannis Chapel (and on to Zaros via Rouvas Gorge) on E4 Trail

Walk P3 in reverse

Grade	D
Start	Nida taverna 1420m (4658ft)
Access	By road from Anoyeia or via Walks P3, P5, P8
Finish	Ay. Ioannis chapel 950m (3116ft)
Access to finish	Fom Zaros via the Rouvas Gorge (Walk P2) or by road from Gergeri
Height loss	Nida to Ay. Ioannis 470m (1541ft); Ay. Ioannis to Zaros 600m (1968ft)
Approx distance	12km (7.5 miles); Ay Ioannis to Zaros 7.5km (4.7 miles)
Time allowance	Nida to Ay. Ioannis 6hrs 45mins; Ay Ioannis to Zaros 3hrs 30mins; total: 10hrs 15mins

For trekkers who are in no hurry to leave the mountains this challenging section of the E4 Trail, which leads down to the Rouvas Gorge (for Zaros) could be the best route southwards, since at different levels it takes in a wide variety of scenery and vegetation. It is not an entirely easy walk because one quarter of it (as a shepherds' route, not a mule track) traverses the very steep oak-forested mountainside above the Rouvas Valley. As ever, although the path is fairly well waymarked, it would not be easy to follow in poor visibility.

The E4 Trail eastwards leaves the Nida Plain at a point 160°SE from the *taverna*. From the car park follow the shepherds' road (south) along the edge of the plain, for about 20mins. Turn left (east) at a T-junction (E4 waymark on a rock). Follow this road across a level area with thickets of thorny burnet for about 2km, and then over a small pass in amongst very rugged rocks and crags. The road (under construction 2005) descends to a small flat plain, and valley, called **Arulokampos**. Cross this meadow. An E4 pole marks the spot where the trail bears right (south), climbing to a low pass marked by another E4 pole. The Amoudara Valley, a

2km-long 'hidden' valley in the mountainous region south of Piperos and Mavro Koumas peaks is now in front of you.

The road under construction may now serve the whole valley in which case you could just follow the road. Otherwise (preferably) follow the path down the centre of the valley, generally about 100°E, looking carefully for E4 waymarks on rocks. (If you have not seen one for a minute or two, retrace your steps and look again.) There are various sheep trails, but presumably the E4 takes the most direct route through the various rocky outcrops that are a feature of the valley floor. Sparse maple and cypress tree woodland provides shade in places. An E4 pole on a small round rock marks the main landmark – a huge vertical cave, or pothole (no shelter) in an adjacent east-facing crag. Shortly after this, a final low pass brings you to a large flat area, which marks the end of the valley. Cross this in the direction 80°E towards woodland and a V-shape on the skyline.

Beyond the woodland, a long 'corridor' brings you to the top of a rocky gully. The steep and more difficult section

The Rouvas forest and Ay. Ioannis from Duo Prinoi chapel

319

of the route starts here. Waymarks in the gully direct you around thickets of spiny burnet and over large boulders down to a level about 50m (164ft) below the valley. Shady woodland takes over here, and the gully levels out a little before plunging vertically down to the valley floor of the Rouvas forest. As you approach this point look carefully, right, for waymarks and a 'turn the corner' arrow that directs you up and out of the gully towards the start of a traverse of the forested mountainside.

After climbing out of the gully, note the huge cliff that is now seen just below. The cliff is the massive obstacle that necessitates the traverse, but the route is also aiming for Duo Prinoi spur, from where the path down to Ay. Ioannis chapel is easy. Note that Duo Prinoi, a shepherds' workstation, also has a chapel, and this can be seen in the distance as you make your descent.

Directly above the big cliff, the first 'hand to rock' short section is encountered. Since – for those with backpacks – it is rather exposed, note the alternative route around it: retreat a few metres, and then climb above it to re-join the trail by that means. There follows another mildly tricky section across a crag before you reach a forested saddle. Here the path becomes 'normal' again and there are frequent way-marks. This is necessary because the next stage, down a very steep forested spur, needs to be tackled carefully if you are to find the correct route down and, later on, avoid overshooting an essential path T-junction. If you miss seeing a waymark for more than a minute or so, retrace your steps and check again.

During the months when sheep are grazing in this area, flocks pass up and down this forested mountainside. Consequently, the steep path you are on (which may be a sheep route right down to the valley floor) can look more used than the E4 Trail that is found at the T-junction of paths. Keep a careful look out for this junction since it appears to have no warning waymarks. It bears right as a traversing path heading (in the forest) towards a big long cliff, or crag, and a waymark is seen just a short distance along it.

In places, this path needs care because the steep hill-side is carpeted with dead oak leaves that are slippery underfoot, and there are one or two places where the rocky outcrops are not conveniently placed to provide hand-holds. However, after negotiating a final descending crag,

E4 Trail: on the steep path down to Duo Prinoi

the footpath becomes easy again and then it is just a matter of walking down through the forest to the **Duo Prinoi spur** 1155m (3790ft) with its concrete water tank, shepherds' huts, chapel, and access road which connects to the main road by the Vrondisi monastery.

From the chapel enclosure fence the red roof of Ay. Ioannis can be seen just above the trees, 130°SE, in the valley below. In 2005 a pan-Cretan mountain-biking course passed through here linking the Ay. Ioannis and Vrondisi monastery roads. Their route is waymarked with red dots down to Ay. Ioannis (and beyond), but the E4 Trail takes a slightly different route.

Pass through a gate below the chapel enclosure and continue down the spine of the spur, which bears a little to the left. As you approach the next level, note on the left-hand side of the ridge the rare sight of a beautiful lone spurge olive tree (its leaves point upwards to conserve moisture). You have a choice here:

(a) The biking route continues down the main spur to join a car track. If you choose that route, turn right when you reach the track and follow the red dots as they lead you over a small saddle and down to the streambed near Ay. Ioannis, where you turn left to find the path up to the picnic area and chapel.

(b) The E4 Trail is routed down a wooded branch spur now on your right, since that is the most direct route to Ay. Ioannis. It is easiest, when you reach the car track, to also turn right and follow the biking route.

For Zaros via the Rouvas Gorge follow the streambed downhill, reversing Walk P2.

The E4 route to the riverbed is not easy to follow just here. It leads to a crag and therefore finishes with a minor rock scramble – that is, if you can find the right place. For the E4 Trail eastwards follow the road uphill from **Ay. Ioannis chapel**. ◄

Note The Rouvas Gorge streambed, or watercourse, includes a ravine section just north of the Ay. Ioannis area, passable as a walking route to the flat-floored valley of the Rouvas forest (as is the car track you have just encountered). On the northwest side of the valley a sheep trail in the forest leads up to a 'shelf' in the mountainside from where a footpath (or perhaps lately a road) heads for the Skinakas road via a spring and a shepherds' hut. This is a different path from the sheep trail you have seen going straight down through the forest (and disappearing from view) on the E4 Trail traverse.

WALK P16
Nida to Kamares via Kamares Cave

Walks P5 and P4 in reverse

Grade	D
Start	Nida taverna 1420m (4658ft)
Access	By road from Anoyeia or via Walks P1, P3, P8
Finish	Kamares 600m (1908ft); via Kamares cave 1524m (5000ft)
Access to finish	KTEL bus from Zaros or Heraklion or taxi from Mires
Height loss	Undulating route: 1580m (5177ft)
Approx distance	6.5km (4 miles) to cave; 5km (3.1 miles) cave to Kamares; total: 11.5km (7.1 miles)
Time allowance	Nida to cave 2hrs 30mins; cave to Kamares 2hrs 30mins; total: 5hrs

Although contour maps (which do not mark cliffs and crags) lead you to suppose this could be an easy way down off the mountain from the Nida Plain, this is not really so. The path is waymarked, but the first section is slow going because it is very rocky. After losing height to contour around the main spur, the path has to regain about 100m (328ft) in height, through forest, in order to pass over another spur (holding the Kamares cave). There follows a long, knee-taxing descent to Kamares. It is a fine route offering stupendous views, but it should be tackled as a project day-walk rather than as a quick escape. The only quick escape is a lift down to Anoyeia.

Note Should the shepherds' road from Voriza join up with the road that ends at the south end of the Nida Plain, then that route will become a very long – but easy – road-tramp off the mountain. At present shepherds say they use a 'one-hour' footpath (not walked by author) between the two road-ends. Since the relevant spur or ravine is very steep, it would be best to accompany a shepherd on his way down. Shepherds may use trail bikes to get to work, in which case there would be no ongoing lift at the roadhead.

Follow the shepherds' road south from the **_taverna_**, past the T-junction (E4 Trail) and on to where it cuts through a bank of red earth. From this point, on the right, cairns and faint blue waymarks mark the start of the path (the route is marked with faint blue and newer red dots) which becomes a traverse, high above a steep ravine, towards a descending spur. The road continues on for another 500m but there it ends. Some maps erroneously mark it on the west side of the ravine. The path first heads for **Koutsounares** spring and shepherds' complex of old stone huts.

From there reverse Walks P5 and P4 bearing in mind that, after contouring around the next spur, you must regain about 100m (328ft) in height to get over the spur of the **Kamares cave**.

WALK P17

Nida Taverna to the Arcadi Monastery

Walks P7 and P8 in reverse

Grade	D
Start	Nida taverna car park 1420m (4658ft)
Access	By road from Anoyeia or via Walks P1, P3, P5
Finish	Arcadi monastery 480m (1574ft)
Access to finish	Daily KTEL buses to Rethymnon: first bus 07.10 (from Karvoussi) stops on main road below monastery forecourt; Rethymnon taxi tel: 29310.25000
Height gain	300m (984ft)
Height loss	1220m (4002ft)
Approx distance	27km (16.8 miles)
Time allowance	Nida car park to ski centre 1560m (5118ft) 1hr 15mins; ski centre to Vitsinela pass 1720m (5643ft) 1hr 15mins; Vitsinela pass to old cistern/summit path junction 1580m (5184ft) 1hr 30mins; to Kampos Tigani (for Ay. Konstantinos) 1hr 30mins; Ay. Konstantinos to Aravanes spring 1hr 30mins; spring to Aravanes Kampos and Arcadi monastery 3hrs 10mins; total: 10hrs 10mins

For further information on this route see Walks P7 and P8. It may be easier to walk in the uphill direction because the footpath sections are very rocky and you have to go carefully. Trekking poles are definitely recommended! However, whatever the drawbacks, it is a challenging route that suits those who like being right off the tourist trail. It offers a long, gradual descent off the mountain and ends at the Arcadi monastery, one of Crete's principal treasures and an interesting place to visit. The monastery has a beautiful setting some distance from any village and if you would prefer to avoid an overnight stay in Rethymnon, pleasant camp spots can be found on the road leading up to a large Byzantine-style chapel on a nearby hill.

Follow Walk P12 from the **Nida** car park, taking the road up to the Ideon Andron cave as far as the stone-built chapel.

Walk around to the back of the nearby goats'-pen enclosure to pick up a footpath heading northwards, across the hillside above the main road (there are several sheep paths here). This traverse brings you to the road-end of a vehicular track that branches off the main road, seen below. Take the narrow disused overgrown track that continues the traverse from the road-end; there is a concrete cistern halfway along it. The track evolves as a footpath that leads up to the ski centre, a ruined building in a hollow at the foot of a steep slope. Over time, the slope may have funnelled gale-force winter winds down to wreck the doors and windows of the building, which is now used as a storm shelter for sheep. There is no water supply. Since the mountainside above the Nida main road is blanketed with thorn thickets, this footpath route from the chapel is the easiest way of getting to it (unless you get a lift up the ski-centre road).

Continue by following a track uphill alongside the broken ski-lift. Once above the crag which shelters the building, this road doubles back. There are two more ruined concrete pillboxes here. Turn left off the road – a red arrow directs you along a dirt track heading west. A shepherds' road (from Zoniana) is now in view, heading up to the pass (290°NW) between Kourouna and the summit ridge.

The dirt track joins this road beside a big grey rock. Walk up to the pass, where there is a large concrete cistern, a shepherds' hut and a water trough. Continue to the end of the road, passing another newly built cistern. The road ends at a small flat-floored plain, or doline, where there is a breeze-block hut (shelter) on the far side of a large sinkhole. The sinkhole, which has perpendicular mud walls, is gradually 'swallowing' the mud floor of the little plain.

Rough going on the descent to the 'old cistern' (May)

This interesting sight can also be accessed as a 4hr round walk from the Nida car park, mostly on unmade roads.

The route now continues as a footpath, which bears to the left side of the valley. It takes more than 1hr to get down to the next road-end and old cistern 1580m (5184ft) in about 2km: tackle this descent with patience. The next road, when you reach it, provides temporary respite. Keep straight on down the valley by bearing left after you pass a right-hand junction. The next road-end is marked by an old stone sheepfold and a white metal signboard. This is just beyond a large new concrete cistern.

The path now crosses an area of grey rocks and hollows before reaching more normal terrain. It bears to the left on a traverse down to a thicket of thorny burnet. Continue left, along the edge of this, to reach a small rocky hollow. Climb across this, and continue (patiently) down to **Kampos Tigani**, now in sight far below. First maple trees appear as you lose height. As soon as you have the opportunity, cross to the other side of the valley to join a road. Keep northwest across the *kampos,* and over the next low pass for Halastra (**Ay. Konstantinos chapel**) with its water troughs and seepage wells.

From **Halastra** the path continues down the right-hand side of the valley, which has now become narrow so that once you have climbed to the next pass it is easier to keep to the centre. Make your way down the (dry) watercourse. Oak forest provides welcome shade. As you lose height and the great whaleback ridge nears its end several paths lead up to the left, out of the valley, but keep straight on. The correct trail descends to approx 1070m (3511ft) and this also leads to the left, over a rock and down to the spring. The spring emerges from a crag and there are concrete troughs. **Aravanes Kampos** 940m (3084ft) is a fairly large flat valley, or grazing area, to the west of this watercourse. Even if you missed the right 'exit' path, by keeping west over difficult oak-forested terrain you would arrive at the *kampos.*
From there reverse the notes of Walk 7.

Avasami spring in May – trough and camp spot in the foreground – from the hillside above the path (Walk L5a)

PART 3 THE LASSITHI MOUNTAINS

This large, almost square-shaped, mountain range of eastern Crete lies south of the main road between Heraklion, Hersonissos and Ay. Nikolaos. The Lassithi Plain (also called 'plateau') is well known. It is not only the largest of the high mountain plains but also the largest flat area in Crete. About 820m (2690ft) in altitude, it is oval in shape, more than 9km across west–east, and 5km north–south. Since parts are very fertile; with a reliable water-table about 3m below ground, up to the 1980s Lassithi was irrigated in summer by means of hundreds of 1920s American-style white-sailed windmill water pumps, which replaced 'medieval' dipping wells. In turn the windmills have been dropped for easily maintained diesel-fuel pumps that are more practical for somewhere that has suffered acute depopulation. However, the traditional business of the plateau partly sustains, and the older generation at least can be seen proudly loading big transport trucks with their fine produce of potatoes, carrots and other vegetables, and fruits such as apples and pears.

At the far western end of the plain there is a sinkhole called the Khonos. A meandering river heads for this, draining snowmelt from the plain and surrounding mountains. In itself it extends from the river of another plain, the Katheros, east of Lassithi and linked to it by the short but rugged Havgas Gorge. During the Venetian occupation when Lassithi was turned over to intensive wheat growing, engineers constructed a grid of drainage ditches at the western end because the Khonos sinkhole did not drain the fields fast enough. The plain still floods at times even though rainfall is much lower nowadays. The meandering river and the ditches still remain so that (even apart from fenced enclosures) walkers cannot take a simple short cut straight across; a route has to be planned using the service tracks. A main rim road linking all the villages circles the plain.

There are several Neolithic and Bronze Age archaeological sites in the Lassithi mountains. One of the most important is the Diktean cave above Psychro ('P'see-crow') on the south side of the plateau. In mythology this cave was the birthplace of Zeus, whilst the Ideon Andron cave, on Mount Ida, was where the infant Zeus was hidden. More certain is that these caves were sacred places of pilgrimage. Votive offerings, such as the clay figurines left in the Diktean cave – and over millennia enveloped by stalactites – are of particular interest. These, and other precious finds, are kept in the Archaeological Museum of Heraklion.

Lassithi is a day-tour destination from the north-coast holiday resorts. In the tourist season the roads are busy with a great number of package tour buses heading for the cave. They may stop briefly at restaurants and shops so that Lassithi saleswomen have learned to be quick, and can seem alarmingly thick-skinned. However, do not be entirely misled; stay a good deal longer than 15mins, be seen to enjoy the area with all its walking potential, and they will respond in kind.

Sheep and goats are kept, and Lassithi shepherds have always practised transhumance, taking their animals

The Lassithi Plain, showing Ay. Georgios with Tzermiado in the distance

down to the lowlands by December. Nowadays, many other residents depart for the coast during the four winter months. Amongst those who remain a strong sense of community is noticeable, contrasting sharply with the tourist trade activities of the summer.

A series of peaks more or less rims the plateau. The two highest are on the south side: Mt Dikti 2148m (7047ft) with Lasaros along the same ridge, and Afendis Christos 2141m (7024ft). Other peaks are: to the west, Afendis 1578m (5177ft), with communications masts on its summit; to the north, Selena 1599m (5247ft), and to the east, Varsami and Katharo Tsivi 1664m (5459ft). Note that cell phones may work on the mountainsides facing the plateau but not, for example, on the remote south side of Mt Dikti.

In between these various high spots are eight passes each of which, in historical times, could be defended against intruders. Lassithi was always a place of refuge, or resistance to authority, causing its inhabitants to suffer from sporadic campaigns of destruction. After the failed 1866 Revolution against the Turks, when many insurgents retreated to Lassithi, the Turkish army successfully invaded on 21 May 1867 through 'an unguarded pass over Mt Afendis'. During World War II partisans and British intelligence agents found shelter on Katharo Tsivi and Selena, high above the Potamos Valley (a reliable water source would have been the first requirement of a hideout). They received supply drops from the Allied HQ in Cairo at Limnakarou and the Katheros Plain.

An attractive feature is the forest cover of evergreen oaks that, in places, grows up to 1500m (4921ft). Shepherds rely more on springs and seepage wells (where these can be made) than rainwater-collecting cisterns. Information from Papa Christoforos (retired) of Ay. Georgios, a keen member of the EOS, is that there are several springs in these mountains, including some at very high altitude. On contour maps, a ruined stone hut shown in rather notional fashion, or when seen near the trail, could indicate the proximity of a spring. Even so, a passer-by might not find it so easily – watching where birds are going sometimes helps. (A permanent spring is called a 'pee-YEE' in Greek.)

Walkers could find numerous paths in the mountains surrounding the plain except that, as it is so large, getting to trailheads is very time-consuming without a car. The EOS, when choosing paths and a route for the E4 Trail, had several elements to consider including the challenging, but fairly popular, ascent of Mt Dikti. Wherever possible, waymarked routes include sections of mule tracks that have escaped the road-making programme.

Since the E4 Trail passes through Ay. Georgios walkers based there are probably in the best position. However, Tzermiado is the largest village. As well as accommodation and restaurants it has banks, a police station and pharmacy. A main rim road links all the villages and, apart from local taxis (often busy) there is a year-round KTEL bus service two or three times daily depending on the season (weekends vary) from Heraklion, and Ay. Nikolaos, with the terminus at the tourist pavilion near the Dikteon cave. The Katheros Plain, which is higher in altitude, is not inhabited year-round and has no bus service. However, there is a surfaced road (17km) from Kritsa, and from springtime one or two of the three *kafeneia* in the hamlet of Avdeliakos should be open for refreshments and light meals.

ROUTE SUGGESTIONS

- For strong walkers, the two-day trek between Kritsa and Lassithi taking in the Katheros Plain, Selakano and the E4 Trail offers such variety that it could be called 'the best of Lassithi'. Those equipped to camp can take it in easier stages. Unusually for a high mountain route, there are *tavernas* at two points along the way, and simple overnight accommodation can usually be found (bring your sheet liner at least). This route has its points whether you start at Lassithi or at Kritsa; since Kritsa is so easily reached from Heraklion starting from there could save time. Alternatively, starting from Lassithi allows you to leave your main luggage at Ay. Georgios and walk the route as a circuit.
- From Lassithi consider following the E4 Trail down to Kastamonitsa, from where buses to Heraklion pass Knossos archaeological site.

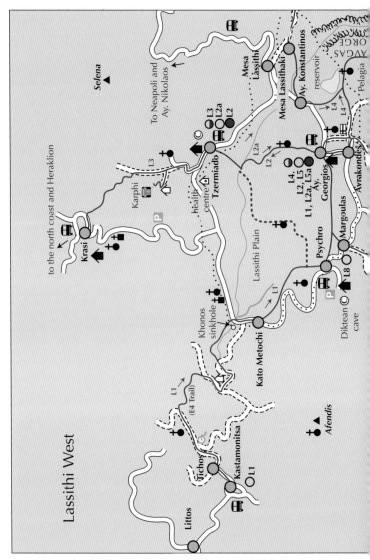

Lassithi West

Selena

To Neapoli and
Ay. Nikolaos

Mesa
Lassithi

Mesa Lassithaki

Ay. Konstantinos

AVGAS
GORGE

reservoir

Pelagia

L3 L2a L2

L3

Tzermiado

health
centre

Karphi

to the north coast and Heraklion

Krasi

L4.
L2, L5, L5a
Ay.
Georgios
L1, L1, L2a, L5a

L2a

L2

Avrakondes

Margoulas

Psychro

L8

Diktean
cave

Lassithi Plain

L1

Khonos
sinkhole

Kato Metochi

L1

(E4 Trail)

Tichos

Kastamonitsa

L1

Afendis

Littos

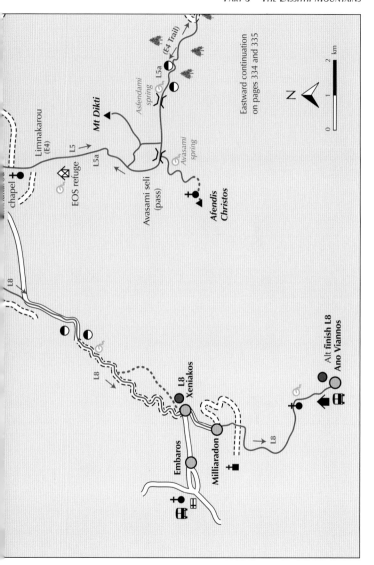

(E4 Trail)

L5a

Asfendami spring

Limnakarou (E4)

L5

Mt Dikti

L5a

EOS refuge

chapel

Avasami spring

Avasami seli (pass)

Afendis Christos

Eastward continuation on pages 334 and 335

N

0   1   2 km

L8

L8

Embaros

L8
Xeniakos

Milliaradon

L8

Alt finish L8
Ano Viannos

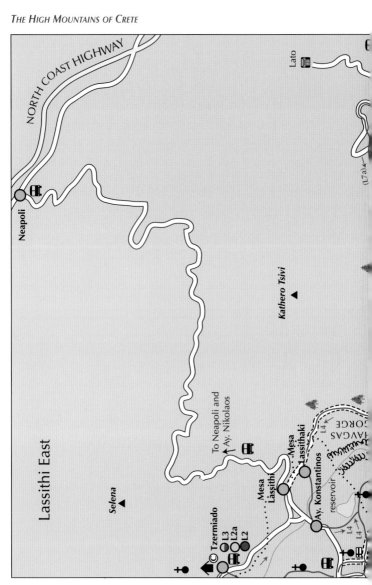

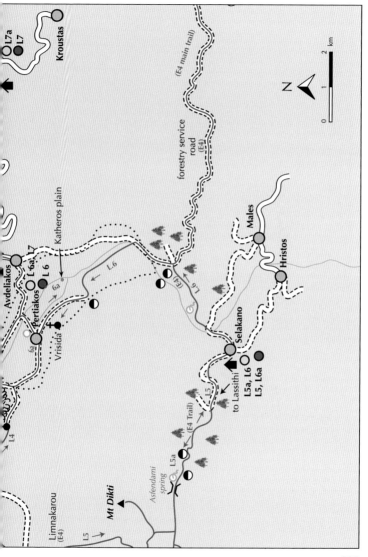

335

WALK L1

Kastamonitsa to Ay. Georgios (E4 Trail)

Grade	B
Start	Kastamonitsa 480m (1574ft)
Access	KTEL bus from Heraklion via Kastelli
Finish	Ay. Georgios, Lassithi 820m (2690ft)
Access to finish	KTEL bus to/from Heraklion or Ay. Nikolaos; local taxi tel: 28440.31523
Highest point	1000m (3280ft)
Height gain	520m (1706ft)
Height loss	180m (590ft)
Approx distance	14km (8.7 miles)
Time allowance	Kastamonitsa to plateau rim 1000m (3280ft) 3hrs 15mins; to Ay. Georgios 2hrs 15mins; total: 5hrs 30mins

Walkers, or backpackers travelling light, who want to start purist-style by climbing to the Lassithi Plain on foot, can approach from the west on the E4 Trail via the lowest of the eight mountain passes. This follows part of an impressively well-built Venetian *kalderimi*, or old road, which climbs the mountainside not far from Kastamonitsa. This is not a particularly demanding climb and there are fine views across the sparsely populated hill country to the west. As you reach the pass, first glimpses of the plain, with the great cliffs of Mt Dikti beyond, are quite memorable. On the final section to Ay. Georgios you are introduced to the plain and its activities as the E4 is routed on tracks beside the fields.

If you want to return to Heraklion the same day check the bus timetable since the last bus from Lassithi to Heraklion may depart from Psychro at 16.45. Note also that the area around Kastelli is the site of the new Heraklion airport, planned to open about 2010. A new road to it is under construction (2006). Access to Kastamonitsa will therefore change and so, most certainly, will the view as you climb the old trail.

Check timetables at the main bus station in Heraklion before taking the Kastelli bus for the ongoing connection to Kastamonitsa ('Kasta-mon-eet-sa'). The bus is likely to depart at 09.00 and pass through Knossos village at 09.15. This could be useful if, alternatively, you have visited Knossos site before tour buses arrive (highly recommended); the site opens at 8am. The Knossos bus stop serves both KTEL and the town bus service; for the town bus buy tickets at the nearby kiosk.

At Kastelli – Kastelli Perdiadon ('Per-the-ar-thon') is its full name, since there are other places called Kastelli in Crete – the bus to Kastamonitsa will be waiting and anyone will direct you to it. Alight at a T-junction where a well-constructed bus shelter advertises the village's proximity to the E4 Trail and the remains of a big Roman wall at the hamlet of Toichos.

Walk straight through the village keeping east-northeast, ignoring a junction beside a corner *kafeneon*. Note blue-painted arrows and dots in places. These indicate a pilgrimage route – along the same route as the E4. The E4 Trail here is poorly marked, even though it was well announced at the bus shelter.

The road gains height at a bend. About 500m after leaving the village arrive at a pass 500m (1640ft). A chapel marks a remaining piece of the old Roman wall. The surfaced road continues left to **Toichos** ('Tee-hoss') hamlet, where a long section of the wall can (as you gain height) later be seen from across the valley. The Venetian *kalderimi* taken by the E4 can now be seen in the distance zigzagging up the hillside. To get to the foot of this trail you must now lose height on dirt tracks. Keep straight on downhill. At the first Y-junction, beside a concrete shed, note an E4 tin flag on a short pole; also blue arrows pointing downwards are seen on the shed. A shepherds' access road climbs in long loops from the shed, but do not take this road – bear left downhill as far as another junction where there is a small spring with a stone bowl marked '1933' (the last drinking water until you get to habitations on the plateau). Keep right, along this track, to arrive at a stone-built chapel, **Ay. Georgios** 540m (1772ft), which has a canopy and picnic table (water taps may be turned off).

You now have a choice of routes:

For the E4 Trail official route, keep straight on.

However an old mule track also joins the E4 *kalderimi* after having tackled the first part of the ascent more gradually. To find it, note a short uphill slip road just before the chapel. A few metres up this, on the left, a stony track runs parallel to the road for a short distance before turning uphill beside a fence. This old trail is used by shepherds and is not

E4 Trail: on the Venetian 'old road' above Kastamonitsa

too overgrown. There are a couple of 'gates' to open and close but otherwise, after passing through oak forest, you soon reach a steep gully. There are no waymarks but the zig-zags can be seen. The trail gains a little height before crossing to the other side of the gully where, rounding a crag, it joins the well-built *kalderimi* at a spot marked with an E4 pole at 640m (2100ft).

The ascent now continues on the *kalderimi*, with its impressive paving and retaining wall, until the hillside levels out and the route becomes much less well defined but still easy to follow as a footpath. When you reach the top – a pass on the mountainous rim of the plateau – large boulders from a newly built service road block the passage of the old road. The new road is fenced. A roofed modern picnic/viewpoint/storm shelter features above it. Clamber over the boulders, keeping to the old road since, as it ends (over on the right) there is a wire 'gate' in the fence, which brings you to a crossroads of modern tracks. ◄

Blue waymarks mark the pilgrimage route to the chapel of St George Honos, downhill towards the plateau.

The uphill track leads, after 2km, to a footpath for the summit of **Asfendis** (which is also reached by road from Plati). Down below, part of Lassithi can now be seen, with the long line of cliffs on the northwest-facing slopes of Mt

Dikti in the distance. If you have been studying available contour maps, which do not show any rugged features, this may be your first sight of what truly to expect from these mountains.

Walk down the road from the pass for a short distance, looking out for a red arrow waymark on the left. This directs you back onto what is left of the old road, which can be followed as a pleasant short cut down the centre of the valley. Although the E4 is mapped as reaching the plain by this means, at a junction with the main rim road, a newer version shown on an information panel appears to use an old trail that goes to Kato Metochi more directly. (Perhaps it is found if you continue down the road from the pass.) At the road junction note the bridge over the riverbed; Khonos, the sinkhole of the plateau is near here. Tramp the road for 1km to **Kato Metochi**, where there are two minimally stocked *kafeneia*. (The afternoon bus does not reach this small village.) The dirt track of the E4 Trail short cut between Kato Metochi and Psychro is easy to find on the left as you walk through the village.

Psychro does a busy short-stay tourist trade since it is sited under the hillside of the Diktean cave. There is an hotel, shops and restaurants. Keep straight on through the village to a Y-junction just beyond the last restaurants. The main rim road goes to Magoulis. However, bear left for the straight overland 3km short cut to Ay. Georgios. These two dirt tracks used by the E4 make pleasant enough walking. In the latter part of the year, abandoned fruit trees provide windfall apples and pears.

As you enter **Ay. Georgios** from the west, note the schoolhouse and the war memorial at a crossroads (the village main street and the Lassithi plateau rim road). The corner *kafeneon* on your left serves as the bus stop. During term time, as part of the KTEL timetable, a school bus passes here at 06.30am (enquire), useful for an early transfer to Heraklion. The main rim road skirts the north side of the village leaving the main street pleasantly free of heavy traffic. In, or near the main street, accommodation includes the Hotels Rhea and Maria's (tel: 28440.31453/69782.72905) and *Pension* Dias (tel: 28440.31207), which has four modest rooms and is open all year. After snow has cleared from Mt Dikti walking groups may fill all the accommodation at certain times, so it would be advisable to book in advance. Ay. Georgios also has two museums worth a visit, three groceries, and a large modern bakery which produces a variety of breads including a rough brown type ('hory-atty-kee') which, although heavy, lasts well for several days.

WALK L2

Ay. Georgios to Tzermiado

Grade	A
Start	Ay. Georgios, Lassithi 820m (2690ft)
Access	KTEL bus from Heraklion or Ay. Nikolaos
Finish	Tzermiado 820m (2690ft)
Access to finish	KTEL bus from Heraklion or Ay. Nikolaos
Approx distance	4km (2.5 miles)
Time allowance	1hr

Northeast of Ay. Georgios an isolated rocky hill rises 100m (328ft) above the surrounding fields. The main road skirts the east side of this hill, but on the west side a more direct overland track links Ay. Georgios with Tzermiado.

Starting at **Ay. Georgios** war memorial, walk north on the main road, following it as it curves around the outside of the village. Tzermiado is the largest of the villages that can be seen on the other side of the plateau. At a crossroads marked with a sign for Maria's Hotel, turn left (north) on a road that is surfaced as far as a chapel, cloister, garden and water tanks, at the foot of the rocky hill. Keep straight on – the road bears a little to the left at first. This track reaches **Tzermiado** main street just beside the Pankriti Bank (ATM). Look right to see two petrol stations and the Kourites Hotel (tel: 28440.22194) just down the road but turn left for the narrow, centre village crossroads that serves as the KTEL bus stop. Taverna Kronio, which does a deservedly busy trade in the tourist season, is also here. It is closed in winter but during those months at least one *psistaria* will be open.

WALK L2A
Tzermiado to Ay. Georgios

Walk L2 in reverse

Grade	A
Start	Tzermiado 820m (2690ft)
Access	KTEL bus from Heraklion or Ay. Nikolaos
Finish	Ay. Georgios, Lassithi 820m (2690ft)
Access to finish	KTEL bus from Heraklion or Ay. Nikolaos
Approx distance	4km (2.5 miles)
Time allowance	1hr

To cross the plain from Tzermiado to Ay. Georgios, walk southwest down the main street from the Taverna Kronio crossroads and bear right down a track just after the Pankriti bank. From here, reverse the notes of Walk L2.

WALK L3
Tzermiado to Karphi and back

Grade	B/C
Start/finish	Tzermiado 820m (2690ft)
Access	KTEL bus service from Heraklion or Ay. Nikolaos
Highest point	1100m (3608ft)
Height gain/loss	280m (918ft)
Approx distance	8km (5 miles)
Time allowance	3hrs 10mins (plus extra for exploring the site)

Karphi 1100m (3608ft) is the best known of several remote, high-mountain settlements built by Late Bronze Age peoples known as the Eteocretans – true Cretans – or 'the last of the Minoans'. The site was excavated in the 1930s by John Pendlebury, the Knossos-based archaeologist and World War II intelligence agent who lost his life during the 1941 Battle of Heraklion. A strong walker, his research of the ancient Minoan road network, before modern development, was unfortunately cut short.

341

Karphi archaeological site and 'the Nail' crag

Starting at the Kronio restaurant crossroads, in the centre of **Tzermiado**, walk around the next corner (or through a lane) to the village church. Continue northwest along the main road to where, just before the health centre building, a road junction is signed both for 'Karfi' and for **Timios Stavros**, a viewpoint and pilgrimage chapel on the **Nissamos Plain**, a flat grazing area about 80m (262ft) above Lassithi. The road is surfaced, and there are no short cuts on the way up (30mins). ◀

On the way down you have the choice of leaving this road at a bend and heading for the back streets of Tzermiado on a path that crosses the hillside high above the main road.

Follow the central track across Nissamos to a crossroads where a sign for Karphi directs you west. A purpose-built concrete picnic/sun/storm shelter can be seen at the foot of the path up to the site. The path traverses the spurge-covered slope of a wide gully as it climbs, passing a spring on the way up. When you arrive near the top, where there is a Y-junction of paths, bear 300°NW. The site at **Karphi**, which is not extensive, is on a slope sheltered to the northwest by a great pointed crag – (the) 'Nail' – which gives the place its modern name. Cliffs border the north-facing rim from where a footpath to Krasi can be seen crossing a scree slope on the mountainside below. It is easy to see why this place was such a good natural fortress (perhaps with a sentry stationed on top of the Nail) but they must have been a hardy lot to endure this draughty spot for a period of apparently 150 years.

Return by the same route.

To walk on to Krasi Return to the Nissamos Plain and climb to the pass on the north rim. At a Y-junction of paths near the top bear left for Krasi. The right-hand path is for a long descent, which includes lots of road-tramping, to Vrahasi on the main Malia–Ay. Nikolaos road.

WALK L4
Ay. Georgios to the Katheros Plain and back

Grade	B/C
Start/finish	Ay. Georgios, Lassithi 820m (2690ft)
Access	KTEL bus from Heraklion or Ay. Nikolaos
Highest point	1200m (3937ft)
Height gain/loss	Undulating route: 380m (1246ft)
Approx distance	17.5km (10.9 miles) for round walk
Time allowance	Ay. Georgios to Pelagia chapel 30mins; Pelagia to Stavros chapel 1hr 35mins; Stavros to Katheros (north side of plain) 1100m (3608ft) 30mins; Katheros to Mesa Lassithaki 2hrs; Mesa Lassithaki to Ay. Georgios 1hr 20mins; total: 6hrs
	Shorter walk: Ay. Georgios to Stavros chapel and return 3hrs 20mins

Geographically speaking Ay. Georgios is almost due west of the gorge that links Lassithi to the Katheros Plain; the gorge, although passable, is too narrow and rugged to take a mule track. Instead, mule tracks were built over the mountainous rim either side of it, one from Mesa Lassithaki and a less demanding one serving Ay. Konstantinos and Ay. Georgios.

The Katheros Plain belongs to the Kritsa community. Both a modern surfaced road and a *kalderimi* (Walk L7) link Kritsa to the plain via a pass above the hamlet of Avdeliakos ('Av-dell-yakos').

THE HIGH MOUNTAINS OF CRETE

In 2002 the first modern road link between the Lassithi and Katheros plains was opened, replacing much of the old Mesa Lassithaki (north side) mule track. Walkers based in Ay. Georgios (or Ay. Konstantinos) can walk to the Katharos Plain on the 03 footpath on the south side of the gorge and then, for a circular route, return to Lassithi on this new road and remaining sections of the mule track, easier to follow in the downhill direction.

The Katheros Plain looking east (May)

Walk east along **Ay. Georgios** main street and bear right at the main Y-junction, signed for the museums (uphill, beside a church). However, keep straight on, past the bakery, to arrive at a junction with a dirt track. Just uphill, on the right, is **Ay. Savvas chapel** and old cemetery: pause beside the cemetery wall to get your bearings.

Pelagia chapel is seen 100°E at the foot of the wooded mountainous rim. The modern village cemetery is on a low hill in the near distance. Mesa Lassithaki (Mesa Lassithi village is larger) is seen at 60°NE. The spot where the mule track from the north side of the gorge reaches the plain is just to the left of this village at 55°NE.

A dirt track, heading east (for Limnakarou), leaves from Ay. Savvas chapel. Follow this as far as a small roadside knoll with trees and big rocks – turn left here and keep straight on across a wide riverbed to join a track from Ay. Konstantinos.

A red-painted pole with an 03 flag marks this crossroads and directs you uphill to Pelagia chapel. What is left of the old mule track leaves from beside the chapel and zigzags up to the top of an oak-wooded gully to where there is an area of old terracing at 1130m (3707ft). Just before the terraces the path bears left for the climb up to a pass at 1200m (3937ft) which overlooks a valley bordered, on its north side, by the gorge. Across the valley, **Stavros chapel** is seen on the next spur at 105°E. The mule track contours around the head of this valley for about 1km to the next spur, and then loses a little height to join a dirt road (from the plain) that leads up to the chapel. The junction is marked with a red-painted pole. Pause here, or at the chapel (no water), to get your bearings; for a shorter walk turn around here and retrace your steps to Ay. Georgios.

In the usual way, the **Katheros Plain** 1100m (3608ft) is rimmed with mountains. It is long and narrow, about 7km long and 1km wide. Now above you to the right, to the southwest, the forbidding appearance of the upper slopes of the Dikti and Lazaros massif explains the absence of footpaths to the summit from this side. Across the valley, at 100°NE, the lower slopes of Mt Varsami form a pass, with Avdeliakos hamlet marking the road to Kritsa. The plain has a dirt-track rim road and one or two cross-tracks negotiate the riverbed and tributary streams. Hamlets and field houses are summer or weekend-only bases, mostly fenced off as a protection from goats. Apart from various mature trees around the edge of the plain there is not much shelter, and if no one is about it can be difficult to find water. A stream may be running at the south end of the plain.

You now have a choice of routes:
    For Kritsa (Walk L7) head for Avdeliakos via the south-side rim road.
    For Selakano (Walk L6a) also follow the south-side rim road.
    For a return to Lassithi (and your starting point) via the north side of the gorge Cross to Kopraki hamlet, 60°NE, by bearing left as you reach the plain from Stavros chapel. At

The overland track from Ay. Konstantinos to Pelagia chapel

Kopraki a modest dirt track (2004), informally signed (in Greek) for Lassithi, heads uphill, left. This is the new road. The broken-up old mule track offers a short cut or two as you gain height to reach a pleasantly level stretch of the road. This passes meadows here and there and Afendis, with its communications masts, is in sight to the west.

It follows that if you had a vehicle (with your extra water supply) and wanted to climb at least some distance up **Mt Varsami** you could nowadays approach it 'off piste" from this road. Companions would be needed because this is a remote, waterless place and the terrain, particularly of the southwest facing slopes of this mountain, involves crags and sinkholes. There are shepherds' workstations, but the footpath to these starts from Avdeliakos. The flanks of the Varsami–Kathero Tsivi massif (and Mt. Selena) are enormously steep, falling 1100m (3608ft) to the east-running valleys below.

The road winds its way past the meadows northwards to a pass 1240m (4068ft) on the steep mountainous rim of Lassithi between Kefala and Varsami. This is a tremendous viewpoint although it happens that your next destination, Mesa Lassithaki, about 300°NW, is hidden under a crag.

The road now bears right (northeast) for a long straight descent across the mountainside. After about 1km it turns a corner, heading away from the view of the plateau. At this point 1080m (4543ft) the hillside is not so steep and a wooded valley descends northwest. You can now take a short cut: follow the footpath (no waymarks) down the centre of this valley. The road, having taken a large loop, can be seen at the bottom. However, after the first part of the descent, the path bears to the left and evolves as a more definite old mule track. Ignore the road below and head for a saddle between the mountainside and another hill. Beyond the saddle the old trail bears right, and after losing more height through sparse woodland evolves as a footpath which heads straight for the road. Follow the road for a minute or two to reach a pass. A mess of newly cut roads spoils the view here.

However, on your left, note a blocked-off dirt track that leads straight downhill. This soon becomes recognisable as the continuation of the old mule track. It can be followed, with one or two interruptions, right down to a T-junction on the road between Mesa Lassithi and Mesa Lassithaki.

Once you are at **Ay. Konstantinos** it is only 2.5km to **Ay. Georgios** along the main road, but this is an unpleasant route because the road is busy and there is no sidewalk. Whether a bus or taxi would pass could be a matter of luck. There are two alternative routes, although both add 3km to this last part of the walk:

Either head for Mesa Lassithaki for an overland track towards the Havgas Gorge and then make your way west to Pelagia chapel;

Or head for Ay. Konstantinos on the track now directly in front of you. Walk through the village, but before leaving it bear left off the main road for the track that leads straight to Pelagia chapel – and the T-junction where you turn right for the return to **Ay. Georgios**.

WALK L5

*Ay. Georgios (for Mt Dikti Summit) to Selakano
(E4 Trail)*

Walk L5a in reverse

Grade	D
Start	Ay. Georgios, Lassithi 820m (2690ft)
Access	KTEL bus from Heraklion or Ay. Nikolaos
Finish	Selakano 930m (3051ft)
Access to finish	Taxi from Males or on foot from Katheros (Walk 6a)
Highest point	Avasami pass 1810m (5938ft)
Height gain	880m (2887ft)
Height loss	990m (3248ft)
Approx distance	17km (10.6 miles)
Time allowance	Ay. Georgios to Limnakarou 1200m (3937ft) 2hrs; Limnakrou to Avasami pass 1810m (5938ft) 2hrs 50mins; Avasami to Asfendami spring 1500m (4921ft) 1hr; Asfendami to Selakano 2hrs 30mins; total: 8hrs 20mins Round walk: Avasami to Mt Dikti summit 2148m (7047ft) 2hrs 30mins Round walk: Limnarkou to summit 8hrs

E4 Trail: Limnakarou and Mt Dikti

The huge mass of Mt. Dikti, combined with Lazaros, dominates both the Lassithi and Kathoros plains and – since this is the highest mountain of eastern Crete – attracts its fair share of 'summit baggers'. Only one place offers relatively easy paths to the summit, as the rest of the mountain is either extremely steep or rendered impassable by cliffs and scree slopes. The summit paths branch off from the E4 Trail, Lassithi to Selakano, which – once it is clear of the villages – is well way-marked. For those equipped to camp, it is possible – since there is a nearby spring – to make a base on Avasami pass, the high pass between Mts Dikti and Afendis Christos, before continuing on to Selakano.

Note Lazaros is 3km along the summit ridge. Although there is, or was, one steep path between Lazaros peak and Selakano village – a height difference of 1235m (4050ft) – it is the type of route that (without a guide) should only be tackled as an ascent so that an escape of returning down again (and getting water) always remains an option.

This is one of the more challenging sections of the E4 Trail because Avasami is a high-mountain pass remote from any roads. Beyond the pass there follows a long, rocky descent on an unfrequented mule track, some parts of which, however, pass through shady oak and pine forest. This brings you to Selakano ('Sell-ak-kan-oh'), the highest of several villages in the fertile pockets that are a feature of these south-facing mountains. Selakano has two *tavernas*, including the charming Stella's, which makes the most of its small terrace beside the church. Stella also keeps the key to the village 'guesthouse', converted from the former 1930s village office. Obviously very basic, it has four bunk beds; tel: 28420.91235 (via OTE landline – possibly not a mobile).

Although remote, Selakano has a beautiful setting and is not exactly 'undiscovered'. Although most visitors arrive by car, the E4 Trail clearly brings a few walkers. From Selakano you can follow the E4/03 footpath to the Katheros Plain, and then head back to Lassithi (or down to Kritsa). Alternatively if you would like to visit Selakano from Lassithi, rather than tackle the high-mountain route, you could follow Walk L6a across the Katheros Plain and reach it more easily from that direction.

Directly south of **Ay. Georgios a**nd Avrakondes there is a ridge, rising to 1220m (3937ft), which encloses the small fertile plain of **Limnakarou** ('Leem-nakka-roo'). There are service roads to Limnakarou and the least rugged option, from Ay. Georgios, is used by those heading for the trailhead by car. There is an EOS refuge sited near a spring on top of a spur about 400m (1312ft) above the plain. This may be a pleasant weekend retreat, but is not convenient to the main trail. Otherwise there is a very old Byzantine chapel (restored) called Panayia Limnakarou, various workstation houses or huts, but no wayside spring. (The traditional-style pump at the roadside would need priming and the spring is some distance across the plain to the east). For drinking water (take 2 litres per person for the next stage) you may have to ask at one of the huts since these have piped water.

The plain, dotted with almond, apple and pear trees, slopes gently downhill northwards. However, to the walker looking south, the most dominant feature beyond the orchards is a great gash in the mountainside where two snowmelt watercourses combine to form a wide riverbed filled with stones. The E4 Trail is routed up the spine of the spur that divides these two watercourses. Once the trail is clear of this feature the remainder of the route crosses, and then climbs the stony mountainside to reach a fairly level area at 1720m (5643ft). Here, the footpath to the summit branches off from the E4. This junction is not far from Avasami pass. The E4 Trail crosses Avasami and then heads east down to Selakano and beyond (Walk L6). E4 poles are supplemented with yellow paint waymarks on the rocks. Even so, it would not be easy to follow the trail in poor visibility.

Since there is road access as far as **Limnakarou**, walkers normally start and finish the summit round walk from there. If you do not have transport arrangements, start as early as possible, in the hope of being given a lift by someone who is working on the plain.

To walk to Limnakarou from Ay. Georgios Walk up to Avrakondes (on the rim-road KTEL bus route). For this, either follow the main rim road (signed for Psychro) from the schoolhouse crossroads, or find a short cut up to it via the road to the museums. Beyond the petrol station there is a development called Lasinthos Ecopark. Bear left onto a road below a hilltop modern housing complex. This joins a car track above Avrakondes – the road to Limnakarou. Keep uphill on this track. It leads to a white church, but before you get there turn uphill again on a short cut (blue arrow) to re-join the Limnakarou road which you can now see climbing the steep hillside of the ridge. Even if you plan to go only as far as Limnakarou, this mountain track to the ridge-top provides stupendous views across the Lassithi Plain. ◄

Note If you start this walk in Avrakondes (on the bus route) note a *kafeneon* on the left. The dirt track beside it, which leads uphill to the white church, is the E4 Trail: this essential turn-off has lost its waymark.

At the ridgetop you have a very different view of Mt Dikti. As seen from Lassithi, this huge mountain provides no clues as to how it is climbed. But at **Limnakarou**, once you know that the path goes up the watercourse, you at last have a bearing on how the route will evolve.

Follow the road down past the chapel and up to the last work hut. A footpath, heading due south up the centre of the riverbed, now takes over. The riverbed is hard going underfoot. The E4 is routed up the opposite bank – you are aiming for a spot that is marked with an E4 pole and lone mop-headed kermis oak. This E4 pole, and the path, connects along a straight sightline with the next pole, which is positioned on the spur – further up the valley – that divides the two watercourses. (You could have continued up the riverbed but the footpath on the bank is easier.) Make your way up to that pole. The path then climbs the spine of the spur before bearing right for a traverse and further ascent up to the skyline, at a spot marked with another E4 pole at approx 1560m (5118ft).

The next E4 pole in the distance (south-southwest), guides you along the path that now crosses a pleasantly undulating area, followed by a short ascent up to the

Mt Dikti from Avasami pass

another E4 pole at approx 1600m (5250ft). A more demanding climb follows, a rocky section that traverses the steep mountainside. An E4 pole, again seen on the skyline at 1670m (5479ft), is your next destination. When you reach the pole, turn east-southeast and cross a small hollow to reach the next pole. This marks the summit path turn-off.

For Dikti summit The path (not walked by author) to the summit (trig point), a further climb of nearly 500m (1640ft), takes an almost direct route up the south-facing flank of the mountain. Return down the same way. **Note** For those on their way to Selakano, there is a more convenient summit path beyond Avasami pass.

To continue the route The E4 now continues along a shallow valley, through thickets of spiny burnet, with the next E4 pole seen 185°SSW. Make your way along the valley and then turn uphill, 105°ESE, for a short distance to reach the area of the **Avasami pass**. As the ground starts to level out, note a crag on your right. Note also at this point two rocks with faded red lettering 'Afendis' (in Greek). The small path between the two rocks is the route to Afendis Christos summit chapel – and also to the spring, reached after a 15min climb. Over on your left there are three low shoulders, or hills. The walled enclosure on top of the central hill might make a good camp spot (for stupendous views), depending on conditions.

To find the spring Take the Afendis path, and after 1min or so climb up to the next level where a rock provides shade if you wish to leave your rucksack(s). The path now climbs the spur above you, bearing to the right just before the hillside gets steeper. A cairn (2007) made with a distinctive pointed rock marks the level of this turn-off. The path passes alongside a crag. Take about 100 paces around the crag to where you overlook a small 'bowl' in the mountainside, then look to your left to see the spring with its large concrete trough at approx 1830m (6004ft). Just below the path a flat place that would take one tent has been made free of stones. Depending on conditions this camp spot, which faces southwest, may be more sheltered than the pass. To the south, the rocky peak of Afendis Christos lies beyond a huge and steep re-entrant. The route to the summit (not walked by author) continues from here. Papa Christoforos (retired) of Ay. Georgios marked it with red dots some years ago.

To continue to Selakano Keep east for a minute or two to reach the top of the pass. The footpath now starts the descent, losing height to a point just above a small, wide gully. There is no E4 pole at this essential turning, but it is marked with cairns. ▸

Turn down the gully, 150°SSE. The path soon bears left, leading to the spine of a spur, and then zigzags down to a sloping, high-level valley. On the descent, note that the route crosses the southern flank of Mt Dikti. There is a pass in the distance at 105°E where a lone tree can be seen on the skyline. You are heading for that spot. Asfendami spring (which runs all year) is found just before you get to the pass.

The sloping valley at the foot of the spur includes a stony streambed draining from Mt Dikti. Keep to the left, and cross the valley towards a second, smaller streambed. There is a steep watercourse in the mountainside above it. Walk up beside the stream to **Asfendami** 1560m (5118ft) where there is a ruined stone hut. The watercourse is now seen to drain, also, to another streambed on the other side of this pass.

Note Just 1min directly downhill, behind a low line of rugged rocks, there is a goatherds' flat-roofed stone-built *mitato* (not disused). In the manner of the high mountains (that so far sustains) this hut is securely fastened, but not locked. Needless to say if a storm obliges you to seek out this shelter, take care to refasten the door and to leave the hut as you found it.

Continue from Asfendami by crossing the hillside towards the east bank of the stream. An E4 pole is seen above the bank. Around 5mins along this path brings you to the spring and water trough. After another 5mins arrive at the 'lone tree' pass that you first saw as you started down from Avasami. There is another stone-built goatherds' hut here. It is not locked (2007) which hopefully will sustain, given the remoteness of this spot.

The descent now continues more steeply. You are leaving the barren high mountains and the forested valley of Selakano is now in sight, although the village is still a long way down. Mt Thripti is seen in the distance at 95°E. An E4 pole marks the path from the hut – bear left and make your way downhill on zigzags before crossing to the edge of the oak forest and another pole. The path now takes up a gradual descent that ends at rocky spur at approx 1410m

Path to the summit
Turn uphill here, towards the summit (more or less in sight 40°NE) for the other 'easy' ascent route of Mt Dikti. The route has been marked with cairns, probably by members of the EOS.

Goatherds' hut near Asfendami spring (May)

(4626ft), the only relatively flat place you will see for some time on this descent. Turn sharp left down the side of the spur to reach an open hillside between two watercourses. A dirt road can be seen in the distance. Near the bottom of the spur the path continues to the left through mixed pine and oak forest at approx 1170m (3839ft). There are yellow paint waymarks and E4 enamelled tin 'flags' nailed to trees.

The path joins a dirt road at 1100m (3609ft) – the road-head of a forest track. Keep straight on, and after a few minutes arrive at a crossroads of tracks where there is a narrow steel service box, and further on, wooden signboards directing you either to Selakano or to Karas spring (distance 300m). Yellow waymarks mark a short-cut track. Continue downhill until you reach a gate. The E4 continues on a rocky short-cut path – this is waymarked just to the right of the gate. Alternatively if you prefer road-walking at this stage, continue through the gate and, after passing two concrete water tanks opposite one another, keep straight on, gaining a little height at the next bend. Bear right at the next downhill junction. Pass through a gate, and at the next junction keep right for the **Selakano** village. Stella's *taverna* is beside the church.

WALK L5A

Selakano to Ay. Georgios (E4 Trail)

Walk L5 in reverse	
Grade	D
Start	Selakano 930m (3051ft)
Access	Taxi from Males or on foot from Katheros (Walk 6a)
Finish	Ay. Georgios, Lassithi 820m (2690ft)
Access to finish	KTEL bus from Heraklion or Ay. Nikolaos
Height gain	880m (2887ft)
Height loss	990m (3248ft)
Approx distance	17km (10.6 miles)
Time allowance	8hrs 30mins

Leave from **Selakano** church, and take the only road out of the village, going west. This is an access road to the forested hillsides above the village. On the way up, cut off a loop by going through a gate across another track. When you re-join the road, keep left and continue to where there are two large concrete water tanks opposite one another on the left side of the road. Walk between these two tanks, and after a minute or so of keeping straight on, pass through a gate. You are now on the E4 Trail. ▶

Keep straight on – the route is waymarked. When you reach a forest road, stay on it as it climbs (there are short-cut options) to a crossroads where wooden signboards with black lettering direct you to the Kavas spring. Pass a roadside rusty steel service box and keep straight on, on a very wide level stretch of dirt road. This ends at an open area with a fenced enclosure and a ruined stone house, or hut. The wooded ravine of the great watercourse system descending from Asfendami is now in sight. The E4 Trail climbs to the right of this.

Just before the road ends, the trail continues as a foot-path, leaving from the left side of the road at 1160m (3806ft) and losing a little height before it enters the forest. When you next leave the trees, waymarks guide you up a steep spur between two watercourses. The route bears to the left near the top and ascends a crag. There is a relatively flat spot here and a fallen tree trunk to sit on 1410m (4626ft). The

Immediately to the left of the gate waymarks indicate a rocky footpath to/from the village.

355

Avasamai pass from Asfendami, October

next section, through forest again, is not so steep. The path climbs steadily until, as the trees thin out, a stone-built hut is seen on a high pass. Waymarks guide you up to this goatherds' hut. You have now left the treeline, and the Selakano Valley, because the pass forms the entrance to the barren high-mountain region between the two huge masses of Dikti and Asfendis Christos. **Asfendami spring**, which runs all year, is now just 5mins along the trail, on a pleasantly level section that continues from behind the hut. Take on water here because the only alternative spring is a 30min round trip from Avasami pass.

Beyond the spring an E4 pole marks the spot where you cross a streambed. (See Walk L5 for further notes on this area and another hut, which is nearby.) Cross a low pass beyond the streambed and follow another stream downhill. Waymarks now guide you to the foot of a spur and from here the path starts the climb to **Avasami pass**. If you need water, see Walk L5 for directions to the spring.

Otherwise reverse Walk L5 route notes – the path is waymarked with E4 poles, although it may not be long before winter storms have blasted off what remains of their yellow/black paint. The rocky footpath that traverses the mountainside as you leave this level area needs care, but otherwise the descent is easy enough underfoot until you get to the stony riverbed above **Limnakarou**. It is best to stay on the east bank, following the E4 recommended route, until you reach a last E4 pole and the mob-headed oak tree.

WALK L6

*Selakano to the Katheros Plain
(for Lassithi or Kritsa)*

Walk L6a in reverse	
Grade	B/C
Start	Selakano 930m (3051ft)
Access	From Lassithi and/or Katheros plains (Walks L5, L6a) or from Males
Finish	Katheros Plain 1100m (3608ft)
Access to finish	Via Pertiakos hamlet, main road down to Kritsa from Avdeliakos (suitable for taxis), or Walks L7, L4 to Lassithi
Height gain	To the Katheros Plain: 270m (885ft)
Approx distances	To Katheros (Avdeliakos) 10km (6.2 miles); to Lassithi (Ay. Georgios) 16km (10 miles)
Time allowance	To Katheros (Avdeliakos) 3hrs 30mins; to Lassithi 5hrs 15mins

The E4 Trail loses height around the south side of Mt Dikti. To get back on course – because it is designed to follow (more or less) the spine of Crete – it now follows an old path linking Selakano to the Katheros Plain. This unfrequented but pleasant footpath climbs the wooded hillside surrounding a large watercourse.

From **Selakano** church, take the village main road downhill northeast for a couple of minutes. You now overlook the next valley. At the head of the valley note the watercourses either side of Koureli peak. The E4 Trail/03 path climbs the hillside just to the right of the east, or main, watercourse.

Now turn left off the main road at the first junction. This

unsurfaced (2007) road contours around the hillside towards the head of the valley, passing through a hamlet). Follow the road around the head of the valley and cross the water-course. Ignore the gated track immediately after the water-course, but take the next uphill dirt road on the left, which is marked with a red dot. Red dot waymarks occur infrequently and there are no E4 waymarks (2007). The track serves one or two huts and some terracing.

At a Y-junction, keep right. This overgrown track leads to a point where, behind the terracing, the footpath is squeezed between a fenced enclosure and a small crag with a spring. Further on, a very faded E4 tin flag is nailed to a tree 970m (3183ft). This is not a well-tramped path and in places you have to look carefully for cairns and/or red dots. However, by keeping more or less in the same direction as you climb, you will be inevitably arrive at the unmade road that leads (east) to the Katheros Plain. Once you are on the road, which at this point passes through forest, you have the choice of either following it east on the E4 Trail to Prina and beyond, or north to the Katheros Plain, for ongoing routes to either Lassithi or Kritsa.

On the Katheros–Selakano path

For Katheros (and Lassithi) Turn left on the road, and after about 5mins arrive at the southern end of the plain, where undulating terrain surrounds a streambed. There are one or two shepherds' workstations here. You are still about 2km from the flat part of the plain. The road now gains height. However, walkers can take a short cut by following the 03 footpath route: just before the road starts to gain height note a fairly indistinct Y-junction of tracks. Bear left here, to cross a flat area. This track winds its way through the low hills and evolves as a path beside the streambed. When you get to a fenced enclosure, pass around this and walk up to a dirt road. This road serves the southwest side of the plain – keep straight on.

When you have a good view of the plain, pause on the road to get your bearings: identify Avdeliakos as the group of houses about halfway along the north side below the lowest part of the mountainous rim. (There are houses on a high knoll but that spot is southeast of Avdeliakos.) A dirt track crosses the plain from Pertiakos, a hamlet on the south side. Stavros chapel, perched on the southern side of the Havgas Gorge, is in sight at 320°NW and the 03 footpath to Lassithi (for Ay. Georgios or Ay. Konstantinos) passes near this chapel.

Note Avdeliakos is named Katharo on some maps.

The road now loses height and continues to the cross-roads at **Pertiakos** where there is a huge oak tree, an old cistern or well, and a *kafeneon* that is usually closed.

For Avdeliakos, Kopaki, and for Kritsa Turn right (north), following the road across the bridge over the riverbed. Turn left (west) on the north-side rim road for Kopaki (Walk L4) or turn right for Avdeliakos.

For Lassithi and Ay. Georgios Keep straight on, but as the road nears the end of the plain keep right at a junction for the road that leads up to **Stavros chapel**.
From there reverse Walk L4.

WALK L6A

Katheros Plain via Pertiakos to Selakano

Walk L6 in reverse	
Grade	B/C
Start	Katheros Plain 1100m (3608ft)
Access	Via Walks L4, L7a or by vehicle from Kritsa to Avdeliakos
Finish	Selakano 930m (3051ft)
Access to finish	Via Walks L5, L6a, or taxi from Males
Height loss	230m (754ft)
Approx distance	From Pertiakos 8km (5 miles)
Time allowance	2hrs 30mins

From the **Stavros chapel** road (Walk L4) keep straight on along the south-side rim road (03 route) to Pertiakos where a huge oak tree marks a crossroads of tracks. Left is for Avdeliakos via the bridge over the riverbed; right is for Vrisida – a few houses and an old chapel on the hillside above. Straight on is for the eastern end of the plain (and **Selakano**). ◄ Just before this road ends, walk downhill to a fenced enclosure beside the streambed. Pass around this and keep straight on, on the footpath beside the stream. This brings you to the north-side rim road. It has now turned south on its way out of the plain.

The unmade road makes pleasant walking as it continues east, gaining height as the flat part of the plain ends in low hills surrounding the riverbed, which has now become a streambed.

Follow this road for about 3mins, looking out for three red-painted arrows below the road, which mark the start of the footpath down to Selakano. This spot is just opposite an uphill dirt track on the left. From there, make your way down through the forest, looking carefully for cairns and faded red dots. In general the path bears to the left for an easier descent away from the steep watercourse. After leaving the treeline the path continues the descent alongside a spindly fence that encloses a disused workstation, old terracing and an open concrete cistern. ◄ When you reach the unmade road that contours around the head of the valley, turn right to cross the watercourse. Keep straight on past a few houses (ignore an uphill junction) for the main road up to **Selakano**.

There is a spring very near – the path crosses it.

WALK L7

Katheros Plain to Kritsa (for Ay. Nikolaos)

Walk L7a in reverse	
Grade	C
Start	Avdeliakos hamlet 1150m (3772ft)
Access	Via Walks L4, L6 (or by car from Kritsa)
Finish	Kritsa 400m (1640ft)
Access to finish	KTEL bus service from Ay. Nikolaos or taxi
Highest point	1240m (4068ft)
Height gain	90m (295ft)
Height loss	840m (2755ft)
Approx distance	10km (6.2 miles)
Time allowance	To rim of plain 1240m (4068ft) 35mins; to restored kalderimi 30mins; to Kritsa 2hrs 15mins; total: 3hrs 20mins

The width of some remaining sections of the 'old road' from the Katheros Plain to Kritsa suggests how busy it must once have been, with ample space for two mule trains to pass. Although the winding new road (17km) has replaced about 2km of the old trail at either end, most of it still makes an attractive walking route. There is shady oak forest above 900m (2953ft), whilst lower down there are wide open views of adjacent mountains and coast. The old trail is not all waymarked at present (2007) but the most well-preserved section of it, through the oak forest, has been repaired and developed by the Forestry Service for recreational use.

Avdeliakos has three *kafeneia*. At least one should be open as soon as the road from Kritsa is free of snow. Simple meals of home-grown produce are offered, and a room for overnight shelter might be available. Kritsa people working on the plain are generous with lifts down to their village, but otherwise there is no escape from tramping about 2km up the modern road to the top of the pass. If a lift is offered you could try asking to be taken just to the top of the pass, because you like walking and want to walk the old road ('pal-yo thromo'). However, thanks to the new road, not every driver will know where it starts and you may be discouraged from trying to find it. Alternatively you may be put off at the starting point of the repaired section now that this has been developed as an attraction.

The cistern on the 'old road' between Kritsa and the Katheros Plain

As you walk over the pass above **Avdeliakos** hamlet and approach the view down to the north, note that the modern road has been cut through solid rock in places, and includes parts of the old road. Pass a culvert as you walk downhill. On the right (2007) there is a small path heading downhill (south). Ignore this (unless it has lately – check – been developed as a connection to the repaired recreational route).

Above the road, on the right-hand side, look out for a section of old walled mule track (the old road). Note its passage to where it is again cut by the new road. This gives you a good indication of where to look (below the crash barrier) for the spot where you can get onto it. There is a permanent marker in the form of a rough concrete 'mess' of about 5m in length, poured down off the side of the road, outside the crash barrier. This feature marks the start of the trail. Also at this point the new road is seen making a very long loop around the steep hillside. The *kalderimi* route enables you to avoid this by taking a short cut down through the oak forest. When it re-joins the new road, you only have to walk downhill for a minute or two before you can get onto it once again. This is the 'reclaimed' section that, following an easy gradient, passes through oak forest and across open *phrygana-*

covered hillsides. The only two water sources on the whole trail are on this section. When it ends (at a shrine) the route continues on/off the main road until, directly above the village, there is no escape from a downhill road-tramp of about 2km.

Below the poured concrete the hillside is very steep, but with care you can make your way down to the forest floor by negotiating what is left of the zigzags of the old mule track. Spoil from the new road has battered this section, but it is not long. Next, follow what is left of the old trail (where there are cairns) as it passes down through the forest. It soon joins the main road where you turn downhill towards a right-hand bend. Just beyond the bend note the continuation of the old road on your left. This is the reclaimed section and the spot is signposted.

Both old and new roads now follow a wide spur almost all the way down to Kritsa. There is a deep ravine on your left. A long straight section of old road, 3m or 4m wide, continues down through the oak forest on an easy gradient until, after passing a house up on the right, it turns sharp left to zigzag down a gully. The gully becomes narrow; just before it ends note an old cistern on your right, covered (2007) with an old car tyre. Opposite the cistern a small path leads up to what is an attractive picnic spot: a shady viewpoint on a rocky spur. The main path turns right at the foot of the gully and soon passes the second cistern, which is beside a low crag. From the cistern keep straight on, to gain a little height. The mule track then turns downhill on the *phrygana*-covered hillside dotted with trees. Halfway down an old stone hut with a small canopy (shelter) is seen over on the right. It is close to the new road, which can be seen continuing downhill in series of loops.

The 'old road' eventually joins a dirt track. Turn right here for the new road. The junction is marked with a shrine and a small fenced garden, marking the end of the repaired 'recreational route'. Walk downhill on the new road – sections of old road can be seen, but it is easier to walk on the new road. The next landmark is a roadside shrine dated 1997 (700m/2297ft) with a stone seating bench opposite and a small olive grove just below. A few minutes further on, where the hillside levels out, bear right on a short length of track to find the next short cut.

When you reach the main road again, look to the left for the next section, which is well worth taking because, after crossing heathland, it descends a wooded ravine, cutting off two big loops in the road. When you emerge from the woodland turn left on the main road and walk 2km down to the village – you are now on top of the huge crag directly above it. **Kritsa** has shops, supermarkets, restaurants and accommodation. The *plateia* is more than halfway down the main street.

WALK L7A
Kritsa to the Katheros Plain

Walk L7 in reverse

Grade	C
Start	Kritsa 400m (1640ft)
Access	KTEL bus from Ay. Nikolaos or taxi
Finish	Avdeliakos hamlet 1150m (3772ft)
Access	Via Walks L4, L7 or by car
Highest point	1240m (1640ft)
Height gain	840m (2427ft)
Height loss	90m (295ft)
Approx distance	10km (6.2 miles)
Time allowance	Kritsa to start of *kalderimi* 500m (1640ft) 45mins; to rim of plain 3hrs 25mins; to Avdeliakos 20mins; total: 4hrs 30mins

The frequent KTEL bus service (1hr 30min journey time) Heraklion to Ay. Nikolaos may make an approach to Lassithi from this direction more convenient than from Kastamonitsa (Walk L1). Kritsa, a busy mountain village getting spin-off from coastal resorts, mixes tourist facilities with workaday amenities. It is also just 4km from the important and interesting archaeological site of Lato, an Iron Age walled mountain settlement variously described as 'the first town plan in Europe'. For taking on supplies (there is no shop beside the Ay. Nikolaos bus station/taxi rank) there are supermarkets near the Kritsa *plateia* (bus stop). In the upper village there is another small shop beside a terrace, where a restaurant or *kafeneon* can provide a last 'indulgence' before you start the climb. Proprietors here could also find rooms for you. Take on drinking water here since there are no springs on the trail.

Kritsa has a long main street heading uphill (west). Follow this up to a Y-junction, signed for Katheros, and bear left. As you leave the village note a steep ravine on your left. The road climbs the spur for 1km or so, then doubles back to cross this ravine again at a higher level. This is where the first remaining section of the 'old road' is found.

When you get to this spot at 500m (1640ft), which has a concrete culvert, leave the road on a footpath that heads up through the woodland of the now-shallow ravine. Keep a look out for the retaining wall of the old road, which soon appears up to the right, beside a spindly fence. An open, flat area follows. A workstation is seen over on the left, beside the new road, which makes a big loop before continuing the climb. The old trail, now a footpath, can be followed uphill as a short cut across this loop. Cross the crash barrier and look left for the continuation of the trail, which cuts off another big loop. This brings you up to another flat area where you re-join the road and continue on to pass a stone seating bench and a shrine, dated 1997, above a small olive grove (which appears to flourish, even at this altitude). This spot is about 1hr 30mins walk from the village. Continue up the new road as far as another white shrine, with a small fenced-off garden attached. This marks the start of the Forestry Service 'recreational route' reclaimed section of the 'old road'.

Walk for 2mins along the track behind the shrine. A footpath, with paving here and there, leads left off this track and heads uphill about 250°SW. This soon evolves as a wide section of the old road, easily seen because red earth between the stones contrasts with the surrounding vegetation.

About 25mins from the shrine note an old stone hut over on the left. The trail now climbs more steeply before making a sharp turn to the right. It loses a little height to pass a concrete-topped cistern sited under a crag. Beyond the cistern it turns up a gully. About 10mins from the cistern, note another small old-style cistern on your left. Opposite this, a small path leads up to an attractive natural flat terrace. However, the main trail keeps on up the gully. Part of the surface damaged by road works has been repaired. After gaining height with a couple of zigzags the old road takes up a long straight traverse though the oak forest. There is a wide, deep ravine on your right and the

The reclaimed section of the 'old road' between Kritsa and the Katheros Plain

pass on the rim of the Katheros Plain is in sight, as is part of the modern road.

Re-join the modern road and walk uphill around a left-hand bend. Ignore a dirt track leading to a hut – the continuation of the old trail is about 1min further on, marked with a cairn or two. Follow this up through the woodland until you are directly below the modern road. Here, the old *kalderimi* has been broken up by road works. Climb up to the road on what is left of the old zigzags and now keep on it, straight over the pass and down to **Avdeliakos** hamlet.

Margoulas to Xeniakos and Ano Viannos

Grade	B/C
Start	Margoulas 840m (2755ft)
Access	Lassithi rim road KTEL bus or on foot from Ay. Georgios
Finish	Xeniakos 500m (1640ft)
Access	KTEL weekday bus, or main road at Embaros for more frequent service
Highest point	1150m (3772ft)
Height gain	310m (1017ft)
Height loss	650m (2132ft)
Approx distance	10km (6.2 miles)
Time allowance	3hrs 25mins
Extension	Xeniakos to Ano Viannos 640m (2100ft); Height gain 550m (1084ft); Height loss 410m (1345ft); Approx distance 6km (3.7 miles); Time allowance 3hrs 20mins

This route, over a mountain pass southwest of Margoulas, is nowadays largely a downhill road walk apart from one remaining section of mule track, which crosses the pass. The great west-facing cliffs of Afendis Christos form an impressive backdrop as you make your way downhill. From Xeniakos ('Ks'en-yakos') there is a sparsely waymarked footpath over the next mountain pass and down to Ano Viannos.

On the south side of Lassithi there are several villages. **Margoulas** can be identified as the village on a hill east of Psychro. Walk up the main street to where there are two *kafeneia* opposite one another. Turn uphill here (south), on the lane that serves the upper village and then joins a track that continues the climb. At the top of the hill there is a chapel 'decorated' with bright red pointing. You now overlook a pleasantly wooded 'hidden' valley with old terraces and various workstations. You are heading for a spot on the mountainous rim at 220°SW (ignore the road on the east-facing mountainside). Keep on this main track of the valley

The 'hidden valley' behind Margoulas

as far as a line of plane trees beside the road. Bear left, downhill, and follow this lesser track to where it ends at the foot of a gully. What is left of the old mule track starts from here – look to your left to find the path which zigzags up the pleasantly vegetated hillside. Cross the pass and make your way down the right-hand side of a big gully to the surfaced road in sight far below at a place called **Stena** 1095m (3593ft), where there is a small parking place.

Walk down the road, passing a bend cut out of solid rock, to reach **Kampos Mani**, where (2006) the road is (mercifully for walkers) unsurfaced. The valley, which drains eastwards to a ravine, has some holm oak woodland but is otherwise blanketed with spiny spurge. There are one or two workstations. Follow the road as it loops around the valley. Maps mark the mule track as continuing down the gorge on a route that is seen as you climb to the next pass. Keep a look out for red waymarks if you want to try this option (not walked by author). There is a spring-fed water trough beside the road on the way up to the pass.

As you descend from this pass and approach a workstation in a walnut grove, note a short cut on the right that cuts off a big loop in the road – a section of old mule track routed down a rocky gully. Otherwise there is no escape from the road loops, but they are not too bad and before long you arrive to overlook the Xeniakos Valley.

The large building now seen under a big cliff across the valley is a modern monastic retreat. From that spot, follow the view of the cliff around to the left, east, to where it joins 'normal' hillside and note a shepherds' road above it at that point. If you plan to walk over to **Ano Viannos**, it is useful to know that the footpath leaving from Milliaradon first climbs the spur above that village, and by bearing right, heads directly up the hillside to that spot.

At the first workstation hut in the hillside directly above **Xeniakos**, the road turns sharply to the right to continue the descent. The owner of the hut uses what is perhaps his own direct path down the hillside to the village. Otherwise tramp the road which leads down to olive groves where you double back to enter the village. From the terrace of the *kafeneon* the pass that leads over to Ano Viannos is in sight on the skyline, almost due south. Locals (of the older generation) will point it out to you.

For Heraklion Xeniakos has a skeleton bus service. Alternatively, the more frequent daily Ano Viannos–Heraklion service passes on the main road beyond Embaros. Two roads from Embaros lead to the main road. Buses will stop on request at either junction. However, should the timetable not suit, note that Embaros has no tourist facilities. Your choice could be to ask the Xeniakos *kafeneon* proprietor to call a taxi for you, or (during the months of long daylight hours) to continue on to Ano Viannos, a much larger village with all facilities including a twice-weekly bus to Ierapetra.

For Ano Viannos Make your way over to **Milliaradon** ('Meel-ya-rar-thon'), in sight as it is very near. (The shopkeeper can rustle up simple meals of home-grown produce.) Walk up the village street to the last house where, on the left, a narrow track leads steeply uphill. This serves olive groves and joins another service track, which in turn would lead you around the hillside to join the shepherds' road you saw on the way down from Kampos Mani. However, bear in mind that the footpath follows the spine of the spur you are on. You need to look carefully for where this path leaves the track and continues the climb because, at that level, there is fairly dense vegetation or low-growing woodland. At the top of the spur, with the big cliff over on your right, leave the woodland and cross the hillside to complete the climb up to the road, which crosses a watercourse at this point.

Since Ano Viannos is southeast of this spot, ignore the rest of the road and follow the (waymarked) footpath as it gains height up the watercourse valley. The mountaintop is fairly rugged with a steep drop to the south, but the way-marks guide you eastwards on a traverse that brings you to a place where you can make a safe descent to a service road. The Ano Viannos Valley is in full view. Note a patch of green woodland that marks the position of Ay. Ioannis chapel and spring. To the envy of the surrounding district, a great volume of water gushes out of the mountain at this place. The footpath continues from the rear of the chapel, crossing the hillside to join an unmade road. Look out for footpath short cuts off this road as you continue the descent to **Ano Viannos** where there are shops and all other facilities. The bus stop is beside a restaurant (enquire).

APPENDIX 1
Glossary

SOE	Special Operations Executive (a handful of Allied Army intelligence agents who lived in the mountains and fought with the Cretan Resistance from 1941 to 1945).

Food-related words

Estiatorio	Offers oven-cooked meals, usually in towns and waterfronts where there is a fast customer turnover.
Kafeneon (pl. kafeneia)	Coffee house serving refreshments; village coffee house sometimes able to provide salad, omelette and chips.
Psistaria	Serves freshly roasted meats, chips and salads.
Taverna(s)	Serves a variety of cooked meals and refreshments.

Water-related words

Lastico	Long black water pipe
Neraki	Diminutive for drinking water
Nero	Water
Pigarthi	Seepage well
Potami	River
Reeaki	Stream
Sterna	Rainwater collecting cistern
Vrisi	Spring and/or water tap

Other useful words for walkers

Fragma	Fence
Hora	Village
Kalderimi (pl. kalderimia)	Stone-built mule track
Madares	Mountain grazing pastures of the Lefka Ori
Metochi	Small hamlet
Mitato (pl. mitata)	Shepherds' hut in the White Mountains (called *koumi* or *mandra* in the other mountain ranges of Crete)
Monopatti	Footpath
Oropethio	Mountain plain (for example, Askifou, Niato, Nida, Lassithi)
Oros (pl. ori)	Large mountain(s) or range
Plateia	Village (or town) main square; ask for the *plateia* and you will find the *kafeneon* and bus stop
Thromos	Road
Vouno(a)	Mountain(s)
Yeffira	Bridge

APPENDIX 2

Further reading

Scene of the first Bronze Age civilisation in Europe, Crete has attracted the interest of archaeologists, scientists and scholarly travellers at least since the 18th century. Dozens of books in Greek, English and other languages have been produced on every subject relevant to the island. A few of these, long out of print in the UK, are reissued by the Efstathiades Group, Athens, as economically priced paperbacks available locally for interested visitors. Imported books are available, but expensive. Foreign bookshops in the towns, and at Matala (central Crete) may stock a last copy or two of out-of-print books. Visit www.west-crete.com for a range of relevant books.

Countryside

O. Rackham and J. Moody *The Making of the Cretan Landscape* (Manchester University Press, 1996, ISBN 0 7190 3647 X/36461)
   Historical ecology: based for a period in Kambia, Anopolis, a botanist and an archaeologist joined forces to produce an in-depth study covering everything to be seen in the Cretan countryside.

Stephanie Coghlan *A Birdwatching Guide to Crete* (Arlequin Press, Chelmsford 1996, ISBN 1 9001 5910 4)
   Birds seen in Crete, and birdwatching areas throughout the island. Amongst places relevant to this walking guide Chania town, Omalos, the Samaria Gorge and Lake Kourna are featured.

Oleg Polunin *Flowers of Greece and the Balkans* (Oxford University Press, reprinted 1997, ISBN 0 1928 1998 4)
   Useful glossary of Latin and popular names. See Chapter 2, Western Crete, for plant-hunting itineraries: Omalos (Walks 1, 2), Samaria Gorge (Walk 3), Imbros Gorge (Walk 23) and the Madares from Anopolis (Trek 8). Use of digital photography has resulted in several new books on flowers to be found in the local shops – take your pick.

George Sfikas *Birds and Mammals of Crete* (1987) and *Wild Flowers of Crete* (Efstathiades Group, Athens 1978)
   Unassuming but useful guides. The latter a book for more advanced botanists, but dozens of illustrations. Also *Trees and Shrubs of Greece* (1979) and (outdated) *The Mountains of Greece*.

Cultural and Travel Guides

Johan de Bakker *Across Crete, Part 1: From Khania to Heraklion* (World Discovery
Guide Books, 2001, ISBN 90 806150 13))
A selection of writings by early travellers in Crete. Since travels were often made
on foot, on old trails which may still exist, many passages are of particular
interest to walkers.

Pat Cameron *The Blue Guide: Crete* (A & C Black Ltd, 7th edition 2003, ISBN 0 7136
4676 4)
Specialising in facts, rather than the author's opinions, the top cultural guide
restyled to be useful also as a 'companion' guide. Walkers will appreciate the
mention of the E4 Trail and other footpaths wherever these are encountered near
places of interest. The Psiloritis and Lassithi mountain ranges are particularly rich
in less-visited archaeological sites and historical points of interest, all of which
are described in detail.

David MacNeil Doren *Winds of Crete* (John Murray, 1974, reprinted Efstathiades)
Living and travelling in the Cretan countryside before modern tourism arrived.

Sonia Greger *Village on the Plateau* (Brewin Books, Studley 1985)
An ethnographic study of the Magoulas community of Lassithi (Walk L9) in the
early 1980s.

Adam Hopkins *Crete, its Past, Present and People* (Faber & Faber [OUP] paperback,
1977, ISBN 0 5711 1361 3)
Observations, history and sociology. Two young shepherds (now in their 50s and
living in a different era) lead the author up the garden path (to Katsiveli, Trek 8).

H.T. Hionides *Greek Dictionary* (Collins Gem series, Harper Collins, reprinted 1997,
ISBN 0 00 458548 8))
A good mini-dictionary.

Sabine Ivanovas *Where Zeus Became a Man* (Efstathiadis, translated by Maria
Stratigati, ISBN 960 226 584 1)
The text is in Greek, German and English. The author observes the work of the
shepherding families of the Milopotamos Valley and their love for Psiloritis. A
quality souvenir of Mount Ida and the people you may meet working on the
mountain.

Archaeology

Costis Davara *Guide to Cretan Antiquities* (Eptalogos S.A, Athens, 1976)
>   Helpful quick-reference directory.

Dilys Powell *The Villa Ariadne* (Efstathiadis, 1973)
>   Essential memoirs concerning Sir Arthur Evans' villa, which overlooks the site of
>   Knossos, and its occupants over the years, including the period of World War II.
>   As a young woman the author was married to archaeologist Humphrey Payne,
>   who died aged 37 of an infected insect bite. She wrote several memoirs of their
>   time in Greece together before forging a new career as a film critic for *The
>   Sunday Times*. In the 1950s (when there were few roads and mountain walking
>   was much tougher), in her late 50s, with a thick head cold and wearing
>   unsuitable shoes (don't do this!) she was guided by an ex-partisan on one very
>   long walking day over the summit of Mount Ida on the route taken by the
>   General Kreipe kidnap party. With no such thing as our modern-day walking
>   routes, the only easily identifiable spot in her account is the Analipsi spring,
>   with its stone-carved bowl (Walk P12).

World War II

To those who walk the high mountains, the (currently out of print) memoirs of the SOE
Intelligence agents who lived and worked with shepherds and partisans are of particular interest, not only for accounts of daring deeds, but as valuable records of the Cretan
way of life before emigration, roads and other amenities changed it so drastically.
Lately Internet searches have enabled New Zealanders in particular to enthusiastically
mop up secondhand copies, but it is worth knowing relevant titles because books like
this always reappear. Of the bunch, currently only *Ill Met by Moonlight* and *The Cretan
Runner* are in print.

>   Agents belonging to Secret Service units such as MI5 have unfortunately not writ-
ten similar memoirs. Both groups contributed to the Resistance effort during the Nazi
Occupation and their work overlapped. If anything, the SOE was assigned to co-ordi-
nate Cretan partisan bands, whilst the Inter Services Liaison Department (ISLD) was
assigned (for the purposes of Commando raids and other strategies) to relay, by wire-
less, intelligence information to the Allied HQ in Cairo.

Antony Beevor *Crete, the Battle and the Resistance* (John Murray, paperback, 1991,
ISBN 0 7195 4857 8)
>   The full coverage of this disastrous campaign by the author of *Stalingrad* and *Berlin*
>   included newly researched material to mark the 50th anniversary of the battle.

Murray Elliot *Vassili, Lion of Crete* (Efstathiades, reprinted 1992)
>   The story of Dudley Perkins, the New Zealander who led a Resistance group in
>   the mountains above Koustoyerako (Walk 6).

Xan Fielding *Hide and Seek* (Secker & Warburg [OUP] 1950)
   The wartime memoirs of the tough and competent SOE intelligence agent assigned to the White Mountains region. Although he settled in Andalucia after the war, he requested that his ashes be scattered in the Lefka Ori. His surviving former comrades chose a viewpoint at Kallergi refuge.

Xan Fielding *The Stronghold* (Secker & Warberg [OUP] 1955)
   The countryside in the 1950s: the author's return, revisiting the people and places he had known during the war. Of particular interest to those who walk the northern foothills of the Lefka Ori.

George Pyscoundakis (trans. by Patrick Leigh Fermor) *The Cretan Runner* (various editions, lately Penguin 1998 and Efstathiades, Athens)
   The World War II memoirs of a young, talented, Cretan shepherd from Asi Gonia who ran messages between all the Special Operations Executive (SOE) mountain hideouts. This translation work was Patrick Leigh Fermor's lasting tribute to the courage of the Cretan Resistance volunteers who assisted and protected Allied forces intelligence agents – he was one himself.

W. Stanley Moss *Ill Met By Moonlight* (various editions; lately Efstathiadis)
   This memoir of the kidnap of General Kreipe by the author together with Patrick Leigh Fermor and members of the Cretan Resistance, notably Manouli Paterakis of Koustoyerako, describes their successful escape over Mount Ida and across the hills of Rethymnon to Rodakino. Patrick Leigh Fermor's account of this venture is included in *Words of Mercury* (John Murray 2003), edited by Artemis Cooper. Observations and thoughts on his time in Crete are covered in chapter 3 of *Roumeli* (John Murray 1966).

A.M. Rendel *Appointment in Crete* (Allan Wingate [OUP], London 1953)
   Sandy Rendel's interesting and impressive memoir of his service as the SOE agent assigned to the Lassithi region.

Mathew Woodbine Parish *Aegean Adventures* (The Book Guild [OUP], 1994)
   Includes a separate chapter by Myles Hildyard, describing his experiences as an escaped prisoner of war hiding, with Australians, in the northern foothills of the White Mountains. The spring near Volikas EOS refuge is easily recognised in this memoir, as are the corbelled huts nearby (Walk 13).

Sean Damer and Ian Frazer *On the Run*: *Anzac Escape and Evasion in Enemy-occupied Crete* (Penquin Group [NZ], 2006, ISBN 0 14 302030 7)
   Experiences and memoirs of Allied Army soldiers, particularly New Zealanders, hiding in the mountains after the Battle of Crete 1941.

Efstathiadis, and others, publish several other memoirs of the Battle of Crete and the Resistance years – take your pick in the local bookshops.

Novels

Nikos Kazantzakis *Zorba the Greek* (Faber & Faber, reprinted 1987, ISBN 0 571 05265 7))
  Timeless character studies, remade 1960s as a memorable film starring Anthony Quinn, Alan Bates and Irene Papas. The film was shot at Vamos, near Vrisses, and on the Akrotiri peninsula at Stavros.

Nikos Kazantzakis *Freedom and Death* (Faber & Faber, reprinted 1983, ISBN 0 571 06679 8)
  1890s Crete: revolutionaries, who sense that victory is at last in sight, continue the struggle against Turkish rule.

Ioannis Kondylakis *Patouchas* (Efstathiadis, 1987)
  Traditional shepherding life: young men forced parental decision by abducting their (hopefully willing) brides.

APPENDIX 3
Useful information

General

Information, accommodation, photographs, links
www.gnto.gr Greek National Tourist information
www.interkriti.org
www.sfakia-crete.com
www.west-crete.com

Mountain guiding
Jean Bienvenu jean@west-crete.com

Archaeological survey
www.sphakia.classics.ox.ac.uk (the work of the team that produced *The Making of the Cretan Landscape*)

Travel/Transport
Buses
www.ktel.org Greek public bus association (lists mainline bus schedules)

Greek ferryboat schedules
www.greekislandhopping.com (Thomas Cook)
www.ferries.gr

Cretan ferryboat schedules
www.minoan.gr
www.anek.gr
www.bluestarferries.com

Airlines and airports
www.aia.gr Athens International Airport
www.olympicairlines.com International and internal flights
www.aegeanair.com Internal flights
www.easyjet.com For flights from the UK to Athens

Many other airlines fly to Athens and several charter flight companies fly to Crete. Try www.airflights.co.uk (tel: 0800.083.7007) for timetables and prices.

Useful telephone numbers

General
The international dialling code for Greece is 0030.

Area codes are as follows:
Athens 210
Chania 28210
Sfakia 28250
Selino 28230
Rethymnon 28310
Heraklion 2810
Ay. Nikolaos 28410
Lassithi 28440

Medical
The expatriates' association of western Crete recommends the following (2006,) all of whom speak fluent English:

Dentist: D. Railakis, 5 Papapastiou, Chania tel: 28210.45600
Eye specialist: Eleni Pavlidou, 46–50 Sfakion str. Chania tel: 28210.20399
Osteopath: Christina Kakavelaka, 10–12 Sfakion str. Chania tel: 28210.23248
Doctor: General Practitioner Dr 'Elizabeth', Vamos tel (clinic): 28250.22184; tel (home): 28250.22764; tel (mobile): 6976 881647

Tourist Police
Chania tel: 28210.53333
Rethymnon tel: 28310.28156
Heraklion tel: 2810.289614/283190

Emergency
Forestry Service (for example reporting a fire) tel: 191
Police/emergency tel: 100; ambulance tel: 166

Tourist Information
Chania tel: 28210.36204/29210.92000
Rethymnon tel: 28310.29148
Heraklion tel: 2810.228225

Transport
Bus transport enquiries (not always successful but sometimes worth a try):
    KTEL Chania tel: 29210.93306/93052
    KTEL Rethymnon tel: 28310.22212
    KTEL Heraklion (main) tel: 2810.245017/245019
    Heraklion (Chania Gate) tel: 2810.255965

Walking
The Hellenic Alpine Association (EOS) (evenings only)
    Chania tel: 28210.44647
    Heraklion tel: 2810.227609

These clubs run walking meets; newcomers are welcome.

LISTING OF CICERONE GUIDES

For full and up-to-date information on
our ever-expanding list of guides,
please check our website:
www.cicerone.co.uk.

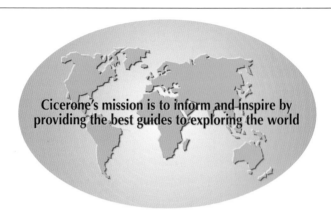

Cicerone's mission is to inform and inspire by
providing the best guides to exploring the world

Since its foundation over 30 years ago, Cicerone has specialised in publishing guidebooks and has built a reputation for quality and reliability. It now publishes nearly 300 guides to the major destinations for outdoor enthusiasts, including Europe, UK and the rest of the world.

Written by leading and committed specialists, Cicerone guides are recognised as the most authoritative. They are full of information, maps and illustrations so that the user can plan and complete a successful and safe trip or expedition – be it a long face climb, a walk over Lakeland fells, an alpine traverse, a Himalayan trek or a ramble in the countryside.

With a thorough introduction to assist planning, clear diagrams, maps and colour photographs to illustrate the terrain and route, and accurate and detailed text, Cicerone guides are designed for ease of use and access to the information.

If the facts on the ground change, or there is any aspect of a guide that you think we can improve, we are always delighted to hear from you.

Cicerone Press
2 Police Square Milnthorpe Cumbria LA7 7PY
Tel: 01539 562 069 Fax: 01539 563 417
info@cicerone.co.uk www.cicerone.co.uk

CICERONE